VOICE OVER IP

ISBN 0-13-065204-0

Prentice Hall Series in
Advanced Communications Technologies

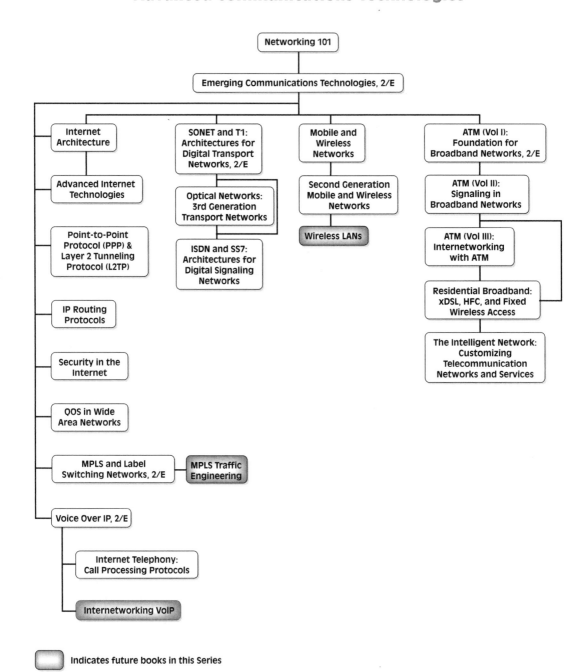

Networking 101

Emerging Communications Technologies, 2/E

Internet Architecture

SONET and T1: Architectures for Digital Transport Networks, 2/E

Mobile and Wireless Networks

ATM (Vol I): Foundation for Broadband Networks, 2/E

Advanced Internet Technologies

Optical Networks: 3rd Generation Transport Networks

Second Generation Mobile and Wireless Networks

ATM (Vol II): Signaling in Broadband Networks

Point-to-Point Protocol (PPP) & Layer 2 Tunneling Protocol (L2TP)

ISDN and SS7: Architectures for Digital Signaling Networks

Wireless LANs

ATM (Vol III): Internetworking with ATM

IP Routing Protocols

Residential Broadband: xDSL, HFC, and Fixed Wireless Access

Security in the Internet

The Intelligent Network: Customizing Telecommunication Networks and Services

QOS in Wide Area Networks

MPLS and Label Switching Networks, 2/E

MPLS Traffic Engineering

Voice Over IP, 2/E

Internet Telephony: Call Processing Protocols

Internetworking VoIP

Indicates future books in this Series

Voice Over IP

UYLESS BLACK

Prentice Hall PTR
Upper Saddle River, New Jersey 07458
www.phptr.com

Library of Congress Cataloging-in-Publication Data

Black, Uyless D.
    Voice over IP / Uyless Black. -- 2nd ed.
      p. cm. -- (Prentice Hall series in advanced communications technologies)
    Includes index.
    ISBN 0–13–065204–0
    1. Internet telephony. 2. TCP/IP (Computer network protocol) I. Title. II. Series.

  TK5105.8865 .B53 2001
  004.6—dc21

                                                  2001050048

Editorial/production supervision: *Laura Burgess*
Acquisitions editor: *Mary Franz*
Editorial assistant: *Noreen Regina*
Cover designer: *Nina Scuderi*
Cover design director: *Jerry Votta*
Manufacturing manager: *Alexis R. Heydt*
Marketing manager: *Dan DePasquale*

© 2002 by Uyless Black
Published by Prentice Hall PTR
Prentice-Hall, Inc.
Upper Saddle River, New Jersey 07458

Prentice Hall books are widely used by corporations and government agencies for training, marketing, and resale.

The publisher offers discounts on this book when ordered in bulk quantities. For more information contact:

        Corporate Sales Department
        Phone: 800-382-3419
        Fax: 201-236-7141
        E-mail: corpsales@prenhall.com

        Or write:

        Prentice Hall PTR
        Corporate Sales Department
        One Lake Street
        Upper Saddle River, New Jersey 07458

Printed in the United States of America
10 9 8 7 6 5 4 3 2 1

ISBN: 0-13-065204-0

Pearson Education LTD.
Pearson Education Australia PTY, Limited
Pearson Education Singapore, Pte. Ltd.
Pearson Education North Asia Ltd.
Pearson Education Canada, Ltd.
Pearson Educación de Mexico, S.A. de C.V.
Pearson Education — Japan
Pearson Education Malaysia, Pte. Ltd.
Pearson Education, Upper Saddle River, New Jersey

This book is dedicated to Brad Waters

For the first edition of this book, I chose the parrot for the cover because of its ability to utter parts of a human language. As you can see, for this second edition, the parrot remains on the cover, and now has a companion (it appears VoIP is increasing its clientele base).

Regardless of the number of parrots on the cover, my original analogy of the parrot to VoIP still holds, so I repeat this description for the second edition, with some small changes that reflect the progress made in VoIP since the first edition of this book was published.

On several occasions, I have had an opportunity to listen to some of the utterances of a parrot, and on the whole, I found this bird's speech about equal in audio quality to that of a human's conversations over the public Internet during periods when the Internet is busy. I am being a bit harsh, because speech quality on the Internet varies. Sometimes it is acceptable, but some of the time it is not very good, and it is not the quality we expect in a conversation through the telephone network.

Why is it difficult to understand the parrot's "speech"? Why is it sometimes difficult to understand speech over the Internet? The problem with the parrot is the bird's lack of a vocabulary, and its inability to form phonemes, and of course its inability to know what it is uttering.

The problem with the Internet is the (sometimes) very long delay in delivering the speaker's voice image to the listener, and its tendency to lose or discard some of the speech traffic. In addition to the long delay in hearing the speaker's voice, it may turn out that the delay is variable, something like talking . . . then not talking . . . then talking . . . then not talking . . . and so on.

Then why is VoIP a topic of widespread interest? The excitement is not because of the ability of IP to carry voice traffic, but because of the more general ability to place voice traffic over data networks. IP just happens to be part of the picture because it is a prevalent protocol used in data networks.

The parrot will never improve its human speech capabilities unless DNA manipulation reaches new heights (or lows). But the Internet will upgrade its ability to support speech traffic, and is improving its "speech capabilities" almost weekly.

As you read this sentence, the Internet is being re-worked to support voice traffic. Eventually, the Internet and the telephone network will be one and the same. It is only a matter of time.

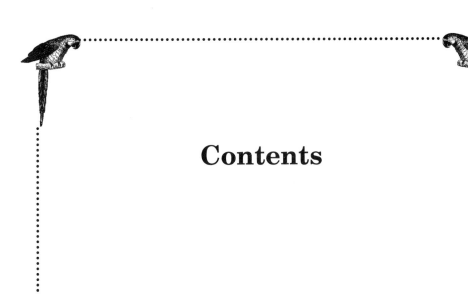

Contents

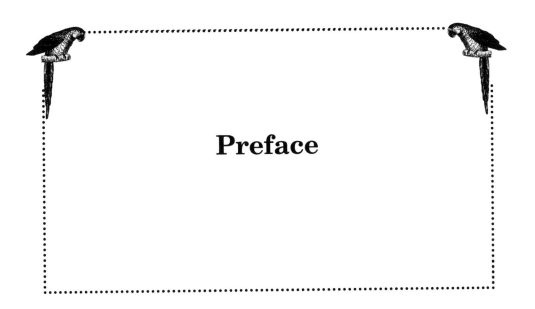

Preface

This book is one in a series of books called "Advanced Communications Technologies." As the name of the book implies, the focus is on the Internet and the Internet Protocol (IP) in relation to the support of voice traffic.

The subject matter of this book is vast and my approach is to provide an introduction to the topic. In consonance with the intent of this series, this survey also has considerable detail but not to the level needed to design a system. For that, I leave you to your project team and the various specifications that establish the standards for Internet telephony.

This book is considered to be at an intermediate to advanced level. As such, it assumes the reader has a background in voice and data communications and the IP suite. Notwithstanding, for the new reader, I have provided several tutorials and guide you to them in the appropriate parts of the book. I also guide the more experienced reader away from them.

I hope you find this book a valuable addition to your library.

NOTES TO THE READER

In writing multiple books about data and voice communications systems, the author is faced with a question: How much overlap (redundancy of material) should there be among the books in the series? If the overlap is too little, the reader must buy other books in the series to fill the gaps. If the overlap is too great, the reader who has purchased other books in the series may feel cheated by spending additional money to obtain the same information.

My approach is to try to strike a compromise between the two extremes. If another book in the series contains information on a topic that is relevant to the topic of the current book, yet is not a required subject in order to read the current book, I make reference to the book. However, that is not always possible. In a few cases, it is necessary to include material from other books in the series. Otherwise, the book in question becomes a fragmented reference to other books. I have taken this approach with this book. I trust you find this an efficient and useful way to deal with this matter.

To help strike this compromise, I have included appendices that are extracted from some of my other books. A basic knowledge of telephony signaling, the V.34 modem, ISDN, and SS7 will be very helpful as you read some of these chapters about VoIP, and I have included tutorials on these subjects in the appendices at the back of this book.

EXPLANATIONS OF MESSAGES AND PROTOCOL FLOWS

This book is a survey (albeit a detailed one) of the VoIP technology. A wide variety of VoIP control messages and protocols are used to support VoIP, and the standards bodies and the Internet task forces are defining hundreds of messages and scores of protocol flows between VoIP gateways, call agents, and user machines. It is not the intent of this book to explain the contents of each message and each protocol flow, which would simply duplicate the VoIP specifications. Instead, I provide tutorial explanations of these messages and flows, as well as selected examples of each. In each case, I provide you with references to the original specifications. In this manner, the book should provide you with a handy reference tool and act as a pointer toward more information if you so desire.

INTERNET DRAFTS: WORK IN PROGESS

A considerable portion this book is devoted to explaining many Internet-based specifications pertaining to packet telephony.

Keep in mind that the Internet drafts are works in progress, and should be viewed as such. You should not use the drafts with the expectation that they will not change. Notwithstanding, if used as general tutorials, the drafts discussed in this book are "final enough" to warrant their explanations. Indeed, many of my clients use these drafts in their product planning and design.

For all the Internet standards and drafts the following applies:

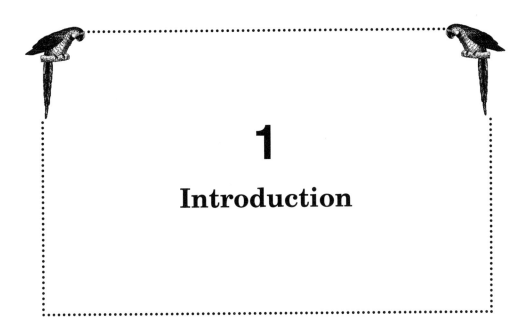

1

Introduction

This chapter introduces the Internet Protocol (IP), voice over IP (VoIP), packetized voice, and Internet telephony. The chapter includes several sections. The first section explains why VoIP is of such keen interest to the industry. The next section explains the prevalent configurations for VoIP. The third section provides a brief introduction to the basic terms and concepts associated with IP-based packet networks, such as the Internet and internets. Following this overview, several key factors that pertain to the support of packetized voice in an internet are evaluated.

INTERNET TELEPHONY AND PACKETIZED VOICE

Voice over IP (VoIP) means the transmission of voice traffic in packets.[1] Several terms are used to describe this process: Internet telephony, internet telephony, IP telephony, packet-voice (packetized voice). Before proceeding further, we need to clarify these terms:

---

[1]For the uninitiated reader, a packet is a small unit of user traffic appended to a routing field. The packet may be variable in length and can vary in its duration. This approach is in contrast to telephony-based, circuit-switched traffic, which is always of fixed length and fixed in time (duration).

1

- *Internet telephony:* Placement of telephone calls over the public Internet; this term implies the use of IP telephony and packet-voice.
- *internet telephony:* Placement of telephone calls over a private network (an internet [note lower case i]). This term also implies the use of IP telephony and packet-voice.
- *IP telephony:* Use of IP to forward voice calls through the Internet or an internet. This term implies the use of packet-voice.
- *Packet-voice (or packetized voice):* Use of a packet network instead of a telephone circuit-switched network to transport telephone calls. The Internet is a packet network, and so are internets. However, packet-voice need not use IP. For example, a packet voice network might run the voice traffic over Frame Relay. Thus, packet-voice is a general term, not necessarily implying voice over IP.

WHY INTERNET TELEPHONY?

IP telephony with VoIP is viewed by some people to be an attractive and effective technology, and by others as nothing more than an irritant. The irritating aspect stems from those people who have used the public Internet to make telephone calls. In many cases, they are not happy with the quality of the speech and the overall ability of the Internet to support voice traffic.

In view of its relatively poor performance in the support of voice traffic, why then is VoIP of such keen interest to the communications industry? There are four major reasons for this interest and for the deployment of IP telephony. The next part of this chapter discusses these reasons in this order:

1. The business case
    (a) Integration of voice and data (and video)
    (b) Bandwidth consolidation
    (c) Inability to negotiate and adapt
    (d) Tariff arbitrage
2. Universal presence of IP
3. Maturation of technologies
4. The shift to data networks

The Business Case

The first reason is a compelling business case for the deployment of the IP protocol suite and associated equipment to support telephony services. This case can be summarized with four suppositions.

Integration of Voice and Data (and Video). First, it is clear that the *integration* of voice, data, and video traffic will be demanded by multi-application software. This integration will result in the evolution to Web servers that are capable of interacting with the customer with attractive real-time data, voice, and video images. Text-only images will become a thing of the past.

Bandwidth Consolidation. The next two suppositions stem from the first. This second supposition is that the integration of voice and data allows for *bandwidth consolidation,* which effectively fills up the data communications channels more efficiently than a conventional voice link. The telephony legacy of channelized voice slots, with the expensive associated equipment (channel banks and data service units (DSUs)), are inefficient tools for the support of data applications.

The common-sense idea is to migrate away from the rigid telephony-based time division multiplexing (TDM) scheme wherein a telephony user is given bandwidth continuously, even when the user is not talking. Since voice conversations entail a lot of silence (pauses in thinking out an idea, taking turns talking during the conversation, etc.), using the data communications (and a packet network) scheme of statistical TDM (STDM) yields a much more efficacious use of precious bandwidth. STDM simply uses the bandwidth when it needs it; otherwise, the bandwidth is made available to other talkers who need it at that instant.

To give you an idea of how wasteful the telephony TDM approach is, consider that about 50% of a normal speech pattern is silence (at least in most conversations). Voice networks that are built on TDM use precious bandwidth to carry those silent periods. Data networks do not. Furthermore, another 20% of speech consists of repetitive patterns that can be eliminated through compression algorithms. The conventional TDM operations do not exploit this technology.

Moreover, modern analog-to-digital operations that use a high-quality STDM, packet-based speech channel can operate at about 4.8 to 8 kbit/s, in contrast to current TDM telephony channels that operate at 64 kbit/s. In the future, it is expected that the packet voice rate will be reduced further. Let's assume a 6 kbit/s speech channel rate for purposes of comparison. The bandwidth consumption ratio is just over 10:1 in favor of the packet-based method.

Inability to Negotiate and Adapt. The telephone infrastructure is based on technology that was developed decades ago. At that time, software-based switches were a thing of the future. Almost everything was hardwired, resulting in a rigid structure, not amenable to change. This infrastructure was also very expensive to build. With regulations from the Federal Communications Commission (FCC) and the State Public Utility Commissions, change was not encouraged (for example, long depreciation schedules of equipment discouraged rapid deployment of new technology).

Thus, as technology shifted and improved, the telephone networks tended to remain static, with limited abilities to adapt. With this rigidity, came the inability to negotiate certain services and accommodate advances in technology. For example, even though low bandwidth codecs[2] operating in the 5 to 8 kbit/s range have been in the industry for many years, the telephone switches and other telephony components could not take advantage of them because of the rigid time division multiplexed (TDM), 64-kbit/s architecture of the telephony equipment.

One of the key aspects of VoIP rests on the idea of an infrastructure that supports change and on the ability to negotiate services, as well as different levels of technology. For example, in a typical VoIP call scenario, users can negotiate the use of different data rates, different coding technologies, IP addresses, port numbers, and increasingly, quality of service (QOS) operations, such as delay requirements.

For the telephone networks to assume this posture, they would essentially have to be scrapped and redone. Thus, with their adaptability, VoIP systems allow the graceful, rapid transition to new technologies, as well as the support for different technologies.

Tariff Arbitrage. The fourth supposition regarding the business case is based on a concept called *tariff arbitrage*. This term means the bypassing of the toll services of public switched telephone networks and instead, using an internet backbone. This approach avoids the costly long distance charges incurred in the tariffed telephone network in contrast to lower costs of the untariffed Internet.

---

[2]A codec (coder/decoder) translates an analog voice signal into digital samples for transport across a packet network. At the receiver, the process is reversed. See Chapter 5 for more details.

Some people believe that VoIP will not be attractive if or when the FCC removes the enhanced service provider (ESP) status granted to Internet service providers (ISPs). The effect of this status is that ISPs are not required to pay local access fees to use the telephone company (telco) local access facilities. There is no question that this status gives ISPs huge advantages in competing for voice customers, because access fees are the most expensive part of a long distance call. Table 1–1 reflects a study conducted by Merrill Lynch and available in [STUC98]. Access charges make up almost 50% of an interchange carrier's (IXC) costs for a switched long distance call. The other major costs are sales, general and administrative (SG&A), and network expenses (equipment, personnel, software, etc.).

Studies indicate (and common sense dictates) that the removal of the ESP status will certainly level the playing field to a great extent, and indeed, if this does occur, there will surely be less hype about VoIP. But the fact remains that, even without this special status, conventional circuit-switched telephony cannot compete with packet-switched telephony on cost. This fact stems partly from the concept of bandwidth consolidation and speech compression, discussed earlier.

Figure 1–1 illustrates a few facts and predictions from a study by Level 3 that compares the cost performance of telephony-based TDM circuit switches and data-based STDM packet switches [SCHM98]. The figure compares the rate of improvement in throughput of these switches, measured in bits per second (bit/s) per $1. It is obvious that packet switching is a more cost-effective approach, and the gap between the two switching approaches will widen. The circuit-switch vendors understand this fact, and they are migrating their TDM circuit-switch architectures

Table 1–1   Long distance cost and profit structure [STUC98]

	Cost per Minute (in $)	Percent of Revenues	Percent of Cost
Average rate	.140	100.0	—
Access	(.050)	(35.75)	45.5
Network operations	(.015)	(10.7)	13.6
Depreciation	(.010)	(7.1)	9.1
Sales, general & administrative	(.035)	(25.0)	31.8
Total Cost	(.110)	(78.6)	100.0
Net Profit	.030	21.45	

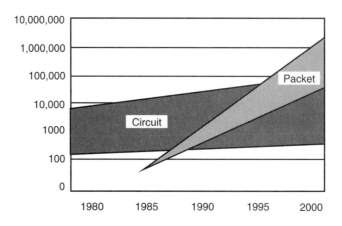

Figure 1–1   Cost performance: bit/s per $1 [SCHM98]

to STDM packet-switch technologies. The asynchronous transfer mode (ATM) is the leading technology in this migration.

Those Who Disagree.   Not all people in the industry agree with the studies that I have just cited. Some believe that, in the long run, the telephone TDM, circuit-switched technology will prove to be the winner over the data STDM, packet-switched technology. Some people disparage the movement to packet-voice, with the complaint that the industry is "Reinventing the telephone network." This latter statement is true in that the telephone technology is being reinvented to run over packet networks. I do not agree with the former statement because circuit switches are being phased out. Anyway, let's examine the other issues.

Universal Presence of IP

The second major reason for IP telephony is the universal presence of IP and associated protocols in user and network equipment. Of key importance is that IP resides in the end-user workstation (in contrast to potentially competitive technologies such as asynchronous transfer mode (ATM) and Frame Relay that operate as user-network interfaces [UNI]). Figure 1–2 shows where these technologies are placed (the term packet switch in this figure is used generically; Frame Relay or an ATM switch could be used).

Make no mistake; the existence of IP in personal computers and workstations gives IP a decided advantage over other existing technologies that are not resident in the user appliance. This "location" of IP

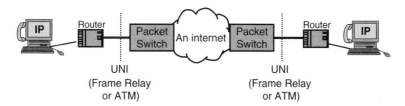

Figure 1–2   Location of IP vs. ATM and Frame Relay

makes it a very convenient platform from which to launch voice traffic. Moreover, IP operates in both wide area and local area networks, whereas Frame Relay operates only in wide area networks and ATM is predominately a wide area network technology. The issues surrounding voice over IP, Frame Relay, and ATM are covered in Chapter 12.

But it is not that simple. Figure 1–2 is part of the picture regarding ATM, Frame Relay, and IP with regard to supporting telephony services, but it is not the entire picture. The reason is that the telephone service providers have implemented ATM in many of their backbone networks. By backbone, I mean the network components that operate between the telephone company nodes; that is, they do not operate on the local loop to the customer. The backbone extends to the telephone Central Office, where the local loops connect to the customer. Figure 1–3 shows this arrangement.

ATM has been deployed by the telephone service providers because it provides several tools for managing traffic in a network. It is also designed to operate gracefully with conventional telephone network technology.

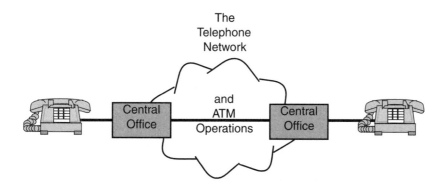

Figure 1–3   ATM in the picture in the network

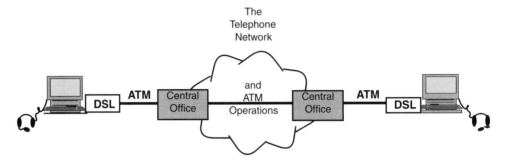

Figure 1–4   ATM in the picture on the local loop

Moreover, as depicted in Figure 1–4, ATM is finding wide deployment in several local loop technologies, such as DSL. Many DSL modems run ATM between the user device and the service provider's node (entrance to the network).

ATM has many detractors as well as many supporters, and later parts of this book will address this subject. For this introduction, keep in mind that the implementations shown in Figures 1–2, 1–3, and 1–4 are all widely deployed. Of course, this book is about VoIP, which is depicted in Figure 1–2; that will be our focus.

Maturation of Technologies

As noted, we will deal with the VoATM versus VoIP situation later in the book. For now, let's consider the third major reason for the deployment of internet telephony: the maturation of technologies that now make IP telephony feasible. Many aspects of VoIP are supported by the wide-scale deployment of digital signal processors (DSPs), discussed in Chapter 4. The DSPs are found in codecs and high-speed modems. Their tailored operations and high-speed performance have opened the way for the support of applications that were unthinkable just a few short years ago. DSPs are now mass-produced and relatively inexpensive, and they are finding their way into many consumer appliances.

Applications: The Next Revolution.   Another aspect of the maturation of technologies (or perhaps the maturation of expectations and demand) is the increased sophistication of user applications. The days are passing when end users will be satisfied with browsers that retrieve and display text-only images. Increasingly, we will use applications supporting three-dimensional images, real-time operations, full-motion video, and data displays.

Indeed, we are witnessing the maturation of three key technologies that will foster a revolution in information technology. They are (a) the increased capacity of communications links, (b) the increased capacity of computers (CPUs), and (c) the advent of reusable, intelligent plug-and-play software code. The convergence of these maturing technologies will at last lay the groundwork for a new generation of user-friendly applications. And you will see the results of this remarkable revolution in your browser package in a few short years.[3]

The real challenge of today does not lie in providing bandwidth and computer capacity. The real challenge lies in the ability to manage, retrieve, and display (in milliseconds) information stored in databases throughout the world—information in thousands of places, consisting of billions of bytes, much of which is fragmented and not correlated with other information. I said during a lecture recently, "In today's society, knowledge is power, if you know where the bytes are stored." I would also add: and if you know how to retrieve those bytes and display them to the consumer.

The Shift to Data Networks

The fourth major reason for the assured success of voice over IP and other data networks is the fact that the world is experiencing a shift away from circuit-based networks (telephony networks) to packet-based networks (data networks). Some market forecasts place the ratio of data networks to circuit networks at 4-to-1 by 2005.

This shift is occurring for two reasons. First, the data industry is more a growth industry than is the voice industry. More people have access to telephones than to computers; thus, there are more people amenable to buying a computer.

Second, the bandwidth requirements for a voice conversation and its quality of service requirements do not change. As long as a telephony circuit is up and running between the two conversants, nothing else is needed. This basic requirement has not changed since the invention of the telephone.

---

[3]This prediction is based on the assumption that this capacity will be pushed out of the network onto the local loop to the residential consumer on a mass basis (many businesses already have this capacity); unfortunately, most residences do not.

On the other hand, the bandwidth for a computer "conversation" and its quality of service requirements continue to grow, with the resultant need to expand the data networks to meet this growth. So, the second reason for the shift is to support new computers and enhanced applications. As computers become faster and as computer users demand more sophisticated services (interactive Nintendo across the Internet, etc.), the demand for increased data services and data networks will continue.

WHY USE IP FOR TELEPHONY TRAFFIC?

But why use IP for telephony traffic? Why not use AppleTalk, IBM's Systems Network Architecture (SNA), or some other protocol? IP is the chosen protocol for internet telephony because, as the mountain climber says, "It is there." IP is not a particularly attractive protocol for telephony because it was designed to transport data traffic. However, its universal presence in PCs, servers, and workstations makes it a convenient platform for the support of telephony traffic.

However, IP is only one part of the overall technology. When one says, "I am using voice over IP," the sentence means much more than just placing voice signals into the IP packets. The VoIP platform encompasses a vast ensemble of technologies and protocols. As you read this book, I will introduce them to you. As a brief precursor, VoIP cannot deliver effective speech images by itself. It needs the Real-Time Protocol (RTP), Megaco, the Session Initiation Protocol (SIP), the Resource Reservation Protocol (RSVP), H.323, and many others to provide a "VoIP platform" to the user.

BARRIERS TO SUCCESSFUL DEPLOYMENT OF IP TELEPHONY

It is the view of many that IP telephony (and voice over other data networks) is a given because of the reasons just cited. However, the deployment of voice over IP is not a trivial matter. The principal reason for this statement is that the Internet protocol suite (and other data networks) is not designed to accommodate synchronous, real-time traffic, such as voice. In addition, the traffic loss experienced in IP networks, as well as the amount and variability of delay, militates effective support of voice and video traffic.

Variable delay is onerous to speech. It complicates the receiver's job of playing-out the speech image to the listener. Furthermore, the delay of the speech signal between the talker and the listener can be excessively long, resulting in the loss of information (the late-arriving samples cannot be used by the codec).

Another factor of voice to be considered in the public Internet is its "uncooperative nature." The Internet is an amalgamation of disparate networks and service providers who have formed associations in an evolutionary and somewhat fragmented manner. Unlike most telephone networks, the Internet never had a "Ma Bell" or a PTT (Postal, Telephone, and Telegraph Ministry) to define the network's behavior, such as guaranteed bandwidth for the telephone call. Indeed, the Internet makes no such guarantees. It need not grant the user's bandwidth needs. Sometime you get the service you need and sometime you do not (after all, you get what you pay for . . .).

Some people believe the connectionless nature of the internet makes it more difficult to offer effective support of voice traffic. These critics point to the connection-oriented operations of telephony networks and cite how its architecture imposes more predictability and discipline in the networks' support of the users' traffic. I agree with this point to some extent, and there is no question that connectionless networks provide a bigger challenge in supporting synchronous voice traffic. But the configuration of an internet to use priority scheduling, upper layer resource reservations, and fixed (constrained) routing can effectively simulate many aspects of a connection-oriented technology. So, I do not think the connectionless argument has much merit.

RELIABILITY OF THE TELEPHONE NETWORK

The telephone network has been engineered to provide continuous, almost-instant, and robust connections for its customers. It is quite rare when telephony service is denied; it is rare when our conversations are anything less than crystal clear.

The telephone network rests on three principles: (a) no traffic loss is permitted, and therefore, (b) retransmissions of lost (or errant) traffic are neither needed nor supported, (c) in any case, the retransmission would take too long because the telephone network is engineered to provide instant response time. All in all, the telephone network makes it seem as if two parties have a direct line to each other.

Data networks (and the Internet) have been designed with the exact opposite philosophy: (a) traffic loss is permitted, and therefore (b) retransmission schemes support the resending of lost (or errant) traffic,

(c) data applications are usually immune from retransmissions, due to their (with some exceptions) non-real-time requirements.

At the risk of overemphasis: Retransmission of voice traffic cannot be done effectively. Retransmission creates long and variable delays in the delivery of the speech traffic, an unacceptable situation for interactive voice conversations.

To summarize, VoIP is not a panacea for the problems encountered in the legacy telephone network. Running voice over a data network is not an easy mix because the two operations are diametrically different in how they operate.

VoIP IN THE INTERNET AND IN PRIVATE INTERNETS

From a technical standpoint, the deployment of synchronous traffic over a *private* asynchronous internet offers the same challenges as just described for the public Internet.

However, there is one big difference between IP telephony in a public Internet and in a private internet: An internet can be designed to be much more "cooperative" than the Internet. Private networks can be more readily tuned than the public Internet. Therefore, they provide much better support of VoIP than does the public Internet, at least for the time being. Eventually, I believe the public Internet will perform well enough to support toll-quality (telephone quality) traffic.

THE QUESTION: NOT IF, BUT HOW?

Even with the uncooperative nature of the public Internet and data networks in general, the question is not if IP telephony will be implemented; the question is how. Many issues surround this question. Let me cite four examples that are explained later in more detail.

First, what happens to the current telephone network? This is not a trivial issue, and VoIP systems must be able to internetwork with the current telephone company (telco) network. Is the linchpin of the telephone network, Signaling System Number 7 (SS7), going to be eliminated? No, VoIP will interwork with SS7 so that a user will have all the features, such as call hold and calling party ID, that are taken for granted today in telco-based SS7 networks.

Second, what happens to telephone key sets and private branch exchanges (PBXs)? They will remain in the inventory, but they will surely evolve away from the circuit-switched technology to one that is packet based.

Third, which bearer services will be used to support VoIP? We will shortly see that IP operates in layer 3 of the classical layered model. What is to be in the lower layers? Will it be Frame Relay, Ethernet, or ATM, at layer 2, and SONET, or wave division multiplexing (WDM) at layer 1? In all likelihood, it will be combinations of all of these technologies.

Fourth, what supporting upper layer protocols will be used? Will it be the Real-Time Protocol (RTP), Differentiated Services (DiffServ), the Resource Reservation Protocol (RSVP), Megaco, SIP, or others? No one knows yet, and once again, it will likely be all of these protocols, and many more.

These four questions are examples of the many issues surrounding VoIP. A great deal remains to be worked out to migrate to a cohesive, cost-effective, and efficient VoIP infrastructure. But that infrastructure is being built this very moment. And things are changing so quickly that some of these questions may be answered by the time this book is published.

CONFIGURATION OPTIONS

We have discussed the issues that surround VoIP. Let us now look at some VoIP configurations and topologies. Several configuration options are available to support VoIP operations. Figure 1–5 shows four examples.

In Figure 1–5(a), conventional telephones are employed as is the telephone network (you may have noticed that the term telco is used in this book as a shorthand notation for the telephone network). The VoIP gateway provides the translation functions for the voice/data conversions. On the transmit side, the gateway uses a low-bit-rate voice codec and other special hardware and software to code, compress, and encapsulate the voice traffic into data packets (IP datagrams). It accepts conventional telco traffic (usually encoded by the telco Central Office into digital 64 kbit/s DS0 signals) and uses the codec to convert these signals into highly compressed samples of the telco signal, usually about 6–8 kbit/s. At the receiving VoIP gateway, the process is reversed. The gateway converts the low-bit-rate speech back to the telco DS0 signals. These signals are converted to conventional analog signals before they are passed to the user's telephone.

This gateway is an n:1 machine because it accepts n telephone connections and multiplexes them into IP datagrams onto one link to the In-

(a) Telephone connection with gateways

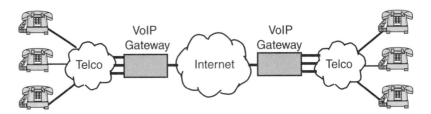

(b) PC connection with router

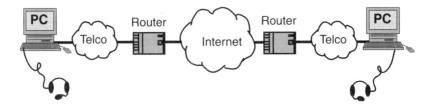

(c) Telephone-to-PC connection

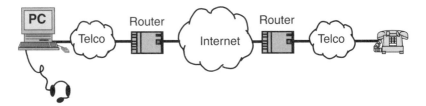

(d) Connection with 1:1 VoIP gateway

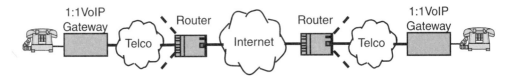

Figure 1–5   Configuration options with the Internet

ternet or an intranet.[4] Chapters 10 and 11 examine these machines in more detail, and we will see that they are capable of delivering high-quality voice traffic. The limitation of this configuration is not within the gateways, but with how efficiently (or inefficiently) the Internet transports the traffic to the receiver gateway.

Figure 1–5(b) shows the use of a personal computer (PC) and the employment of a router. With this operation, the encoding, compression, and encapsulation operations are performed at the PCs. The router's job is to examine the destination IP address in the datagram and route the traffic accordingly. The router treats the traffic just like any other datagram and is not aware that the bits in the datagram are voice traffic.

This configuration will eventually be one that delivers high-quality voice traffic. But for the present, it is not an optimal approach. First, the generalized processors in PCs are not designed to code (analog-to-digital [A-D]) and decode (digital-to-analog [D-A]) voice signals as efficiently as do VoIP gateways.

The VoIP layout depicted in Figure 1–5(c) uses a PC at one end and a conventional telephone at the other end. With this arrangement, the routers are out-fitted with additional capabilities and take over some of the functions of a VoIP gateway. One of my friends in North Carolina uses this arrangement to call me at my home in Virginia. He uses his PC to call my conventional telephone. It is completely transparent at my end of the connection (except for the quality of the call).

A simple and low-cost approach to VoIP is the 1:1 VoIP gateway, shown in Figure 1–5(d). The 1:1 ratio means that only one voice connection is supported by the gateway. The 1:1 gateway sits beside the telephone. It is an unobtrusive device, about half the size of the telephone. It accepts the speech analog signals and performs A-D operations (at this time, typically G.723.1 or G.729, explained in Chapter 5) on the signals. At the receiver, the reverse operation takes place.

There is a wide array of 1:1 gateways in the industry, and gateways are relatively easy to use. The configuration can be a bit of a hassle, since you must use the telephone dial-pad to enter the configuration parameters, such as IP addresses, ISP phone numbers, etc. In addition, both parties must have the same 1:1 gateway device in order to use this configuration.

---

[4]The convention in this book is to use the term Internet (with an upper case I) to identify the public network. The terms internet (lower case i) and intranet identify private networks that use the IP suite of protocols.

Problems with the Configurations

The configurations shown in Figure 1–5 represent low-function systems. These are bare-bones operations when compared to the services taken for granted by most telco users that have access to SS7 and advanced intelligent network (AIN) services. The configurations shown in Figure 1–5 might not include the equipment to support call forwarding, call holding, caller ID, or other telco services voice users expect. These services are provided by machines (such as key sets, PBXs, Centrex, etc.) absent from the Figure 1–5 configurations. (In fairness, the high-end gateways now offer some of the PBX type of functions.) Additionally, these configurations use the public Internet, which is not set up to deliver toll-quality voice traffic.

Using a LAN Connection into the Telephone Network

Another configuration option is shown in Figure 1–6. The users are attached to a local area network (LAN) at one site, and local calls on the LAN are managed by the gateway. Inside the gateway (or inside another machine on the LAN) is a call manager that performs the management functions. The PCs and workstations run VoIP and thus execute the low-bit-rate codec. If the telephone call must go outside the LAN, the gateway performs the necessary conversion of the signals to meet the telco's requirements. Once the traffic is given to the telco, it is handled like any other call.

This configuration is one that is gaining considerable attention in the industry, because the local LANs (such as Ethernet) can be used for

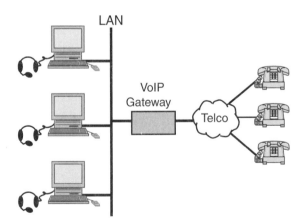

Figure 1–6   Connecting with the LAN and the telephone network

both voice and data traffic. Also, for simple telephone calls, there is no expensive key system or PBX in the network.

PRIVATE VoIP NETWORKS: THE VPN

There is yet another way. It incorporates the attractive features of the IP platform with those of the PBX and a virtual private network (VPN). The five configurations described in Figures 1–5 and 1–6 use the public Internet and/or the public telco to convey the voice signals between the two users. Another configuration, shown in Figure 1–7, uses a private intranet and/or leased lines instead of the Internet. This configuration also includes the PBX and key sets.

This configuration offers substantial cost benefits to the IP telephony user. First, the long distance toll network is avoided. Second, the

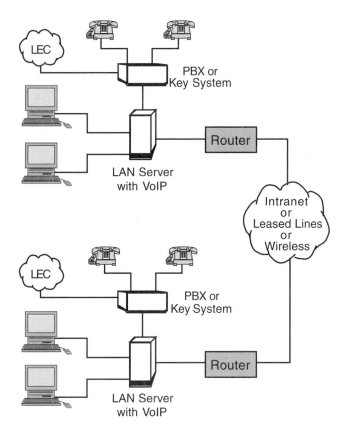

Figure 1–7   VoIP configurations through a private network

integration of voice and data can occur with servers and routers for bandwidth consolidation. Third, the use of these components obviates the installation of potentially expensive voice components such as channel banks. Fourth, the approach provides high-quality voice signals, just as good as those of the plain old telephone service (POTS).

Companies that have opted for this approach are saving money and finding that the careful selection of a VoIP gateway vendor can result in toll-quality voice traffic in the network. These enterprises are also deploying company call centers, using the VoIP technology. For example, in Figure 1–7, the top part of the configuration might be a remote office that is connected to the call center, shown at the bottom part of the figure.

This type of network is often called a virtual private network (VPN). The idea is to provide service to the customer such that the customer perceives that the service is coming from a private network, one tailored to the customer's needs, when in fact the network is used by many other customers.[5]

PRIVATE INTERNET AND PUBLIC INTERNET CONFIGURATIONS

In some situations, VoIP is implemented by internetworking the public Internet with private networks (internets), as shown in Figure 1–8. I use this configuration quite often in my day-to-day work in which I multicast lectures to my students. A VoIP server residing in a private network receives my speech and multicasts it to my students, who are logged on to this private network, other private networks, or the Internet. I can dial in to the multiconference server from anywhere in the world through my ISP and the public Internet. The server (and the software in the PCs of the conference attendees) allows an interactive dialogue between my students and me.

This dialogue is controlled from my end. When a student (say, Mary) wants to ask a question or make a point, she clicks on a "raise hand" icon on her PC. This results in the sending of a message through the server to my PC, where my screen shows that a student has a question. The name and location of the student are provided as well. I can then grant this student permission to speak by clicking on a microphone icon next to her name. I say something like "OK, we have a question from Mary in Lon-

---

[5]A VPN displays other attributes, such as security, IP address assignments, and QOS features.

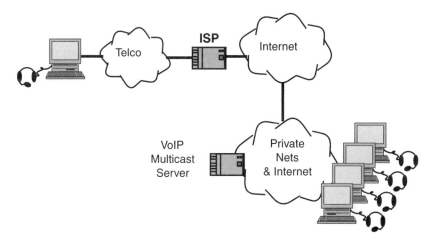

Figure 1–8   Private and public VoIP configuration

don. Go ahead Mary, I have granted you the mike." All conference attendees can hear Mary's question and my response.

Additionally, I can show slides, draw pictures, use chat rooms, give
the "podium" to a student, set up breakout rooms, share spreadsheets, or
bring up a Web site during my presentation.

Some students are shy, and reluctant to ask questions. In that case,
they can use a private chat room where no one sees their question but
me. In return, I respond by simply saying, "One of our private chat partners has this question. . . ."

It is a very powerful communications tool. I like it because I do not
have to get on an airplane to reach my students; well, not entirely true. The
airline trip might take me to Vail or St.Thomas, from where I can multicast
my lecture to any location in the world that has an Internet connection.

I don't like one aspect of this technology: I cannot see my students,
and my students cannot see me. But that will change. As more bandwidth is made available at the local loops, I will add real-time video to
my lectures. The software already supports video, but the local loops do
not have the capacity for its use.

THE NEXT STEP

VoIP is proving to be effective in private enterprises. The technology is
still in its infancy, and as it grows, it will require a rethinking of the traditional role of channel banks, PBXs, key systems, data service units

(DSUs), and even Centrex. As you are reading this paragraph, several Internet task forces are developing standards that provide the interworking of the traditional telco technology with the IP platform, and vendors are already writing the code and building the hardware for these systems. A general view of these systems is provided in Figure 1–9, and the systems are described in more detail in later chapters.

The key components to this operation are the VoIP Gateway and the VoIP Call Agent, also called a Gatekeeper, and a Controller. We use the initials (CAG) to identify these terms, since all three are used extensively. The Gateway is responsible for the connection of the VoIP devices (on the left side of the figure) to the networks (on the right side). The Gateway is also responsible for signal conversions between the systems. For example, a 64-kbit/s digital voice image coming from the telephone network might be translated into a low-bit 8-kbit/s voice image for transfer to a personal computer on a LAN, and vice versa.

The overall controller of the system is the CAG. Indeed, the Gateway is a slave to the master CAG and does not do much until the CAG gives the orders. For example, the CAG might direct the Gateway to

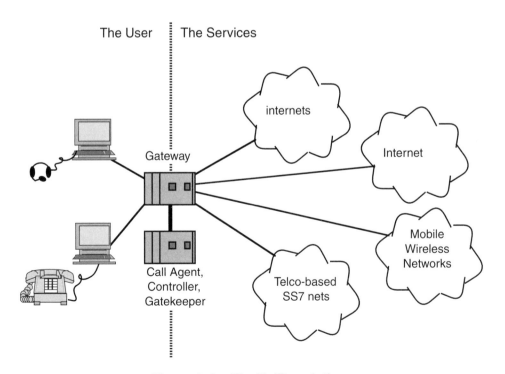

Figure 1–9   The VoIP evolution

monitor a particular interface for off-hook, and then instruct the Gateway how to collect the dialed digits, and then how to forward the call to the next node.

To follow up immediately and examine more information on this subject, refer to Chapter 10. For now, we must leave the subject of configuration options to later discussions and turn our attention to an emerging technology called electronic commerce (E-com)[6] and the way in which VoIP with IP-based call centers are being deployed to support E-com.

E-COM AND IP-BASED CALL CENTERS

E-com is the use of computer networks to support financial transactions. Common examples are on-line shopping, electronic funds transfer (EFT), commercial videoconferencing, and airline/car rental reservations. Companies like Amazon.com and e*Trade are examples of E-com enterprises.

Many companies are experiencing large increases in their Web site inquiries. Even though the inquiry may not result in a specific financial transaction at that time, it is known to enhance the company's marketing position. Figure 1–10 reflects a study conducted by the International Data Corporation (IDC) of the growth of software implementations for email and Web response applications [POLE98].

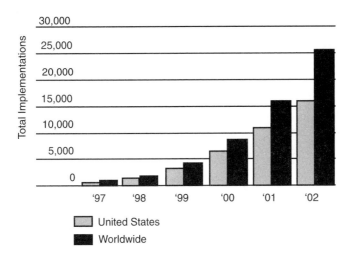

Figure 1–10   Email and Web response software implementations [POLE99]

---

[6]Most publications refer to electronic commerce as e-Commerce or eCommerce.

But we should make clear that setting up E-com in a company is a big job. It requires all the resources of a conventional commercial endeavor (such as catalog shopping), plus the ability to integrate on-line, real-time interfaces with the customer. Those industries that do it routinely (the airline, for example) are exceptions. Most companies will require major changes to their culture and infrastructure in order to move to E-com. Moreover, many companies using E-Com are not yet turning a profit.

We learned earlier that some companies have already migrated to IP-based call centers. The call centers are not using the public Internet; it is too slow and unreliable. Their approach is to use private intranets and/or leased lines to support VoIP. Private VoIP networks are proving

(a) On-line Households in United States

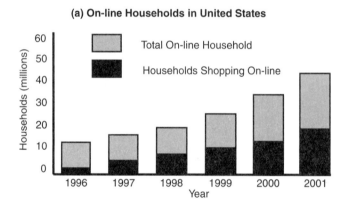

(b) Percentage of Households Buying On-line

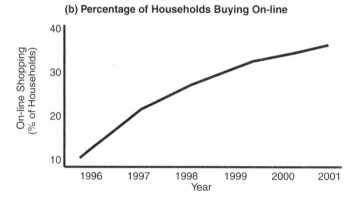

Figure 1–11   On-line shopping [RAPP98]

to be cost effective. At the same time, they provide high-quality voice signals.

In addition to IP-based call centers, many companies are betting that on-line shopping will be as big a success as catalog shopping. If so, the revenue for on-line shopping will be very high. Without question, the potential market for on-line shoppers is big and still growing. Prudential Securities has published a study of the number of the number of households in the United States that are, and will be shopping online [RAPP98]. Figure 1–11 summarizes some of the findings of Prudential Securities, which indicates a substantial growth in the online shopping industry.

At this point in this evolving marketplace, no one really knows how big the market will be for E-com and on-line shopping. Most agree that it will be a big market. There is less ambiguity about the role of VoIP-based call centers. As I stated, they are already proving to be a big success. We discussed this system earlier in this chapter (see Figure 1–7).

CONFIGURATION AND TOPOLOGY CHOICES

Let us return to the subject of the supporting technologies for VoIP. Figure 1–12 shows some of the technology choices to answer the how question. It is unlikely that IP telephony will operate over a single bearer service. Moreover, as the Internet task forces continue to refine multiservice Request for Comments (RFCs), it is also unlikely that only one teleservices protocol stack will be used.[7] A more likely scenario is the existence of a multiplicity of support options. Here are some examples:

- VoIP over PPP over twisted pair
- VoIP over PPP over SONET
- VoIP over Fast or Gigabit Ethernet
- VoIP over AAL1/AAL2/AAL5 over ATM over SONET
- VoIP over Frame Relay
- VoIP over FDDI
- VoIP over RTP over UDP, then over IP, and layers 2 and 1

---

[7]For the uninitiated reader, the term bearer service refers to the lower three layers of the OSI Model, and the term teleservices refers to the upper four layers of the Model. And bearer channels refer to user channels (in contrast to signaling channels).

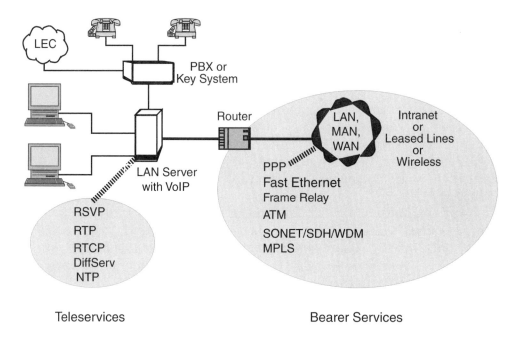

Figure 1–12   Technology choices to support VoIP

We could go on, for there are other choices and combinations. The purpose of this discussion is to emphasize that different bearer and teleservices products will be available to meet diverse customer requirements. Later chapters provide overviews of some of these technologies, but the main emphasis in this book is VoIP itself. Other books in this series are dedicated to the detailed discussion of these supporting technologies.

BASIC TERMS AND CONCEPTS

Some of the readers of this book are familiar with the Internet and others are not. I use the next part of this chapter to provide a tutorial on some basic Internet terms and concepts. The experienced reader can skip to the section titled "Evaluating the Factors in Packetized Voice."

The Internet is an association of thousands of user computers that communicate with each other through networks. These user computers are called "hosts." The networks are connected together through another machine that relays the host computer traffic between user applications (such as email and file transfer) that are running on the hosts. In Internet parlance, the term *router* describes the machine that performs the re-

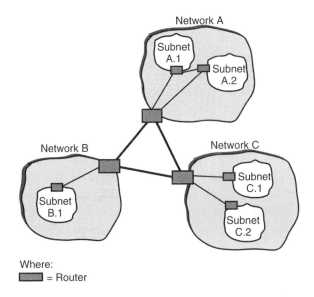

Where:
■ = Router

Figure 1–13   Internetworking and internets

laying functions between networks. Figure 1–13 shows a router placed
between networks A, B, and C. The routers are said to be *internetworking* machines, since they connect networks together.

Networks are often grouped together, and the individual networks
are called subnetworks. They are full networks unto themselves, but the
idea allows a set of subnetworks (subnets) to be associated with one organization or some type of administrative domain, such as an Internet service provider (ISP). The organization can identify each network with a
subnet identifier (ID) and can group these IDs (networks) together (or
treat them separately). The grouping concept is called address aggregation. In Figure 1–13, Subnets A.1 and A.2 can be collectively identified
with address A.

This approach is useful because, like the telephone system approach, it allows the Internet components to be identified with a hierarchical address. For example, in a telephone system, you can reach
someone by dialing first an area code, then an exchange number, and
then a subscriber number. In the Internet, addresses are managed by a
form of hierarchical aggregation called address prefixes.[8]

---

[8]The concept of a network address in the Internet is based on the use of class-based
IP addresses. With prefixing, address classes are no longer important. For more information, see [BLAC98].

An internetworking router is designed to remain transparent to the end-user application. Since the end-user application resides in the host computer, the router need not burden itself with application protocols and can dedicate itself to fewer tasks, such as managing the traffic between networks.

ATTRIBUTES OF THE INTERNET

The Internet was developed to support the transfer of data traffic (packets) between computers and workstations with the use of adaptive routing features; see Table 1–2.

Adaptive routing means the traffic can take different routes through the Internet depending on network conditions such as congestion, a failed link, etc., at a specific time. The possible result of adaptive routing is that the destination user may receive the packets out of order. An Internet protocol (the Transmission Control Protocol, TCP) at the receiver can be used to reorder the packets into the proper sequence. The other possible result of adaptive routing is that the arrival rate of the packets at the receiver may vary; some packets may arrive with little delay, whereas others take longer.

The Internet is designed as a connectionless system. This means that no "affiliations" are established between the machines in the Internet. As a result, the Internet does not maintain an ongoing knowledge of the user's traffic and does not build a fixed path between the switches from the source to the destination host machines. In effect, Internet Protocol (IP) traffic routing is stateless; that is, it does not build tables to maintain information about a connection because there is no connection.

The connectionless aspect of the Internet goes hand in hand with the adaptive routing concept. But in the telephone network, the opposite architecture is employed: connection-oriented fixed paths between the calling and called parties. The telephony approach is needed to support

Table 1–2   Attributes of the Internet

Attribute	Consequence(s)
Data applications	Not "tuned" for voice or video
Adaptive routing	Path may vary during traffic transfer, and packets may arrive out of order
Connectionless	Circuits are not set up between users
"Best effort" delivery service	Traffic discarded if problems occur

the real-time, nonvarying delay requirements of speech. The Internet, on the other hand, is a data network, and most data applications do not require the real-time transport service.

The Internet is a "best effort" delivery network. The term best effort means that the Internet will attempt to deliver the traffic, but if problems occur (damaged bits due to noise, congestion at a router, etc.) or the destination host cannot be found, the traffic is discarded. In most instances, TCP in the originating machine can resend the lost or damaged packets.

Internet Attributes with Respect to Voice Traffic

It is evident from this brief examination of the Internet and our previous discussions about the requirements for toll-quality voice that the Internet is not a particularly good choice for the transport of voice traffic. However, this is a moot point, since it is the anointed technology for packetized voice. And as stated before, the Internet will eventually evolve to support toll-quality voice.

THE INTERNET LAYERED ARCHITECTURE

Many of the concepts in this book are explained with the layered protocol concept. This section provides a brief review of the Internet layers, and Chapter 2 gives more detailed information. Figure 1–14 provides a review of the Internet protocol suite layers.

With some exceptions, the Open Systems Interconnection (OSI) Model layer 6 is not used. Layer 5 is not used at all.

The physical and data link layers are (as a general rule) also not defined. The philosophy is to rely on existing physical and data link systems. One notable exception to this practice is at the data link layer, where the Internet task forces have defined the Point-to-Point Protocol (PPP).

For the newcomer, here is a summary of the functions of the layers:

- *Physical layer:* Defines the media and physical aspects of the signals (voltages, etc.). Defines clocking and synchronization operations. Defines physical connectors. Also identified as layer 1 or L_1. Examples are T1, E1, SONET, and L_1 of Ethernet.
- *Data link layer:* Supports the transfer of traffic over one link. Might perform error detection and retransmission, depending on

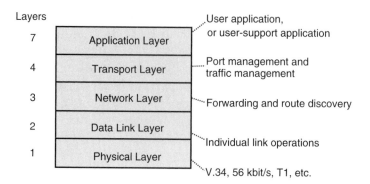

Figure 1–14   The Internet Protocol suite layers

the specific link layer protocol. Also identified as layer 2 or L_2. Examples are PPP, LAPD, and L_2 of Ethernet.

- *Network layer:* Performs forwarding operations and route discovery. Supports some limited diagnostic functions, such as status reports. Also identified as layer 3, or L_3. An example of forwarding is IP. An example of route discovery is Open Shortest Path First (OSPF).

- *Transport layer:* Supports end-to-end acknowledgment of traffic as an option. Supports the identification (with a port number) of the layer 7 protocol to be invoked to support incoming traffic. Also identified as layer 4 or L_4. Examples are TCP and UDP.

- *Application layer:* Contains the end-user application or another application that directly supports the end-user application. Also identified as layer 7 or L_7. Examples are file transfer and email.

EVALUATING THE FACTORS IN PACKETIZED VOICE

Now that we have a general understanding of the Internet attributes and the Internet protocol suite, it is appropriate to evaluate how to place speech traffic on an internet or any data network. The VoIP designer must evaluate three key factors: packet time, bandwidth requirements, and computational effort.

Packet time deals with two performance operations. The first operation deals with the length of time to send the VoIP traffic from the sender to the receiver. The second is the variation in time of the arrival of the successive packets at the receiver. This interrarrival time is called *jitter*.

For the first factor, if the packet is delayed excessively, its arrival will be too late for use by the codec; after all, voice conversations are real time and cannot tolerate the long delays in the delivery of the VoIP packets. Jitter is also important because the VoIP conversing parties do not talk in spurts, where one word or syllable is uttered, then a variable pause occurs, then another, and another, and so on. As far as possible, it is desirable to feed the receiving codec (and the receiving listener) nonjittered traffic, resulting in a smooth continuous flow of speech.

The second factor deals with how much bandwidth is required to support the transmission. The bandwidth calculation must factor in the bits required to represent the speech signal as well as the overhead headers (protocol control information) that support the signals. All told, they add significant overhead to the voice packet, and until we have all the bandwidth we need (if we ever do), this protocol control information is a big drain on the bandwidth bucket.

The third factor is the computational effort needed to support the coding, transport, and decoding of the speech images in each machine in the network. The term computational effort refers to the expense and complexity involved in supporting the audio application. In simple terms, it refers to the millions of instructions per second (MIPS) required to support the operation, as well as the amount of memory needed; that is, the complexity and expense of the voice coder/decoder (codec).

As examples of computational efficiency, a conventional 64-kbit/s voice signal can be produced in a high-quality manner by the use of a 2-MIPS machine. If an 8–10 MIPS machine is employed, the signal can be reduced to 16 kbit/s. Furthermore, a 15–to-20 MIPS machine can produce a high-quality signal of 8 kbit/s. Currently, the ITU-T is examining a standard for a 4 kbit/s machine that is expected to require 40–45 MIPS.

ACCOMMODATING THE VOICE AND DATA REQUIREMENTS IN A NETWORK

In "Barriers to Successful Deployment of IP Telephony," I made some general comments on the difficulty of supporting speech traffic in the Internet. This section provides more information in the context of how the requirements for voice and video traffic differ.

Tolerance for Errors

Voice transmissions exhibit a high tolerance for errors. If an occasional voice packet is distorted, the fidelity of the voice reproduction is not severely affected. In contrast, data packets have a low tolerance for errors; one corrupted bit is likely to change the meaning of the data. Furthermore, voice packets can afford (on occasion) to be lost or discarded. In the event of excessive delays in the network, the packets may be discarded because they are of no use if they arrive at the receiver too late. Again, the loss does not severely affect voice fidelity if the lost packets are less than approximately 5% of the total packets transmitted. As discussed before, data packets can ill afford to be lost or discarded.

Tolerance for Delay

Yet another difference between voice and data transmissions deals with network delay. For packetized voice to be translated back to an analog signal in a real-time mode, the two-way delay for voice packets must be constant and generally must be low—usually less than 300 ms. Why is low delay important? If it takes a long time for the voice packets to be sent from the speaker (person A) to the listener (person B), when speaker A stops talking, receiver B is still receiving the speech packets. Person B cannot start talking until all the speech signals have arrived. In the meantime, person A hears nothing for a while.

The two-way delay measures how long it takes (a) for A's speech to reach B, (b) for B to hear the speech, (c) for B to talk back, and (d) for A to hear B's response. If the delay becomes long (say, over 400 or 500 ms), the conversation appears phony, almost like a half-duplex connection where the two people are taking turns talking, but waiting awhile before taking the turn. All in all, delay can be quite annoying.

For data packets, the network delay can vary considerably. Indeed, the packets can be transmitted asynchronously through the network, without regard to timing arrangements between the sender and the receiver.

Tolerance for Delay and the Effects on Queues.

Voice packets require a short queue length at the network nodes to reduce delay, or at least to make the delay more predictable. The short voice-packet queue lengths can experience overflow occasionally, with resulting packet loss. However, data packets require longer queue lengths to prevent packet loss in overflow conditions.

Tolerance for Variable Bit Rates and Constant Bit Rates

A useful method to describe the nature of applications traffic is through two concepts known as *variable bit rate* (VBR) and *constant bit rate* (CBR). An application using VBR schemes does not require a constant and continuous allocation of bandwidth. These applications are said to be *bursty,* which means they transmit and receive traffic asynchronously (at any time with periods in which nothing is sent or received). Examples of VBR applications are almost any type of data communications process.

These applications permit the queuing of traffic in a variable manner from the standpoint of time, and they do not require a fixed timing relationship between the sender and the receiver. Therefore, if traffic is sent from the sender and is buffered (queued) for variable periods of time, the receiver is not disturbed. Typical applications using VBR techniques are interactive terminal-to-terminal dialogues, inquiry/response operations, client-server systems, and bulk data transfer operations.

In contrast, an application using CBR schemes requires constant and continuous (or nearly so) allocation of bandwidth. These applications are said to be nonbursty. The term nonbursty has to be used carefully with these applications because some of the applications will tolerate a certain amount of burstyness.

Typical CBR-based applications are voice transmissions. These applications require guaranteed bandwidth and a constant and near-continuous timing relationship between the sending and receiving devices. They also require a predictable delay between the sender and the receiver.

Packetized Voice: It's VBR Traffic. Interestingly, packetized voice is classified as VBR traffic, not a CBR-based telephony network, because it is transported over a VBR-based data network. So, the challenge is to receive the data network's bursty voice packets at the receiver and smooth the VBR behavior to that of CBR, and in that way permit conventional CBR digital-to-analog operations to take place.

Examples of Voice, Video, and Data Applications Requirements

The need to support multiapplication traffic requires the Internet to extend its capabilities far beyond what it can do now. It must support the diverse needs of different types of traffic. As examples, Tables 1–3, 1–4, and 1–5 show the performance requirements for several audio, video, and data applications [RADI94]. Tables 1–3 and 1–4 show the mean opinion scores (MOS) for the technologies. A MOS is a rating system devised by

Table 1–3   Audio bandwidth and MOS performance applications [RADI94]

Coders	Uncompressed bit rates in kbit/s	Transmission mode	Expected in kbits** Peak	Average	MOS
CD audio (propri- etary algorithm)	1411.4–1536	CBR	192	192	*
		VBR	384	192	*
FM stereo audio	1024–1536	CBR	128	128	*
Wideband audio (G.722)	128	CBR	64/ 56/ 48	64/ 56/ 48	*
PCM audio (μ-law, G.711)	64	CBR	64	64	4.3
		VBR	64	32–21	*
ADPCM audio (G.721)	64	CBR	32	32	4.1
LD-CELP audio (G.728)	64	CBR	16	16	4.1

* Expected MOS may be between 4 and 4.5 but is yet to be supported by published results
** Some of the bit rates are compressed

the telephone industry to assess the customer's satisfaction with a service. A MOS of 3.5 is considered to be fair-to-good. A MOS of over 4 is considered to be very good.

Table 1–3 shows several audio applications and the ITU-T G Series Recommendations that use devices to code and decode the analog signals to and from digital images. These devices are called coders, vocoders, or

Table 1–4   Video bandwidth and performance for VBR codecs [RADI94]

Video quality, coding resolution, and format	Transmission mode	Encoder- decoder delay in frames**	Compressed video bit rate/s kbit/s* Peak	Mean	MOS*
Low rate video- conferencing quality	VBR with negligible buffer	0	2562	239.6	4.5–5.0
360 × 288 pixels non- interlaced 4:1:1, 8 bits/sample 30 Hz, p × 64 or MPEG-1 standards	VBR with buffer	1	1400	239.6	4.0–4.5
		2	934	239.6	3.5–4.5
		3	847	239.6	3.5–4.5
		4	822	239.6	3.5–4.5

* Estimated
** Delay increases with the increase in buffer size (one frame delay = 33 ms)

Table 1–5 Bit rates required for data [RADI94]

Data (text, still images, graphics) object size	Uncompressed object size in Mbit/s	Typical compression ratio	Retrieval & transfer of object *	Document browsing *	Retrieval and transfer**		Document browsing**	
					Uncompressed	Compressed	Uncompressed	Compressed
ASCII text, 8.5" × 11" page, (88 char/line × 55 lines × 8 bits/char)	0.029	2–4	2	0.5	0.015	0.008–0.004	0.059	0.029–0.015
8.5" × 11" color page (200 pixels/inch × 24 bits/pixel)	90	10–20	2	0.5	45	4.5–2.3	180	18–9
Medium resolution, 8.5" × 11" color page (400 pixels/inch × 24 bits/pixel)	359	10–20	2	0.5	180	18–9	700	70–35
High resolution, 8.5" × 11" color page (400 pixels/inch × 24 bits/pixel)	1436	10–20	2	0.5	718	72–36	2,872	287–144
Graphics quality, (1600 pixels/inch × 24 bits/pixel)	5744	10–20	2	0.5	2872	287–144	11,488	1152–575

* Typical response time in seconds
** Peak bandwidth requirements in Mbit/s

codecs. The MOS ratings are acceptable, but there is one significant problem: the bit rates are high. The G.722, G.711, G.721, and G.728 coders are not efficient in this regard. Chapter 3 describes other coders that are more efficient.

Table 1–4 shows some MOSs for video systems. Notice the requirements for large bandwidth (kbit/s) needed to obtain an acceptable MOS.

Finally, Table 1–5 shows the bandwidth requirements for several data applications. Once again, it is obvious that the support of high-quality images requires considerable capacity. Moreover, for interactive browsing, the network must provide fast response times.

MAKING THE INTERNET LOOK LIKE THE TELEPHONE NETWORK

It is clear from the AT&T study that application requirements vary, and these variances occur not just between voice, video, and data applications but within these applications as well.

We cannot simply say "The Internet (and a data network in general) should change to support voice, video, and data." Instead, we must say "The Internet should change to support different types of voice systems, different types of video systems, and different types of data systems."

In other words, the challenge is to make the Internet behave more like a telephone network and a CATV system, yet retain its characteristics to support data. And that is precisely what we will turn our attention to for the remainder of this book with regard to voice support.

SUMMARY

Data networks and the Internet were designed to support data traffic. The Internet success stems from its ease of use and its low cost to access and transport traffic. As the need for multiservice networks grows (networks that support voice, video and data), the need to "upgrade" the Internet becomes compelling, and parts of the multiservice architecture are being put in place today. The ultimate challenge is to change the Internet (and other data networks) from a data-only service to a multiservice architecture.

2

Characteristics of the Internet and IP

This chapter is divided into three sections. The first section explains the Internet architecture and the characteristics of the Internet; that is, how it "behaves" (or misbehaves) in the handling of user traffic. This section is a more detailed explanation of the generalized discussion in Chapter 1. The next section provides a brief overview of IP. The last section provides a brief overview of Internet ports and sockets and the major features of TCP and UDP.

The reader who is experienced with the Internet can skip the last two sections, but I recommend that all read this first section.

ARCHITECTURE OF THE INTERNET

The Internet is a complex collage of regional and national networks that are interconnected with routers. The communications links used by Internet service providers (ISPs) are lines leased from the telephone system, such as DS3, and SONET/SDH lines. Other lines are provided by competitive access providers (CAPs), and still others are provided by private carriers, such as private microwave and satellite operators.

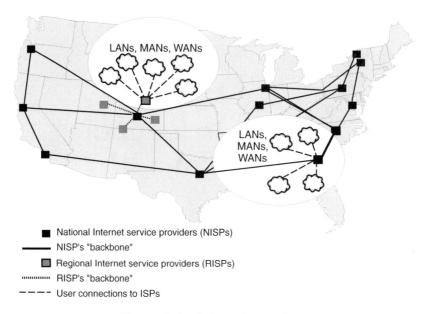

Figure 2–1   Internet overview

The Internet connections and the many ISPs are impossible to depict in one illustration, but Figure 2–1 provides an accurate view of the basic structure of the Internet topology.

ISPs AND THE TELEPHONE NETWORK

The Internet service providers (ISPs) provide the customer's access to the Internet. They provide this access through the telephone network, and the Internet user (say, from the home) uses a dial-up or DSL modem to connect to the ISP through the telco local exchange carrier (LEC), and the LEC Central Office (CO); see Figure 2–2.

Alternatively, the user might connect to the Internet through a mobile phone or through the CATV service provider. Plain old dial-up is the prevalent method in use today.

The telephone companies are required to provide the ISPs with connections to the telephone company's customers. The connections are provided at the telco's plant. These connections from the customer to the CO's main distribution frame (MDF, a physical "patch panel") can be

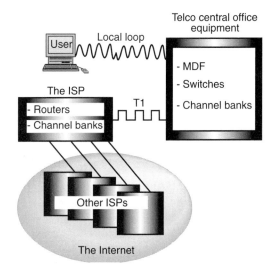

Figure 2–2   Typical telco and Internet service provider (ISP) setup

patched to the local switch (a conventional circuit switch, for example). Alternatively, the line from the customer can be patched to a digital cross-connect (DCS) machine, which is a software-based component that can support leased lines—in this example, leased lines to the ISP.

The trunk connections from the CO to the ISP are at an agreed-upon point of presence (POP), say, at the CO's site. On the trunk side, the signals are of the T1 family or SONET family.

ATTRIBUTES OF THE INTERNET

Before we begin an analysis of IP, TCP, UDP, let's examine in more detail the major attributes of the Internet, introduced in Chapter 1.

As we learned, the Internet was developed for the transfer of data traffic with the use of adaptive routing features. The Internet Protocol (IP) is stateless; that is, it does not build tables to maintain information about a connection because there is no connection.

The Internet is a "best effort" delivery network. The term best effort means that the Internet will attempt to deliver the traffic (it will do its best), but if problems occur, it will discard the traffic.

Finally, the Internet supports either unicasting (one-to-one) or multicasting (one-to-many) operations. The multicasting feature has proved to be a very useful tool for conference calling as well as for the downloading of software or data to multiple sites.

Round-Trip Time (RTT)

Round-trip time (RTT) is a measure of the time it takes to send a packet to a destination node and receive a reply from that node. RTT includes the transmission time in both directions and the processing time at the destination node.

Most RTTs on the Internet are within the range of 70–160 ms, although large variations of RTT do occur. Because of the asynchronous nature of the Internet, RTT is not consistent. During periods when there is a lot of traffic on the Internet, the RTT may exceed 300 ms.

The ITU-T G.114 Recommendation limits RTT to 300 ms or less for telephone traffic. This performance factor is based on many studies and observations, which have shown that longer delays in a telephone-based conversation give the impression to the conversationalists that they are using a half-duplex circuit.

PACKET LOSS

Another Internet characteristic that is important to voice and video applications is packet loss. Two factors are involved: how often packet loss occurs and how many successive (contiguous) packets are affected. Packet loss is masked in a data application by use of TCP to resend the lost TCP segments. Certainly, the loss of many segments and their retransmissions will affect the application's performance, but on the whole, the end-user data application is not concerned with (or aware of) packet loss.

Packet loss is quite important in voice and video applications, since the loss may affect the outcome of the decoding process at the receiver and may also be detected by the end-user's ears or eyes. Notwithstanding, today's codecs can produce high-quality voice signals in the face of about 5% loss of the voice packets (G.723.1 is the example) *if* the packet losses are random and independent. G.723.1 compensates for this loss by using the previous packet to simulate the characteristics of the vocal signal that was in the lost packet.

Traffic loss on the Internet is bursty: large packet losses occur in a small number of bursts. This characteristic of Internet behavior complicates the support of telephony because packetized voice works best if the packet loss is random and independent.

The effect of packet loss can be alleviated somewhat by the use of forward error correction (FEC) schemes, and methods have been devised to compensate for loss bursts [BORE97]. These schemes add extra delay to the process and can result in the loss of the packet because it is made available to the user in a time domain that is too late to be useful.

One FEC approach borrows from the tried-and-true mobile wireless technology: repeat the signal more than once. With mobile wireless systems, this operation interleaves successive copies of the coded voice image across multiple packets (slots in the mobile wireless terminology). With Internet telephony, experiments are underway to send copies of the packet 1 to n times. If one copy is lost, say copy n, it can be recovered from the other copies. However, this operation is only effective if a copy arrives safely and, therefore, implies that one of the copies survives the burst error. If the copies are spaced too far in time to survive the error, they may arrive too late to be useful.

Order of Arrival of Packets

The subject of the order of the arrival of packets at the receiver is not of keen interest to the data application if it is supported by TCP, because TCP can reorder the TCP segments and present the traffic to the application in the correct order. TCP is not used for voice and video, so the order of packet arrival is an important subject to these applications. Several studies show that out-of-sequence arrival is not unusual.

Another factor to note is that Internet delays follow a diurnal cycle. During the hours of 8:00 a.m. to 6:00 p.m., delays are greater. For example, in the middle of the business day, delays are about 20 ms greater than in the late evenings.

Hop Distance

Hop distance is a term used to describe the number of hops (nodes, such as routers and servers) between a sender and a receiver. It is a critical aspect in internet telephony because more hops translate into increased delay and more jitter. Hop distance must consider round-trip time (RTT) because of the interactive, real-time nature of telephone conversations. Figure 2–3 shows several aspects of hop distance and RTT and their potentially deleterious effect on the quality of voice applications.

The traffic is to be sent from a host on Subnet 1 to a host on Subnet 2. The IP datagrams must be processed by both hosts as well as by all the routers (and servers) on the path between the hosts. Let us assume the traffic traverses through the fewest number of hops (a common approach), which means the datagrams are processed by seven routers, numbered Router 1 through Router 7 in the figure. Thus, the datagrams are sent through nine hops. If the routers are not heavily loaded with traffic, then the queuing delay will be short and the interarrival jitter at each router, while variable, will not create a major problem when the traffic arrives at the receiver. However, if traffic is heavy or if the routers are not performing their datagram forwarding operations efficiently, the delay and jitter will result in the inability of the receiver to reconstitute the real-time voice signal into a high-quality speech pattern.

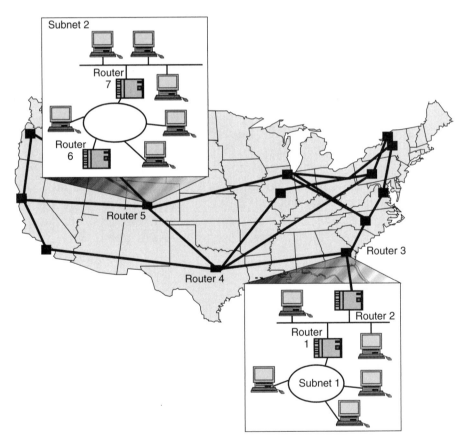

Figure 2–3   Hop distance and round-trip time (RTT)

Several studies also reveal that geographical distance cannot always be correlated to round-trip delay. In one study, a short distance of only 477 miles but with a hop count of 21, resulted in a 500-ms round-trip delay. To emphasize the point, hop distance is a key factor in delay, and geographical distance is less a factor (unless geosynchronous satellites are used, in which case round-trip delay is 240 ms just on the uplink and downlink to and from the satellite).

The telephone network does not have delay problems. First, the path between the talker and listener is fixed during the call setup. Second, the circuit switches do not queue the traffic. Rather, the voice channels are time-division-multiplexed into DS0 channels (TDM slots) and sent directly from the input interface on the switch to a corresponding DS0 slot on a preconfigured output interface. The delay through the voice switch is miniscule (it is not even a factor) and fixed.

Thus, circuit switches provide fixed paths, as well as very low, fixed delay. In contrast, packet switches, such as routers, provide variable paths and variable delay, which is sometimes a low delay and sometimes a lengthy delay.

NEED FOR FIXED ROUTING?

Given that fixed routing is a desirable feature for real-time, delay-sensitive traffic, one can ask: is it needed? That is, does an internet (or more precisely, the Internet) shuffle traffic around frequently, with the routers altering routes often? Studies conducted on the routing behavior of the Internet reveal that most of the traffic between two or more communicating parties remains on the same physical path during the session. In fact, route alteration is more an exception than the rule.

One study on Internet "routing persistence" is summarized in Table 2–1. This information represents a small part of the study that is available from [PAXS97].

Paxson defines routing persistence as the length of time a route endures before changing. Even though routing changes occur over a wide range of time, most of the routes in the Internet do not change much from moment to moment. If, however, an Internet user has a long session on the Net, there is a good chance that the user's traffic will not stay on the same path and might therefore arrive out of order.

A point should be emphasized in Paxson's study. The not-applicable (NA) entries in Table 2–1 represent situations in which frequent routing fluctuations do occur in parts of the Internet. While they are not a factor

Table 2–1   Routing persistence [PAXS97]

Time	% of Total	Comments
Seconds	NA	In load balancing
Minutes	NA	In tightly coupled routers
10's of minutes	9	Changes usually through different cities or autonomous systems
Hours	4	Usually intranetwork changes
6+ hours	19	Usually intranetwork changes
Days	68	(a) 50% of these routes persist for <7 days (b) Other 50% persist for >7 days

in the "big picture," if your traffic flows through that part of the Internet, it will be affected by these changes. The point to remember about this aspect of Internet behavior is that out-of-order arrivals of VoIP packets complicate the job of the codec's decoding operations and can lead to poor-quality speech reproduction.

SIZE OF PACKETS AND KINDS OF TRAFFIC IP SUPPORTS

We continue the analysis of the attributes of the Internet by examining the traffic characteristics relating to average size of the protocol data unit (packet); see Figure 2–4(a). The most common packet size is 40 bytes, which accounts for TCP acknowledgements (ACKs), finish messages (FINs), and reset messages (RSTs). Overall, the average packet sizes vary from 175 to about 400 bytes, and 90% of the packets are 576 bytes or smaller. Ten percent of the traffic is sent in 1500-byte sizes; this percentage reflects traffic from Ethernet-attached hosts.

The other common occurrences are packet sizes of 576 bytes (6% of the traffic) and 552 bytes (5% of the traffic). These sizes reflect common protocol data unit sizes used in the Internet protocols.

In Figure 2–4(b), the type of traffic carried by IP is shown. Almost all the traffic is TCP, followed by UDP, then ICMP. Other traffic encapsulated directly in IP accounts for very little of the Internet traffic.

The significance of these facts to VoIP is as follows. First, it is important to use small packets for voice traffic. If a packet is lost in the network, the small packet is less likely to contain significant parts of a

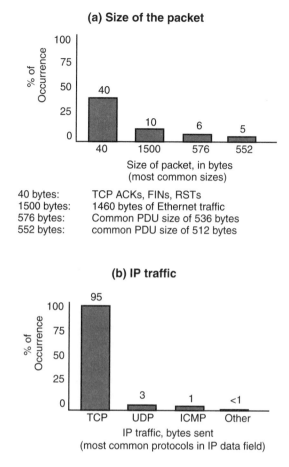

(a) Size of the packet

40 bytes: TCP ACKs, FINs, RSTs
1500 bytes: 1460 bytes of Ethernet traffic
576 bytes: Common PDU size of 536 bytes
552 bytes: common PDU size of 512 bytes

(b) IP traffic

Figure 2–4   Traffic characteristics of the Internet

speech signal. The idea is to divide and conquer. Most low-bit-rate codecs are designed to produce very short voice packets, usually no more than 10–30 ms in duration and 10–30 bytes (of voice traffic) in length.

The other reason for a small packet is that it permits the processing node, such as a router, to examine and operate on a small unit of information quickly: it does not have to wait long for the bits to propagate through the incoming interface. In contrast, a long packet means it takes awhile for the bits of the entire transmission to arrive and therefore to be processed.

The Internet has been calibrated to use relatively large packets. The fact that almost 50% of the packets transported on the Internet are only

40 bytes is not significant. Many of the packets are not for user traffic but for connection management operations for TCP.

If a substantial amount of Internet traffic becomes voice traffic, it will require a concomitant increase in Internet capacity because the smaller packets will consume significantly more of the overall bandwidth: the ratio of overhead to user payload will increase. Some people have expressed concerns about this situation, but I do not think it will be a major problem because the increased use of high-speed SONET links and the migration to wave division multiplexing (WDM) will provide the needed bandwidth.

A potentially bigger problem is the increased load on the routers in the Internet. After all, the router has to spend as much time processing the fixed-length header of a 10-byte packet as it does in processing a header of the same length for a 576-byte packet. One can ameliorate this situation by multiplexing multiple voice samples inside one packet, but taking care not to expand the overall packet size such that it succumbs to the large-packet problem described earlier. Chapter 12 provides more information on voice channel multiplexing.

Moreover, with the migration to high-speed gigabit routers using label switching, I believe the overall latency in the Internet will continue to improve.

Figure 2–4(b) points to another potential problem of supporting voice traffic on the Internet. The vast majority of user traffic is transported with the TCP header. As explained later in this chapter, TCP provides extensive support for traffic integrity operations: (a) error checks, (b) acknowledgments of traffic, (c) retransmissions of erroneous traffic, and (d) flow control.

But voice applications need not use TCP; in fact, they should not use it because the TCP support features introduces too much delay in the overall procedure and it is impractical to achieve real-time performance if some of the erroneous packets are retransmitted. The overall delay would be over 400–500 ms, clearly beyond the RTT that is acceptable for speech.

The potential problem is related to TCP flow-control mechanisms. One feature implemented in many TCP products is the ability of TCP to back off from sending traffic when the Internet is congested and experiencing poor RTT.

In this regard, TCP is a "courteous" protocol. It waits if necessary and does not intrude its presence (its packets) into a congested network. But UDP, on which VoIP operates, has no such qualms. It is a "discourteous" protocol in that is has no back-off mechanisms. It will continue to send traffic even if the network is congested.

So, if the network is congested, TCP stands by the door at the network and does not enter. Indeed, TCP opens the door, and UDP goes through it!

As seen in Figure 2–4(b), UDP accounts for only 3% of traffic that is placed directly in the IP datagram. However, if voice (and video) become heavy users of the Internet, then it is possible that the TCP users will experience degraded performance during periods of high activity of the real-time UDP traffic.

Well, I said it is a potential problem. If the Internet and internets are built with sufficient bandwidth, there will be no problem.

OVERVIEW OF IP

Scores of books are available that describe IP in detail. The approach here is to provide an overview of IP and to emphasize the aspects of IP that are especially important for the support of voice traffic. I recommend any of the Douglas Comer and Richard Stevens TCP/IP books to the newcomer.

IP is an example of a connectionless service. It permits the exchange of traffic between two host computers without any previous call setup. (However, these two computers can share a common connection-oriented transport protocol.) It is possible that the IP datagrams could be lost between the two end-user stations. For example, the IP node enforces a maximum queue length size, and if this queue length is violated, the queues will overflow. In this situation, the additional datagrams are discarded in the network. For this reason, a higher level transport layer protocol (such as TCP) is essential to recover from these problems.

IP hides the underlying subnetwork from the end user. In this context, it creates a virtual network to that end user. This aspect of IP is quite attractive because it allows different types of networks to attach to an IP node. As a result, IP is reasonably simple to install. And because of its connectionless design, it is quite robust.

Since IP is an unreliable, best-effort, datagram-type protocol, it has no retransmission mechanisms. It provides no error recovery for the underlying subnetworks. It has no flow-control mechanisms. The user data (datagrams) can be lost, duplicated, or even arrive out of order. It is not the job of IP to deal with most of these problems. As we shall see later, most of the problems are passed to the next higher layer, TCP.

These low-level characteristics of IP translate into a fairly effective means of supporting real-time voice traffic. Assuming the routers are

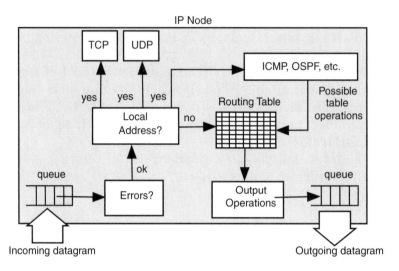

Figure 2–5 Processing an IP datagram [STEVb98]

fast and sufficient bandwidth is available, IP does not introduce significant overhead to the support of VoIP. There are better mechanisms, but as stated in Chapter 1, no other mechanism has the universal presence of IP (and the IP addresses).

Figure 2–5 shows how IP processes an incoming IP datagram [STEVb98].[1]

The incoming packet is stored in a queue to await processing. Once processing begins, the options field is processed to determine if any options are in the header (the support for this operation varies). The datagram header is checked for any modifications that may have occurred during its journey to this IP node (with a checksum field, discussed later). Next, it is determined whether the IP address is local; if so, the IP protocol ID field in the header is used to pass the bits in the data field to the next module, such as TCP, UDP, or ICMP.

An IP node can be configured to forward or not forward datagrams. If the node is a forwarding node, the IP destination address in the IP datagram header is matched against a routing table to calculate the next node (next hop) that is to receive the datagram. If a match in the table to

---

[1] I have added the error check operation, which is not in Mr. Steven's figure on page 112 of his book.

the destination address is found, the datagram is forwarded to the next node. Otherwise, it is sent to a default route or discarded.

Figure 2–6 is an example of a typical routing table found in a router. Individual systems differ in the contents of the routing table, but they all resemble this example.

The entries in the table are:

- *Destination:* IP address of the destination node.
- *Route Mask:* Mask that is used with destination address to identify bits that are used in routing. These parts of the IP address are called the address prefix.
- *Next Hop:* IP address of the next hop in the route.
- *If Index (port):* Physical port on the router to reach the next hop address. You may also know this physical port by the term INT, for interface.
- *Metric:* "Cost" to reach the destination address, such as number of hops, one-way delay, etc.
- *Route Type:* Whether the route is directly attached to router (direct) or reached through another router (remote).
- *Source of Route:* How the route was discovered.
- *Route Age:* Time, in seconds, since the route was last updated.
- *Route Information:* Miscellaneous information.

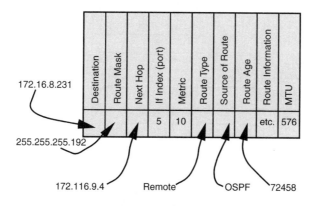

Figure 2–6   Typical IP routing table

The IP Datagram

A productive approach to the analysis of IP is to examine the fields in the IP datagram (PDU) depicted in Figure 2–7.

The *version* field identifies the version of IP in use. Most protocols contain this field because some network nodes may not have the latest release of the protocol. The current version of IP is 4.

The *header length* field contains four bits, which are set to a value to indicate the length of the datagram header. The length is measured in 32-bit words. Typically, a header contains 20 bytes. Therefore, the value in the length field is usually 5.

The *type of service (TOS)* field can be used to identify several QOS functions provided for an Internet application. Transit delay, throughput, precedence, and reliability can be requested with this field.

The TOS field contains five entries consisting of 8 bits. Three bits of the TOS field contain a *precedence* value, which indicates the relative importance of the datagram. Values range from 0 to 7, with 7 as the highest precedence and 0 set to indicate a *routine precedence.* The precedence field can be used to implement flow-control and congestion mechanisms in a network. These mechanisms would enable routers, servers, and host nodes to make decisions about the order of discarding datagrams in case of congestion. Chapter 8 provides considerable information on the use of the precedence bits in VoIP operations.

The *total length* field specifies the total length of the IP datagram. It is measured in bytes and includes the length of the header and the data.

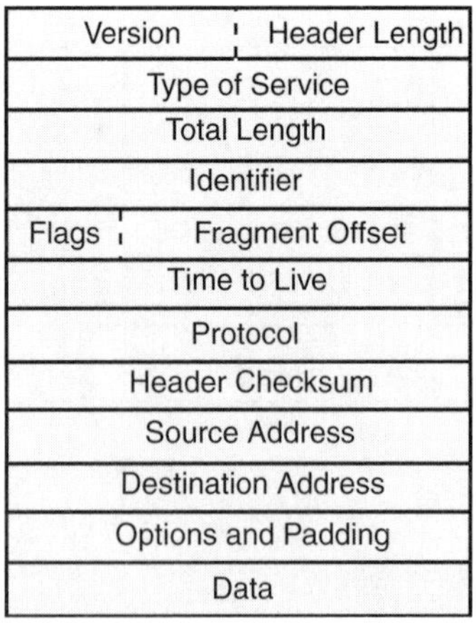

Version	Header Length
Type of Service	
Total Length	
Identifier	
Flags	Fragment Offset
Time to Live	
Protocol	
Header Checksum	
Source Address	
Destination Address	
Options and Padding	
Data	

Figure 2–7   The IP datagram

IP subtracts the header length field from the total length field to compute the size of the data field. The maximum possible length of a datagram is 65,535 bytes (2^{16}). Nodes that service IP datagrams are required to accept any datagram that supports the maximum size of a PDU of the attached networks. Additionally, all nodes must accommodate datagrams of 576 bytes in total length.

Each 32-bit value is transmitted in this order: (a) bits 0–7, (b) bits 8–15, (c) bits 16–23, and (d) bits 24–31. This is known as big-endian byte ordering.

The IP protocol uses three fields in the header to control datagram fragmentation and reassembly. These fields are the *identifier, flags,* and *fragmentation offset.* The identifier field uniquely identifies all fragments from an original datagram. It is used with the source address at the receiving host to identify the fragment. The flags field contains bits to determine if the datagram can be fragmented, and if the datagram is fragmented, one of the bits can be set to determine if this fragment is the last fragment of the datagram. The fragmentation offset field contains a value that specifies the relative position of the fragment to the original datagram. The value is initialized as 0 and is subsequently set to the proper number if an IP node fragments the data. The value is measured in units of eight bytes.

The *time-to-live (TTL)* parameter measures the number of hops the IP datagram has traversed in the Internet. Its value is set at the sender and decremented (by 1) by each processing node. Each node is required to check this field and discard the datagram if the TTL value equals 0.

The *protocol* field identifies the next-level protocol above the IP that is to receive the datagram at the final host destination. It is similar to the Ethertype field found in the Ethernet frame but identifies the payload in the data field of the IP datagram. The Internet standards groups have established a numbering system to identify the most widely used upper layer protocols.

The *header checksum* is used to detect an error that may have occurred in the header. Checks are not performed on the user data stream. The checksum is computed as follows (and this same procedure is used in TCP, UDP, ICMP, and IGMP):

- Set checksum field to 0.
- Calculate 16-bit one's complement sum of the header (header is treated as a sequence of 16-bit words).
- Store 16-bit one's complement in the checksum field.

- At receiver, calculate 16-bit one's complement of the header.
- Receiver's checksum is all 1's if the header has not been changed.

IP carries two addresses in the datagram. These are labeled *source* and *destination addresses* and retain the same value throughout the life of the datagram. These fields contain the Internet addresses.

The *options* field identifies several additional services.[2] It is similar to the option part field of CLNP. The options field is not used in every datagram. The majority of implementations use this field for network management and diagnostics.

TRANSMISSION CONTROL PROTOCOL AND USER DATAGRAM PROTOCOL

Figure 1–14 in Chapter 1 shows that layer four of the OSI Model is the Transport layer. Layer four is where Transmission Control Protocol (TCP) and the User Datagram Protocol (UDP) operate.

UDP does not provide sequencing or acknowledgments. UDP is used in place of TCP in situations where the full services of TCP are not needed. For example, telephony traffic, the Trivial File Transfer Protocol (TFTP), and the remote procedure call (RPC) use UDP. Since it has no reliability, flow control, or error-recovery measures, UDP serves principally as a multiplexer/demultiplexer for the receiving and sending of traffic into and out of an application.

TCP resides in the transport layer of a conventional Internet layered model. It is situated above IP and below the upper layers. It is designed to reside in the host computer or in a machine that is tasked with end-to-end integrity of the transfer of user data. In practice, TCP is placed in the user host machine. TCP is also loaded into the router to enable the router to examine the TCP header and port numbers. This subject is discussed in the next section.

TCP is designed to run over the IP. Since IP is a best-effort protocol, the tasks of reliability, flow control, sequencing, opens, and closes are given to TCP. TCP and IP are tied together so closely that they are used in the same context, "TCP/IP." TCP can also support other protocols.

---

[2]The options field has fallen into disuse with routers because of the processing overhead required to support the features it identifies. The concepts of this field are well founded, and a similar capability is found in IPv6, the new IP version.

The Port Concept

One of the jobs of TCP and UDP is to act as the port manager for the user and application residing in layer seven (these operations are performed in concert with the operating system).

Figure 2–8 reinforces those thoughts once more. It shows how the traffic passes from TCP or UDP to the respective application.

A TCP upper layer user in a host machine is identified by a *port* identifier. The port number is concatenated with the IP Internet address to form a *socket*. This address must be unique throughout the Internet, and a pair of sockets uniquely identifies each end-point connection. As examples:

Sending socket = Source IP address + source port number

Destination socket = Destination IP address + destination port number

Although the mapping of ports to higher layer processes can be handled as an internal matter in a host, the Internet publishes numbers for frequently used higher level processes.

Even though TCP establishes numbers for frequently used ports, the numbers and values above 1024 are available for private use. The remainder of the values for the assigned port numbers have the low-order 8 bits set to zero. The remainder of these bits are available to organizations to use as they choose.

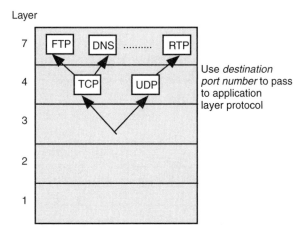

Figure 2–8   The port concept

TCP Traffic Management Operations

TCP acknowledges segments for both interactive traffic and bulk data traffic. However, TCP varies in how these acknowledgements occur. The variability depends on the operating system through which TCP executes, as well as the options chosen for a TCP session. In essence, there is no "standard" TCP operating profile.

Notwithstanding these comments, TCP does use many common procedures that are found in most TCP implementations and versions.

UDP

UDP serves as a simple application interface to the IP. Since it has no reliability, flow-control, or error-recovery measures, it serves principally as a multiplexer/demultiplexer for the receiving and sending of IP traffic.

UDP makes use of the port concept to direct the datagrams to the proper upper layer application. The UDP datagram contains a destination port number and a source port number. The destination number is used by UDP and the operating system to deliver the traffic to the proper recipient.

Perhaps the best way to explain UDP is to examine the message and the fields that reside in the message. As Figure 2–9 illustrates, the format is quite simple and contains the following fields:

- *Source port*: This value identifies the port of the sending application process. The field is optional. If it is not used, a value of 0 is inserted in this field.
- *Destination port*: This value identifies the receiving process on the destination host machine.
- *Length*: This value indicates the length of the user datagram, including the header and the data. This value implies that the minimum length is 8 bytes.

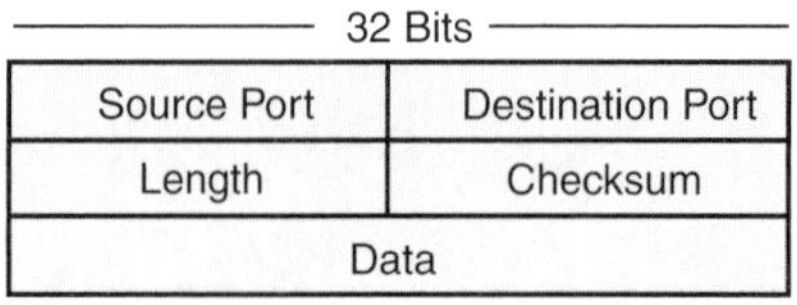

———————— 32 Bits ————————

Source Port	Destination Port
Length	Checksum
Data	

Figure 2–9   Format for the UDP data unit

- *Checksum*: This value is the 16-bit one's complement of the one's complement sum of the pseudo-IP header, the UDP header, and the data. It also performs a checksum on any padding (if it was necessary to make the message contain a multiple of two bytes).

There is not a lot more to be said about UDP. It is a minimal level of service used in many transaction-based application systems. However, it is quite useful if the full services of TCP are not needed.

SUMMARY

Data networks in general, and the Internet in particular, are designed to support asynchronous, non-real-time traffic. The variable delay in data networks is usually not a big problem because of the asynchronous nature of data applications.

The design philosophy of data networks is the opposite of voice networks. Voice networks are designed to support synchronous real-time traffic, with a fixed delay between the sender and the receiver.

UDP and IP are the chosen L_4 and L_3 protocols for VoIP. Their choice has nothing to do with their merit (although they are not poor choices). Rather, it reflects the fact that UDP and IP are found in most workstations and personal computers.

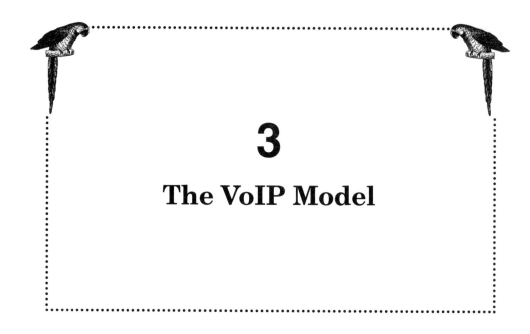

3

The VoIP Model

This chapter introduces the VoIP model, a topic discussed in many parts of this book. The VoIP protocol suite is examined, as well as the placement of the voice traffic in the model. As a precursor to later chapters, brief explanations are provided on several protocols that support voice traffic in an internet. The chapter concludes with a discussion of the three *planes* that exist in the VoIP model.

THE VoIP PROTOCOL SUITE

Figure 3–1 shows several of the Internet protocols and their relation to the conventional Internet layered model. For this discussion, our interest is on the VoIP-related protocols. The other protocols in this figure are certainly important (those in the physical and data link layers, for example), but they are not germane to this specific analysis in this chapter, and they are covered in other books in this series and in Chapters 6, 9, and 12.

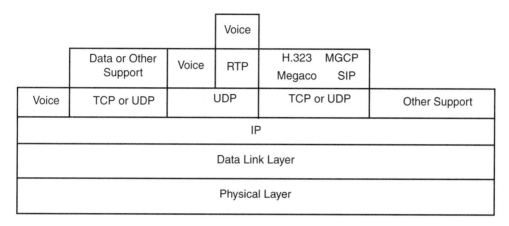

Figure 3–1   The VoIP protocol suite

VOICE OVER IP, VOICE OVER UDP, OR VOICE OVER RTP?

One interesting aspect of Figure 3–1 is the placement of the voice operations in three possible positions in the model. Voice can run directly over IP; or over the UDP then IP; or over the RTP, then UDP, and then IP.

From the technical standpoint, the voice traffic can run on any of these three protocol stacks. However, I recommend the alternative in which voice operates first over RTP and then the subsequent protocols. That being the case, the term voice over IP (VoIP) is not accurate. It should be titled voice over RTP, with the initials of VoRTP! No, let us not make up another term; VoIP will suffice. Rather, let's answer the questions of (a) why there are three alternatives, and (b) why one is better than the others.

Voice Directly Over IP

Running voice directly over IP means placing the voice traffic directly into the user field of the IP datagram. I do not recommend this protocol stack alternative for the reasons cited in the next two sections of the chapter. It is mentioned because, strictly speaking, voice directly over IP is indeed VoIP.

Voice Directly Over UDP

UDP has long been a mainstay in an internet. It is an important tool for VoIP operations because it helps manage Internet port numbers between computers and applications. These Internet ports identify a layer 7 application; that is, the application that runs on top of UDP.

One might ask why bother to use UDP since it does little? As noted, the UDP header contains the Internet source and destination port numbers that are required for proper execution of the layer 7 protocols (as explained in Chapter 2). A UDP upper layer user in a host machine is identified by a *port* identifier. The port number is concatenated with the IP address to form a *socket*. This address must be unique throughout the Internet, and a pair of sockets uniquely identifies each end-point connection.

Although the mapping of ports to higher layer processes can be handled as an internal matter in a host, the Internet publishes reserved port numbers for frequently used higher level processes. They are called *well-known ports*. Sockets are important in an internet; they identify the sessions between applications.

Another point to consider regarding the use of UDP is that some VoIP-based call processing protocols cannot function effectively without the use of ports. For example, one of the SIP functions is to support the passing of port numbers between applications that will be used during the packet telephone call. So, enough said. Use port numbers; thus, use UDP as part of the VoIP protocol stack.

Voice Directly Over RTP

RTP is designed to support real-time traffic; that is, traffic that requires playback at the receiving application in a time-sensitive mode, such as for voice and video systems. RTP also operates with both unicast and multicast applications.

RTP provides services that include payload type identification (for example, the type of audio traffic, such as G.723, G.729), sequence numbering, timestamping, and delivery monitoring. Applications usually run RTP on top of UDP to make use of UDP's port multiplexing and checksum services. RTP supports data transfer to multiple destinations by using multicast distribution if provided by the underlying network (an IP multicast implementation).

The sequence numbers included in RTP allow the receiver to reconstruct the sender's packet sequence, but sequence numbers might also be used to determine the proper location of a packet. All in all, RTP provides functions that are quite useful to a VoIP user.

NOT VOICE OVER TCP

As the VoIP protocol suite shows, the Transmission Control Protocol (TCP) is not invoked for voice operations because its many features create excessive delay of the traffic. In addition, TCP has retransmission capabilities as well as retransmission timers, which do not work well with real-time traffic. In contrast, UDP is a protocol with no retransmissions, no timeouts, no ACKs, no NAKs, and therefore, no delaying services that could hamper voice traffic.

THE CALL PROCESSING (SIGNALING) PROTOCOLS

Several protocols shown in Figure 3–1 provide the control and management of telephony sessions in an internet. They are known as signaling or call processing protocols. These protocols can run over UDP or TCP. The principal job of these protocols is to set up and clear voice or video calls in a packet network. Their counterparts in conventional circuit-switched networks are Q.931 (in ISDN networks) and ISUP (in SS7 networks). Appendices A and B provide information on the circuit-switched network systems.

I have grouped these systems into one part of the model for purposes of this general explanation. In Chapter 10, we will learn that many of their operations vary. For example, SIP supports features to locate parties that are to be part of a call. The other protocols in this group do not have this type of service, at least not to the level of SIP's location abilities.

As another example, H.323, SIP, MGCP, and Megaco all have operations that define how to set up and tear down a call across a data network, but their individual rules for this service are different.

One can certainly wonder why multiple protocols that exhibit redundant operations are published. The answer is that some of these procedures are developed by the ITU-T, and others by the Internet task forces, two different standards bodies with their own views of how to go about developing standards. Another answer is that there are often differences of opinion about how to design a protocol to meet a stated set of objectives, and these differences can lead to multiple efforts.

Considerable coordination has occurred between some of these working groups and task forces. This situation sometimes results in the dovetailing of one standard into another. For example, Megaco is published as part of the ITU-T H Series (H.248).

Nonetheless, the proliferation of multiple protocols that have over-lapping operations can be confusing to an outsider, but one hopes this approach will lead to better specifications.

OTHER SUPPORT FOR VoIP

The notation of "Other Support" in Figure 3–1 is a modest entry (relative to its importance) in the VoIP model. These other protocols provide valuable support functions for the VoIP operations. These protocols are explained in Chapters 9 and 12 and in the companion book to this text, *Internet Telephony: Call Processing Protocols.*

DATA IN A VoIP SESSION

The notation of "Data" in Figure 3–1 means that conventional data applications may be involved in a VoIP session. For example, transferring a file, a slide, a drawing, a spreadsheet, etc., during a packet voice conversation fits into this part of the VoIP protocol suite.

HOW THE WEB FITS IN

A VoIP model includes the Web technology. It is depicted in a general fashion in Figure 3–2. Protocols such as HTTP, markup languages such as HTML and XML, and the use of URLs and the DNS are essential components of VoIP. A CEO of a large telecommunications firm coined the term of "Web tone" to describe the use of the Web to support (and supplant in some instances) conventional dial-tone, telephony services.[1]

Even if the industry does not migrate to a full Web-based telephone network in the future, HTTP, HTML, XML, URLs, and DNS still play a big role in present (and future) VoIP networks. As we shall see in Chapter 10, the Internet-based VoIP Call Processing Protocols rely on the procedures and protocols that are embedded in the Web. Indeed, the IETF has purposely kept its VoIP architecture closely associated with the Web architecture in order to provide a readily available, universal platform for VoIP.

---

[1]Web-tone, wherein Web-based servers function as telephony exchanges.

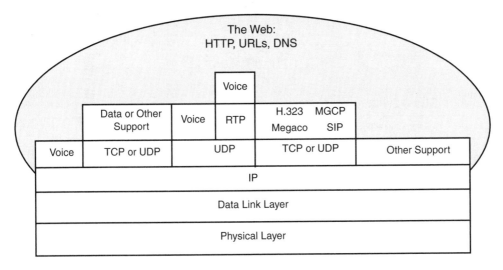

Figure 3–2   Web-based VoIP

GROUPING THE VoIP PROTOCOLS INTO PLANES

To simplify matters, the VoIP model can be redrawn to look like the model in Figure 3–3.

In this depiction, the various protocols shown earlier are grouped into *planes.* The term plane refers to a group of related functions and their associated protocols and interfaces. For VoIP three planes are defined:

- *Signaling plane:* This plane contains the VoIP call processing protocols. It is invoked to set up, tear down, and otherwise manage the calls. As a general statement, the signaling plane is not invoked once the call is set up and running. Exceptions to this statement are situations that require help from this plane during the call, such as adding or dropping a party during a conference call, changing certain operational parameters (perhaps asking for more bandwidth), and similar needs. Recall that these protocols include Megaco, MGCP, H.323, and SIP.

- *Support plane:* This plane contains the VoIP protocols that support the call and the signaling plane. Examples are RSVP, RTP, NTP, and many others explained in later chapters or in the companion book to this text, *Internet Telephony: Call Processing Proto-*

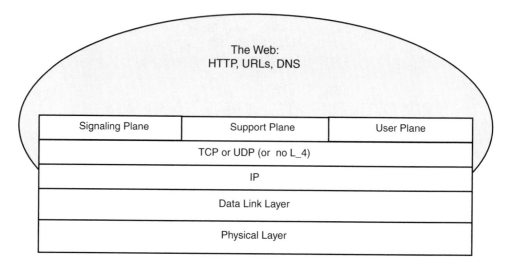

Figure 3–3 Another view of the VoIP model: the three planes

cols. They are not considered signaling protocols; rather, they support the signaling protocols.

- *User plane:* This plane contains the user traffic. Obviously, the principal example is packet voice; that is, VoIP.

SUMMARY

The VoIP model and the VoIP protocol suite provide a helpful, visual view of how VoIP operates with other Internet protocols. We also learned that VoIP can operate in one of three places in the model, but the placement of voice over RTP/UDP/IP makes the most sense. We also learned that the VoIP model can be distinguished by three planes and that it relies heavily on the Web and the DNS.

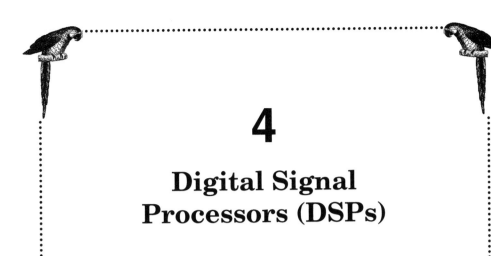

4

Digital Signal Processors (DSPs)

Digital signal processors (DSPs) are the engines for voice coders and modems, and they are finding their way into many other systems, such as answering machines and consumer high-fidelity audio systems. In this chapter, we provide an overview of DSPs and show how they are used to support low-bit rate coders for VoIP.

ROLE OF DSPs IN PACKET-VOICE OPERATIONS

A DSP is a specialized processor that has been in use for many years in other telephony applications such as mobile/wireless networks. They are attractive for internet telephony because they are small, use relatively little power, and are very fast. Packet voice requires computation-intensive operations and special processing, and a standard microprocessor is not up to the task of performing these operations.

In addition, packetized voice requires considerable multiplication and addition functions in a very short period of time. A DSP supports these types of functions. Multiplication operations to estimate the frequency spectrum of a signal are computation intensive and are often performed with a Fast Fourier Transform (FFT) algorithm, a subject discussed shortly.

The DSP is the principal machine that performs voice packetization and compression. It works with other components as depicted in Figure 4–1. The DSP's functions are integrated with other microprocessors. In this example [KRAP98], the DSP supports the voice packet module. It interfaces with a microprocessor containing operations for telephony signaling, network management (the Simple Network Management Protocol [SNMP]), and a packet protocol module, which is used for sending and receiving voice packets.

The DSP component performs compression, voice activity detection, echo cancellation, jitter management, and clock synchronization. The telephony signaling module acts as the communicator between the DSP and the packet protocol module. In turn, the packet protocol module converts the signal information from telephony-based protocols (DS0) to packet-based protocols (IP). The network management protocol monitors the overall activities of the system and allows configuration operations to be performed on various components.

The DSP usually supports more than one telephony channel. The number of channels supported depends on a variety of factors, principally the power of the DSP in millions of instructions per second (MIPS). Another key factor is the amount of memory residing in the DSP. The more memory on the board, the more efficient the operation, but this approach translates into fewer MIPS. Thus, there is a trade-off between MIPS and memory. As a general practice, manufacturers place considerable memory on the DSP chip for implementations of 1 to 8 ports (interfaces).

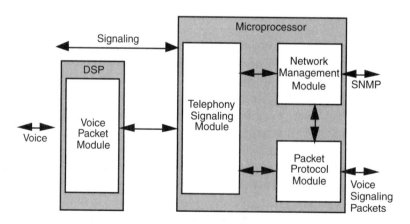

Figure 4–1   Packet-voice module [KRAP98]

DSP Voice Packet Module

Figure 4–2 shows the DSP voice packet module in more detail [KRAP98]. The pulse code modulation (PCM) interface performs conventional G.711 A-D and D-A operations, and this information is used by the voice codec module to perform the compression operations and syntax translations in accordance with G.723.1, G.729A, etc. The PCM interface also contains a tone generator and resampler. The resampler is fed by the comfort noise unit and the packet-loss manager.

On the transmit side, the module employs an ITU-T G.165/G.168 echo canceller, which is fed into gain control, a voice activity detector, and a tone detector. The output from the voice activity detector is processed by an ITU-T G Series codec and then sent to the packet protocol module for assembly and transmission. On the receive side, the packet protocol module receives the traffic and passes this information to the adaptive playout unit, where a packet loss manager monitors and compensates for the loss of packets. This input is fed to the comfort noise converter, which provides noise to the receiver to simulate a telephone line.

The module may contain the fax interface unit consisting of a V-Series fax specification such as V.17, the fax T.38 protocol, and a network driver.

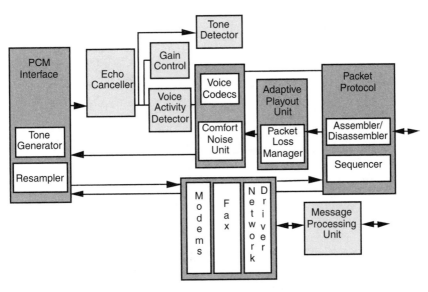

Figure 4–2   Typical DSP-based module [KRAP98]

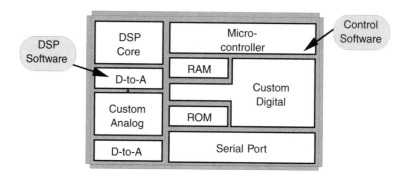

Figure 4–3   DSP–core-based ASICs [LAPS97]

DSP Cores

An approach in the design of a DSP system is to combine the DSP with custom circuits on a single chip. This approach is attractive because it allows the manufacturer to use the high-powered DSP as well as custom circuits in one system. Two approaches are used in this endeavor. One approach uses a DSP–core-based, application-specific integrated circuits (ASIC), and the other approach uses customizable DSP processors. The overall chip contains a DSP as one part of the chip, and an ASIC as another part. Figures 4–3 and 4–4 provide a functional view of these types of chipsets [LAPS97].

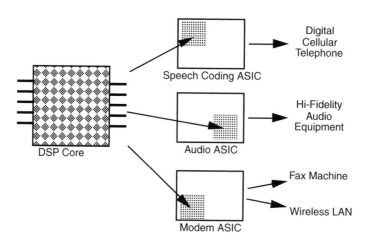

Figure 4–4   Another view of DSP core-based ASICs [LAPS97]

Notice that the DSP core logic is part of the overall system, which can support various types of ASICs, such as a speech coder, a high-fidelity ASIC, or a modem ASIC. The configurations shown in Figures 4–3 and 4–4 are general examples, and the vendors differ in how they implement the DSP-based ASICs. Some vendors provide a complete configuration; others provide a "core" and license the core to the customer. The latter approach allows the customer to customize the circuit to a specific application.

DSP VS. CUSTOMIZED HARDWARE

It is also noteworthy that a DSP implementation may not be as effective as customized hardware. One obvious benefit is that customized hardware can be designed to perform better than a generalized DSP. For example, in systems that need a high sampling rate, customized hardware may be the best approach. For large-volume applications, it may be less expensive to use customized hardware instead of a DSP approach. An application with fewer requirements often does not need the full functionality of a DSP. Therefore, the full operations of the DSP may be too costly for an application with a narrow range of functions. Notwithstanding, the long lead times for the design and manufacturing of customized hardware usually translate into high costs and the inability to meet critical deadlines.

It is not necessary to take an all-or-nothing approach. A variety of hybrid products are available that combine DSPs with application-specific ASICs, customized ICs, and field-programmable gate arrays (FPGAs).

FIXED- AND FLOATING-POINT PROCESSORS

As depicted in Figure 4–5, DSPs are organized around a fixed or floating-point architecture. The fixed-point architecture is the simplest approach and was the original way in which DSPs were designed. The floating-point architecture uses the conventional mantissa and exponent notations. Just like any other processor, fixed-point operations yield more precision but yield a lesser range of fractions. The fixed-point processors are available in 16-bit, 20-bit, or 24-bit word sizes. In contrast, floating-point processors use a 32-bit word length. For efficiency and cost reduction, designers attempt to use the smallest word size to support the

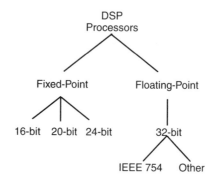

Figure 4–5   DSP arithmetic structure

application. Currently, the most common word size for a fixed point processor is 16 bits. Since most readers will have studied the arithmetic of fixed- and floating-point operations, I will not dwell on these operations here.

One last point is relevant to this discussion. Be aware that as a general practice, the word size of the instruction word size is the same in most processors. However, exceptions do exist, and some implementations support a 16-bit word size and a 24-bit instruction word size.

MEMORY ARCHITECTURES

In traditional processors, shown in Figure 4–6, instructions and data are stored in a single memory area and processed in the processor core, through the address bus and the data bus. In a simple implementation of this architecture, the processor takes one instruction cycle to make an ac-

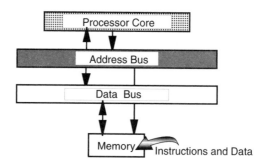

Figure 4–6   Von Neumann architecture

cess to memory without either a read or a write operation. This approach is known as the Von Neumann architecture. Although this architecture is sufficient for many systems today, it is inadequate for processor-intensive, real-time applications.

One example is the implementation of algorithms to support real-time voice and video [the Finite Impulse Response (FIR) filter algorithm, discussed shortly]. In this arrangement, a processor needs multiple memory accesses to perform the operations to support typical FIR operations consisting of multiply and accumulate operations. This statement is true even if the processor is designed to perform a multiply-and-accumulate operation in only one instruction cycle. The fact still remains that four memory accesses are needed to perform the operation.

In contrast to the Von Neumann architecture, DSPs implement a Harvard architecture, shown in Figure 4–7. With this approach, two memory spaces can be partitioned, with one space to hold instructions and the other to hold data, although there are implementations where the two memory locations store both instructions and data. As the figure shows, there are also two bus sets, thus allowing two simultaneous accesses to memory. In effect, this architecture doubles the architecture's capacity (known as the memory bandwidth), and it is quite important in keeping the processor core completely occupied with both instructions and data.

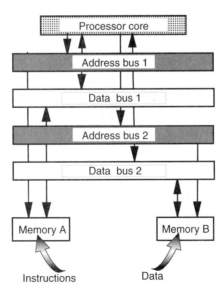

Figure 4–7   Harvard architecture

It should be emphasized that high-performance, generalized processors (the Pentium and the PowerPC) certainly can make multiple memory accesses per instruction, but the generalized processor is just that: a device built for generic, generalized processing. We have more to say about this subject shortly.

SOFTWARE DIFFERENCES

The DSP programmer is involved with *each* instruction that passes through the processor. Generalized processor programmers may not know or even specify the instructions and data that reside in caches. In contrast, the majority of DSP processors do not implement cache, but rather rely on chip memory with the multiple bus sets to allow them to rapidly perform several memory accesses with each instruction.[1]

Moreover, data caches are rare for DSPs because the input data for the DSP is no longer needed once it has been operated on. That is, once the DSP operates on a sample (say, a voice sample), the sample can be discarded because it is not used in subsequent operations. (It is true that a voice sample is used more than once for sample-to-sample correlations, but after it has been processed, it is not used again.)

FAST FOURIER TRANSFORM OPERATIONS

Fast Fourier Transform (FFT) operations are commonly used in DSPs. They were developed in the 1970s to reduce the number of operations in the multiplication of numbers [CRAN97], which is a common operation in digital telephony. Consider two D-digit numbers x and y. The conventional multiplication of x and y consists of multiplying each successive digit of x by every digit of y and then adding the resulting columns. The process takes D^2 operations. FFT reduces the number of operations to D log D. For example, if x and y were 1000-digit numbers, the conventional multiplication would take more than 1,000,000 operations. FFT reduces the number of operations to about 50,000.

---

[1]There are exceptions to this statement. Some DSPs do use a very small instruction cache separate from the on-chip memory banks. That cache stores critical instructions for very small looping operations to obviate the processor having to use its on-chip operations to retrieve these critical instructions.

The numbers X and Y are treated as signals, and FFT is applied to X and Y in order to break X and Y into their spectral components. The spectra are then multiplied together, frequency by frequency. An inverse FFT operation and some other final operations are then used to yield the product of X and Y.

There are variations of FFT. One method treats the digital signals as bipolar so that both positive and negative digits can be used. Another approach is to weight the signals by first multiplying x and y by some other special signal. I refer you to [CRAN97] for more information on FFT, as well some fascinating information on large numbers.

SIGNAL FILTERS AND THE FINITE IMPULSE RESPONSE (FIR) FILTER

One of the main operations of the DSP is signal filtering. The operation improves the quality of the signal, for example, by improving the signal-to-noise ratio.

The Finite Impulse Response (FIR) filter is a common digital filter. It implements a 31-tap filter, which is shown in Figure 4–8. This illustration is the most widely used in the literature, and further information is available from [EYRE98] and [LAPS97]. Both these references use the same examples and identical textual explanations. I quote directly from [EYRE98].

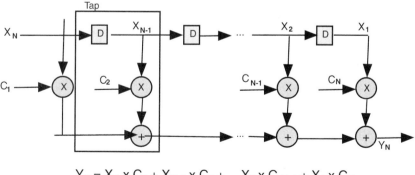

$$Y_N = X_N \times C_1 + X_{N-1} \times C_2 + \ldots X_2 \times C_{N-1} + X_1 \times C_N$$

Figure 4–8   The finite impulse response filter (FIR) [EYRE98]

The blocks labeled D [in Figure 4–8] are unit delay operators; their output is a copy of the input sample, delayed by one sample period. A series of storage elements (usually memory locations) is used to implement a series of these delay elements (this series is called a delay line).

At any given time, N-1 of the most recently received input samples reside in the delay line, where N is the total number of input samples used in the computation of each output sample. Input samples are designated X_N; the first input sample is x_1, the next is x_2, and so on.

Each time a new input sample arrives, the FIR filter operation shifts previously stored samples one place to right along the delay line. It then computes a new output sample by multiplying the newly arrived sample and each of the previously stored input samples by the corresponding coefficient. In [Figure 4–8], coefficients are represented as C_k, where k is the coefficient number. The summation of the multiplication products forms the new output sample, Y_n.

We call the combination of a single delay element, the associated multiplication operation, and the associated addition operation a tap. The number of taps and the values chosen for the coefficients define the filter characteristics. For example, if the values of the coefficients are all equal to the reciprocal of the number of taps, 1/N, the filter performs an averaging operation, one form of a low-pass filter.

To summarize briefly, N represents the total number of input samples used for the specific computation for each output sample. The concept works according to a shift register concept. When a new input sample arrives, the previously stored samples are shifted one place to the right through the delay line. A new output sample is then computed by multiplication of the new sample with each of the previously stored input samples by the corresponding coefficient.

As you can see, the DSP is organized around the multiply-and-accumulate (MAC) operation. Because multiple accumulate operations are quite common in applications such as packet telephony, the efficient design of a DSP to perform multiply-accumulates is quite important. Because MAC is indeed important, DSPs provide specialized MAC operations.

PREDICTABILITY OF PERFORMANCE

Earlier, we discussed the critical need for DSPs to support real-time applications. They must exhibit predictable execution performance because of the tight time constraints involved in real-time execution. In contrast, some generalized processors use code that may consume a different number of instruction cycles depending on what branching operations may take place. Consequently, it is quite difficult with these architectures to predict how long it will take for certain operations to take place. This lack of predictability makes it difficult to optimize code or to predict the timing of the execution of the code in certain situations.

Since the DSP programmer determines the exact set of instructions when the instructions are processed, it is a relatively easy task to predict the time required to execute the code on a DSP. In a nutshell, DSPs do not use the general processor's concepts of branch predictions and speculative execution. The DSP executes highly specialized instruction sets to perform certain functions in a very efficient manner.

An interesting aspect of this situation from a programming standpoint is that the code is certainly less than intuitive and may require some retraining on the part of a conventional application programmer. To illustrate this point, consider this instruction based on the Motorola DSP 56300 system [EYRE98]. X and Y represent two Harvard architecture memory spaces:

$$\text{MAC } X0, Y0, A \text{ } X: (R0) + , X0 \text{ } Y: (R4) + N4, Y0$$

This instruction directs the DSP to do the following:

- Multiply the contents of registers $X0$ and $Y0$.
- Add the result to a running total stored in accumulator A.
- Load register $X0$ from X, pointed to by register $R0$.
- Load register $Y0$ from Y, pointed to by register $R4$.
- Postincrement $R0$ by 1; and
- Postincrement $R4$ by the contents of register $R4$.

It is tight code and is quite specialized. This single line of code encompasses all the operations to calculate an FIR filter trap.

Compilers are available to allow programmers to write in C or C++ for translations for execution on DSPs. Generally, these compilers do not work very well because the use of multiple memory spaces, irregular instruction sets, multiple buses, and memory locations makes it a particularly big challenge to write efficient compilers for DSPs.

ANOTHER EXAMPLE OF DSP CODE

The previous example is a bit difficult to read and takes some thought for a programmer to use. Let us look at another example that may be a bit easier to analyze. The code shown in Figure 4–9 is from an analog de-

```
Entry   fir
fir:    CNTR=30;........................................./Instruction 1
*/
        MR=0, MX0=DM(I1,M1), MY0=PM(I4,M4);................*Instruction 2
*/
        Do sop Until CE;....................................../*Instruction 3
*/
sop:    MR=MR+MX0*MY0, MX0=DM(I1,M1), MY0=PM(I4,M4);......./*Instruction 4
*/
        MR=MR+MX0*MY0;....................................../*Instruction 5
*/
        RTS;................................................/*Instruction 6
```

Figure 4–9   FIR filter routine [STEVa98]

vice's ASP-21xx DSP. I guide you to [STEVa98] if you need more information on these operations.

The example shown deals with the FIT operation introduced earlier. One of the most important functions in communication DSPs is signal filtering. This concept is simple in that the operation manipulates an input signal to improve its characteristics. Examples that come to mind in filtering are improving the signal-to-noise ratio on a telephone line or removing unwanted noise or static from the input signal. Digital filtering has replaced most analog filtering because it is less expensive, makes defining operation tolerances easier, and is not subject to environmental factors (such as temperature).

Here is an explanation of what the code does:

- *Instruction 1:* Load loop counter with the filter length minus 1, so the example is for a 31 tap-FIR filter.
- *Instruction 2:* The accumulator register MR is set to 0, and a prefetch of a sample in memory location (DM) is loaded into register MX0. In addition, a filter coefficient is loaded into MY0 from memory location (PM). I1 and I4 contain the address of the data samples and filter coefficients, respectively. M1 and M4 contain modifier values and are set to 1 here. The code meaning may not be obvious, but each time instruction 2 is executed, I1=I1+M1, and I4=I4+M4.
- *Instruction 3:* A do loop is set up to end at label sop. With each loop execution, the loop counter decrements by 1, and the loop is exited upon counter expiration.

- *Instruction 4:* Perform the multiply-accumulate in MR, then fetch the next data sample and filter coefficient.
- *Instruction 5:* Perform the last multiply-accumulate.
- *Instruction 6:* Exit the routine.

SUMMARY

Digital signal processors (DSPs) are the engines for voice coders and modems and are an important variable in the VoIP equation. They rely on Harvard architectures, very compact code, FFT, and other advanced techniques. It is reasonable to say that the new generalized processors (the Pentiums, for example) will be of sufficient horsepower to compete with DSPs. This may be so, but the generalized processors will likely be tied up with other operations. So, it seems reasonable to say that DSPs and the new chips will both reside in the end-user PC.

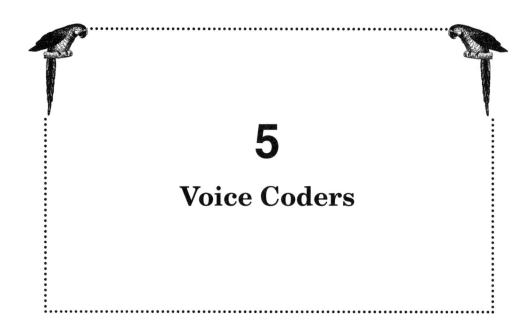

5

Voice Coders

This chapter provides an overview of the prevalent coders/decoders (codecs) used in VoIP. They are also known as codecs, speech, coders, voice coders, or simply coders. There is a wealth of information on this subject, and it is not my intent to rehash these sources. Some recommendations for reading are [MINO98], any of John Bellamy's books, and the *BT Technology Journal*. Several of BT's issues in the past two years have focused on voice coders and the ITU-T specifications.

The approach in this chapter is to provide a brief tutorial on the major coder functions, provide a brief classification of coders, and then explain three coders used for VoIP: ITU-T G.723, ITU-T G.728, and ITU-T G.729 voice coders.

FUNCTIONS OF THE VOICE CODER

The principal function of a voice coder is to encode pulse code modulation (PCM) user speech samples into a small number of bits (a frame) in such a manner that the speech is robust in the presence of link errors, jittery networks, and bursty transmissions. At the receiver, the frames are decoded back to the PCM speech samples and then converted to the waveform.

CLASSIFICATION OF SPEECH CODERS

Speech coders are classified into three types: waveform coding, vocoding, and hybrid coding. Waveform coders reproduce the analog waveform as accurately as possible, including background noise. Since they operate on all input signals, they produce high-quality samples. However, waveform coders operate at a high bit rate. For example, the ITU-T G.711 (PCM) specification uses a 64-kbit/s rate.

Vocoders (voice + coders) do not reproduce the original waveform. The encoder builds a set of parameters that are sent to the receiver to be used to drive a speech production model.[1] Linear prediction coding (LPC) is used to derive parameters of a time-varying digital filter. This filter models the output of the speaker's vocal tract [WEST96]. The quality of vocoders is not good enough for use in telephony systems.

The prevalent speech coder for VoIP is a hybrid coder, which melds the attractive features of waveform coders and vocoders. The hybrid coders are also attractive because they operate at a very low bit rate (4–16 kbit/s). These coders use analysis-by-synthesis (AbS) techniques.

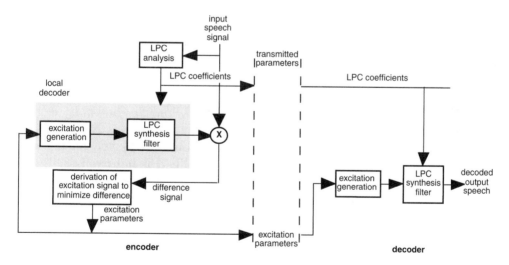

Figure 5–1   Analysis-by-synthesis operations [WEST96]

---

[1]This concept has been around for many years. Homer Dudley of Bell Labs demonstrated it at the World's Fair in 1939.

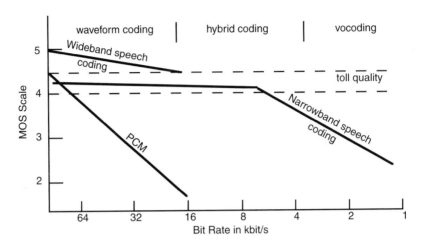

Figure 5–2 MOS ratings versus bit rate for low-bit-rate coders [WEST96]

To illustrate, consider a speech pattern produced by the human vocal tract: voiced sounds (phonemes like pa, da, etc.), and unvoiced sounds (phonemes like sh, th, etc.) are produced during talking to produce the signal. An excitation signal is derived from the input speech signal in such a manner that the difference between the input and the synthesized speech is quite small. The use of LPC, the excitation operation, and the difference checks for AbS are shown in Figure 5–1, and we examined the filter concepts in Chapter 3.

Toll-quality coders easily operate at 8 kbit/s, as shown in Figure 5–2. As explained in Chapter 1, toll-quality speech must achieve a MOS (mean opinion score) of 4 or above. Conventional PCM speech deteriorates significantly at rates less than 32 kbit/s. PCM is not the issue here. Hybrid coding and vocoding exhibit acceptable MOS ratings for fairly low bit rates. At this stage, most VoIP-based coders operate at a range of 5.2–8 kbit/s. Research points to standardized coders that will provide acceptable MOS ratings at 4 kbit/s, and some proprietary systems operate at 4.8 kbit/s with a MOS of 3.8.

Vector Quantization and Code-Excited Linear Prediction

An enhancement to the operation is to use a previously stored codebook of optimized parameters (a vector of elements) to encode a representative vector of the input speech signal. This technique is known as vector quantization (VQ).

Coding performance can be improved further by combining VQ with AbS. The AbS VQ technique forms the basis for code excited linear prediction (CELP) coding. The main difference between VQ and AbS VQ is the definition of the quantization distortion measure in the VQ codebook search [WONG96].

LINEAR PREDICTION ANALYSIS-BY-SYNTHESIS CODERS

The most popular class of speech coders for bit rates between 4.8 and 16 kbit/s are model-based coders that use an LPAS method. A linear-prediction model of speech production is excited by an appropriate signal in order to model the signal over time. The parameters of both the speech model and the excitation are estimated and updated at regular time intervals (e.g., every 20 ms) and are used to control the speech model. Two LPAS coders are discussed next: the forward-adaptive and backward-adaptive LPAS coders.

Forward-Adaptive LPAS Coders

In a forward-adaptive AbS coder, the prediction filter coefficients and gains are explicitly transmitted. To provide toll-quality performance, these two coders rely on a source model for speech. The excitation signal, in the form of information on the pitch period of the speech, is transmitted as well. The coder provides a good model for a speech signal but is not an appropriate model for some noises or for most instrumental music. Thus, the performance of LPAS coders for noisy backgrounds and music is of poorer quality than that produced by G.726 and G.727 coders.

In the next subsections, we take a closer look at the ITU-T G.723.1 and G.729 LPAS coders.

The 6.3- and 5.3-kbit/s G.723.1. ITU-T G.723.1 provides toll-quality speech at 6.3 kbit/s.[2] A lower quality speech coder operating at 5.3 kbit/s is also included. G.723.1 was designed with low-bit-rate video telephony in mind. For this application, the delay requirements are less stringent because the video coding delay is usually larger than that of speech. The G.723.1 coder has a 30-ms frame size and a 7.5-ms look-ahead. When combined with processing delay to implement the coder, it

---

[2]Some of my clients would not agree with this statement. They find the G.723.1 speech signals "tinny." I have found some systems that are good and some that are poor.

is estimated that the coder would contribute 67.5 ms to the one-way delay. Additional delays result from the use of network and system buffers.

The G.723.1 coder performs conventional telephone bandwidth filtering (based on G.712) of the voice signal, samples the signal at the conventional 8000 Hz rate (based on G.711), and converts the 16-bit linear PCM code for input to the encoder. The decoder part performs a complementary operation on the output to reconstruct the voice signal.

The system encodes the voice signal into frames in accordance with LPAS coding. A coder can produce two rates of voice traffic: 6.3 kbit/s for the high rate and 5.3 kbit/s for the low rate. The high-rate coder is based on Multipulse Maximum Likelihood Quantization (MP-MLQ), and the low-rate coder is based on Algebraic-Code-Excited Linear-Prediction (ACELP). A coder and decoder must support both rates, and the coder/decoder can switch between the rates between frame boundaries. Music and other audio signals are compressed and decompressed as well, but the coder is optimized for speech.

The encoder operates on frames (blocks) of 240 samples each to support the 8000 kHz sampling rate. Further operations (a high-pass filter to remove the DC component) result in four subframes of 60 samples each. A variety of other operations occur, such as the computation of an LPC filter, unquantized LPC filter coefficients, resulting in a packetization time of 30 ms. For every subframe, an LPC filter is calculated, using the unprocessed input signal. The filter on the last subframe is quantized with a predictive split vector quantizer (PSVQ). As stated earlier, the lookahead takes 7.5 ms, so the coding delay is 37.5 ms. This delay is a significant factor in evaluation of coders, especially for transporting speech through a data network, since less delay in the coding (and decoding) process means more latitude to deal with the inevitable delay (and variable delay) found in internets.

The decoder operates also on a frame basis. The decoding process occurs as follows (a general summary of G.723.1):

- The quantized LPC indices are decoded.
- The LPC synthesis filter is constructed.
- On each subframe, the adaptive codebook excitation and fixed codebook excitation are decoded and input to the synthesis filter.
- The excitation signal is input into a pitch postfilter and then into a synthesis filter.
- The resulting signal is input into a formant postfilter, which uses a gain scaling unit to maintain the energy at the input level of the formant postfilter.

Silence compression has been used for a number of years to exploit the fact that silent periods in a voice conversation occupy about 50% of the total time of the conversation. The idea is to reduce the number of bits sent during these silent intervals and thus save in the overall number of bits transmitted.

For many years in the telephony network, selected analog speech signals have been processed through time-assigned speech interpolation (TASI). This technology places other speech or data signals into the silent periods of a conversation and so provides additional capacity on multichannel links. Today, the concepts of TASI are applied to digital signals and tagged with new names—one example is TDMA (time division multiple access). To review briefly, TDMA breaks down the conventional signals into small, digitized segments (slots). These slots are time-division-multiplexed with other slots into one channel.

G.723.1 uses silence compression by executing discontinuous transmission operations, which means that artificial noise (at reduced bit rates) is inserted into the bit stream during silent periods. In addition to conserving bandwidth, this technique keeps the transmitter's modem in continuous operation and avoids the tasks of switching the carrier on and off.

G.729. G.729 is designed for low-delay applications, with a frame size of only 10 ms, a processing delay of 10 ms, and a lookahead of 5 ms. This yields a 25-ms contribution to end-to-end delay and a bit rate of 8 kbit/s. These delay performances are important in an internet, because, as we have learned, any factor decreasing delay is important.

G.729 comes in two versions: G.729 and G.729A. The original version is more complex than G.723.1, whereas the Annex A version is less complex than G.723.1. The two versions are compatible but their performance is somewhat different, the lower complexity version (G.729) having slightly lower quality. Both coders include provision for dealing with frame erasures and packet-loss concealment, making them good choices for use with voice over the Internet. Cox et al. [COX98] state that the G.729 performance for random bit errors is poor. They do not recommend them for use on channels with random bit errors unless there is a channel coder (forward error correction and convolutional coding) to protect the most sensitive bits.

Backward-Adaptive LPAS Coding [16-kbit/s G.728 Low-Delay Code Book Excitation Linear Prediction (LD-CELP)]

The 16-kbit/s-G.728 is a hybrid between the lower-bit-rate, linear-prediction analysis-by-synthesis coders (G.729 and G.723.1) and the backward ADPCM coders. G.728 is an LD-CELP coder and operates on five samples at a time.

CELP is a speech-coding technique in which the excitation signal is selected from a set of possible excitation signals through an exhaustive search. The lower rate speech coders use a forward adaptation scheme for the sample value prediction filter, and LD-CELP uses a backward adaptive filter that is updated every 2.5 ms. There are 1,024 possible excitation vectors. These vectors are further decomposed into four possible gains, two possible signs (+ or −), and 128 possible shape vectors.

G.728 is a suggested speech coder for low-bit-rate (56–128 kbit/s) ISDN video telephony. Because of its backward adaptive nature, it is a low-delay coder, but it is more complex than the other coders because the fiftieth-order LPC analysis must be repeated at the decoder. It also provides an adaptive postfilter that enhances its performance.

PARAMETER SPEECH CODERS: 2.4-KBIT/S MIXED-EXCITATION LPC (MELP)

Parametric speech coders assume a generic speech model with a simplified excitation signal and thus are able to operate at the lowest bit rates. All of the speech coders discussed previously can be described as *waveform following*. Their output signals are similar in shape and phase to the input signal.

Parametric speech coders are different and do not exhibit waveform following. They are based on an analysis-synthesis model for speech signals that can be represented with relatively few parameters. These parameters are extracted and quantized, usually on a regular basis, every 20–40 ms. At the receiver, the parameters are used to create a synthetic speech signal. Under ideal conditions, the synthetic signal sounds like the original speech. Under harsh enough background noise conditions, any parametric coder will fail because the input signal is not well modeled by the inherent speech model. The 2.4 kbit/s MELP was selected as the U.S. government's new 2.4-bit/s speech coder for secure telephony.

For multimedia applications, the study from [COX98] states that parametric coders are a good choice when there is a need for low bit rates. For example, parametric coders are often used for simple user games. This keeps down the storage requirements for speech. For the same reason, they also are a good choice for some types of multimedia messaging. They tend to be lower in absolute quality for all types of speech conditions and particularly noisy background conditions. This shortcoming can be overcome when the speech files can be carefully edited in advance. At the present time, most of the parametric coders used in such applications are not standards. Rather, they are proprietary coders that have been adapted to work for such applications.

G.723.1 Scalable Coding for Wireless Applications

Annex C of G.723.1 specifies a channel-coding scheme that can be used with a triple-rate speech codec. The channel codec is scalable in bit rate and is designed for mobile multimedia applications as a part of the overall H.324 family of standards.

A range of channel codec bit rates is supported, ranging from 0.7 kbit/s up to 14.3 kbit/s. The channel codec supports all three operational modes of the G.723.1 codec, namely, high-rate, low-rate and discontinuous transmission modes.

The channel codec uses punctured convolutional codes. Based on the subjective importance of each class of information bits, the available channel codec bit rate is allocated optimally to the bit classes. This allocation is based on an algorithm that is known by the encoder and decoder. Each time the system control signals a change either in the G.723.1 rate or in the available channel codec bit rate, this algorithm is executed to adapt the channel codec to the new speech service configuration.

If a low-channel codec bit rate is available, the subjectively most sensitive bits are protected first. When the channel codec bit rate is increased, the additional bits are used, first, to protect more information bits and, second, to increase the protection of the already protected classes.

Before the application of the channel encoding functions, the speech parameters are partly modified in a channel adaptation layer to improve their robustness against transmission errors.

EVALUATING CODERS

In evaluating the performance of codecs, several factors come into play, as summarized below.

- *Frame size:* Frame size represents the length of the voice traffic measured in time. It is also called frame delay. Frames are discrete parts of the speech, and each frame is updated in accordance with the speech samples. The codecs covered in this chapter process a frame at a time. This traffic is placed in voice packets and sent to the receiver.

- *Processing delay:* This factor represents the delay incurred at the codec to run the voice and coding algorithm on one frame. It is often simply factored into the frame delay. Processing delay is also called algorithmic delay.
- *Lookahead delay:* Lookahead delay occurs when the coder examines a certain amount of the next frame to provide guidance in coding the current frame. The idea of lookahead is to take advantage of the close correlations existing between successive voice frames.
- *Frame length:* This value represents the number of bytes resulting from the encoding process (the value excludes headers).
- *Voice bit rate:* This parameter is the output rate of the codec when its input is standard pulse-code-modulation voice images (at 64 kbit/s).
- *DSP MIPS:* This value specifies the minimum speed for the DSP processor to support the specific encoder. Be aware that DSP MIPS do not correlate to MIPS ratings of other processors. These DSPs are designed specifically for the task at hand in contrast to general-purpose processors that operate in workstations and personal computers. Consequently, achievement of the operations discussed in this analysis requires a much greater MIPS capability from a general processor than from a specially designed DSP.
- *Required RAM:* This value describes the amount of RAM needed to support a specific encoding process.

A key evaluation factor is the time required for the encoder to do its work. This time is referred to as one-way latency or one-way system

Table 5–1   Speech coding standards [RUDK97]

Standard	Coding type	Bit rate kbit/s	MOS	Complexity	Delay (ms)
G.711	PCM	64	4.3	1	0.125
G.726	ADPCM	32	4.0	10	0.125
G.728	LD-CELP	16	4.0	50	0.625
GSM	RPE-LTP	13	3.7	5	20
G.729	CSA-CELP	8	4.0	30	15
G.729A				15	
G.723.1	ACELP	6.3	3.8	25	37.5
	MP-MLQ	5.3			
U.S. DOD FS1015	LPC-10	2.4	synthetic	10	22.5

delay. It is computed as the sum of frame size + processing delay + look-ahead delay. Obviously, decode delays are important as well. In practice, the decode delays are about one-half the time of the encode delays.

COMPARISON OF SPEECH CODERS

Table 5–1 [RUDK97] compares several coders with regard to bit rate, MOS, complexity (with G.711 as the base), and delay (frame size and lookahead time).

CONSERVATION OF BANDWIDTH WITH VOICE ACTIVITY DETECTION

In several discussions thus far in this book, the idea of silence suppression has been explained. The formal term for this operation is called *voice activity detection* (VAD). It is used to cease the sending of packets when voice-level activity falls below a threshold.

This valuable tool, while reducing bandwidth consumption, can be a bit tricky to implement. It can lead to a problem called *clipping*, in which part of the speech is truncated and not carried in the VoIP packets. One approach to combat clipping is to continue to sample and code the speech pattern and allocate the packet to the samples, but drop the packet if the voice energy does not meet a minimum threshold during an allotted time.

BANDWIDTH CONSUMPTION OF THE CODEC AND SUPPORTING PROTOCOLS

The VoIP packets are small. The reasons behind this statement are explained in Chapter 8 when we deal with VoIP traffic engineering. For this discussion, we note that the codec voice samples are encapsulated into the IP datagram, which in turn is encapsulated into the UDP data unit, which then is encapsulated into the RTP data unit. This process is shown in Figure 5–3.

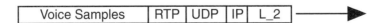

Figure 5–3   VoIP packets and supporting headers

Table 5–2 Cisco support of ITU-T codecs [CISC00c]

	Voice BW Kbit/s	MOS	Codec Delay (ms)	Packet Size (Bytes)	Cisco Pay-Load (Bytes)	Packets Per Second	IP/UDP/ RTP Hdrs (Bytes)	cRTP (Bytes)	L_2	L_2 Header (Bytes)	Total BW No VAD	Total BW VAD
G.729	8	3.9	15	10	20	50	40		Ether	14	29.6	14.8
G.729	8	3.9	15	10	20	50		2	Ether	14	14.4	7.2
G.729	8	3.9	15	10	20	50	40		PPP	6	26.4	13.2
G.729	8	3.9	15	10	20	50		2	PPP	6	11.2	5.6
G.729	8	3.9	15	10	20	50	40		FR	4	25.6	12.8
G.729	8	3.9	15	10	20	50		2	FR	4	10.4	5.2
G.729	8	3.9	15	10	20	50	40		ATM	2 cells	42.4	21.2
G.729	8	3.9	15	10	20	50		2	ATM	1 cell	21.2	10.6
G.711	64	4.1	1.5	160	160	50	40		Ether	14	85.6	42.8
G.711	64	4.1	1.5	160	160	50		2	Ether	14	70.4	35.2
G.711	64	4.1	1.5	160	160	50	40		PPP	6	82.4	41.2
G.711	64	4.1	1.5	160	160	50		2	PPP	6	67.2	33.6
G.711	64	4.1	1.5	160	160	50	40		FR	4	81.6	40.8
G.711	64	4.1	1.5	160	160	50		2	FR	4	66.4	33.2
G.711	64	4.1	1.5	160	160	50	40		ATM	5 cells	106.0	53.0

G.711	64	4.1	1.5	160	160	50		2	ATM	4 cells	84.8	42.4
G.729	8	3.9	15	10	30	33	40		PPP	6	20.3	10.1
G.729	8	3.9	15	10	30	33		2	PPP	6	10.1	5.1
G.729	8	3.9	15	10	30	33	40		FR	4	19.7	9.9
G.729	8	3.9	15	10	30	33		2	FR	4	9.6	4.8
G.729	8	3.9	15	10	30	33	40		ATM	2 cells	28.3	14.1
G.729	8	3.9	15	10	30	33		2	ATM	1 cell	14.1	7.1
G.723.1	6.3	3.9	37.5	30	30	26	40		PPP	6	16.0	8.0
G.723.1	6.3	3.9	37.5	30	30	26		2	PPP	6	8.0	4.0
G.723.1	6.3	3.9	37.5	30	30	26	40		FR	4	15.5	7.8
G.723.1	6.3	3.9	37.5	30	30	26		2	FR	4	7.6	3.8
G.723.1	6.3	3.9	37.5	30	30	26	40		ATM	2 cells	22.3	11.1
G.723.1	6.3	3.9	37.5	30	30	26		2	ATM	1 cell	11.1	5.6
G.723.1	5.3	3.65	37.5	30	30	22	40		PPP	6	13.4	6.7
G.723.1	5.3	3.65	37.5	30	30	22		2	PPP	6	6.7	3.4
G.723.1	5.3	3.65	37.5	30	30	22	40		FR	4	13.1	6.5
G.723.1	5.3	3.65	37.5	30	30	22		2	FR	4	6.4	3.2
G.723.1	5.3	3.65	37.5	30	30	22	40		ATM	2 cells	18.7	9.4
G.723.1	5.3	3.65	37.5	30	30	22		2	ATM	1 cell	9.4	4.7

Cisco provides guidance on how a network designer can assess the overhead associated with the use of various ITU-T codecs in conjunction with Cisco's VoIP products [CISC00c]. Part of this information is provided in Chapter 8 (see "Guidance on Fragmentation"). For our discussion now, Table 5–2 shows Cisco's VoIP bandwidth consumption statistics for the prevalent ITU-T codecs.

The table is mostly self-descriptive, but the following additional comments should prove helpful.

- *Voice Bandwidth (BW) kbit/s:* Bandwidth consumption of the codec.
- *MOS:* Mean opinion score of the quality of the codec. Recall that 5 is the highest and 0 is the lowest, and anything above 4.0 is considered very good.
- *Codec Delay (ms):* Processing delay at the codec.
- *Packet Size (Bytes):* Sample size for the packet.
- *Cisco Payload (Bytes):* Cisco overhead (and the samples), used to identify and manage the voice samples. This value includes the bytes cited in the previous column.
- *Packets Per Second:* Number of packets sent per second. This emission rate is a function of the codec and payload size.
- *IP/UDP/RTP headers (Bytes):* Number of bytes in these headers.
- *cRTP (Bytes):* Use of Cisco's compression algorithm (see "Compressing the Headers" in Chapter 8).
- *L_2:* Type of layer 2 bearer service.
- *L_2 Header (Bytes):* Headers at layer 2.
- *Total Bandwidth (BW) (kbit/s) no VAD:* Bandwidth required with no VAD.
- *Total Bandwidth (BW) (kbit/s) with VAD:* Bandwidth required with VAD.

The column labeled "Total Bandwidth bit/s with no VAD" is calculated as follows: linefeed (Cisco payload (bytes) + IP/UDP/RTP headers (bytes) [or cRTP header (bytes) + Layer2 header (bytes)) × 8 [bits per byte] × Packets per second.

The exception to this calculation is when ATM is used at layer 2: linefeed (number of cells × 53 [bytes per cell] × 8 [bits per byte] × Packets per second.

Using the VAD operation, the total bandwdith of the VoIP session is half the bandwidth consumed when VAD is not executed.

SUMMARY

Speech coders are the engines for the creation and processing of the VoIP packets. They, in turn, are driven by DSPs, discussed in Chapter 3.

The old DS0, TDM G.711 coder of 64 kbit/s will eventually be phased out of the industry and replaced with the low-bit-rate coders.

6

Modems, LAPM, PPP, and the V.100 Series

In this chapter, we examine the newer high-speed modems, with an emphasis on V.34 and V.90 (the 56-kbit/s modem). Some Internet users are using the layer-2 link protocol, Link Access Procedure for Modems (LAPM), so we will examine LAPM as well. The Point-to-Point Protocol (PPP) is used in most dial-up connections to the Internet, so we must examine the PPP also. Some PPP-based products do not use LAPM, and instead use a similar protocol, named Link Access Procedure, Balanced (LAPB); it, too, is covered. Since ISDN services are available in most cities today, we take a look at how the V.100 Series supports the ISDN user.

You may wonder why I am including information on modems in a VoIP book. After all, modems are designed to transport data over analog links, and VoIP is voice. We need to keep in mind that VoIP voice samples are represented as data bits, and these data bits are contained in data packets. Therefore, if a telco analog local loop or a CATV cable is used by the VoIP customer, the modem is the instrument used to get the VoIP data packets across these links. If the local loop is ISDN based, the modem may be still involved at the customer site.

Of course, if the VoIP packets are being transported across a native digital network such as an Ethernet, then the modem is not employed.

But for point-to-point dial-up links, the modem is quite important, and the VoIP gateways stipulate the types of modems the customer must use for the gateway interface.

One other point before we proceed into the chapter. I have chosen to explain outboard modems in this chapter; that is, modems that are not housed inside the user's terminal. These examples are relevant to an installation that has a modem pool, with banks of modems in use. An inboard modem may not implement all the operations that are described in this chapter, specifically the use of some of the V.24 interchange circuits.

ANOTHER LOOK AT THE LAYERED ARCHITECTURE FOR VoIP

We have now assimilated enough information to have another look at the VoIP protocol stack that was introduced in Chapters 1 and 3, as depicted in Figure 6–1. In this chapter, we will adjust the model described in the introductory chapters and provide some more details. For this part of the book, we focus on layers 1 and 2 of this model.

In Chapter 7, the roles of ISDN, ADSL, and HFC are explained. This chapter examines the V Series modems, as well as the layer-2 protocols shown here. You might wish to refer back to Figure 6–1 as you read this chapter.

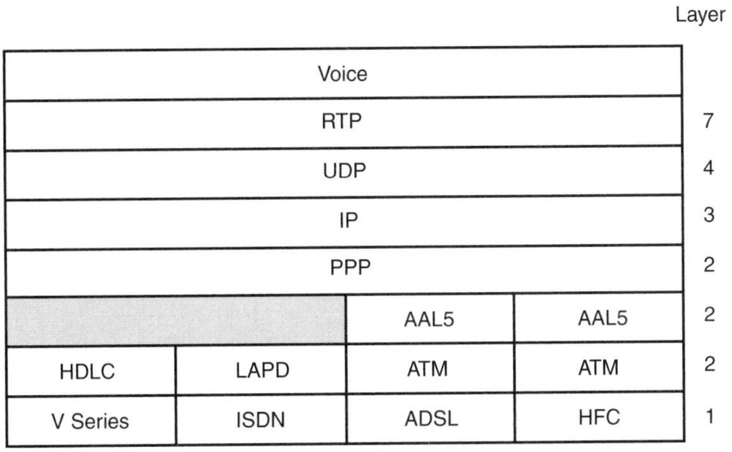

Layer

Voice			
RTP			7
UDP			4
IP			3
PPP			2
		AAL5	AAL5	2
HDLC	LAPD	ATM	ATM	2
V Series	ISDN	ADSL	HFC	1

Figure 6–1 The VoIP layered protocol suite

PREVALENT MODEMS

The ITU-T is the prevalent standards organization for the publication of modem specifications. Indeed, I doubt a commercial modem can be purchased which does not adhere to ITU-T specifications. These modems are published under the ITU-T V Series recommendations.[1]

The architecture for the recent V Series modems is based on the V.34 specifications. More recent variations of V.34 are published in V.90 (more commonly known as the 56-kbit/s modem). A later section in this chapter describes the architectures of these modems.

ROLE OF DSPs IN MODEM OPERATIONS

Chapter 4 was devoted to a discussion of DSPs. Modern modems employ programmable DSPs. Previously, modem DSPs were based on read-only-memory (ROM). This approach required new hardware for any upgrade or for the support of a new modem standard. Programmable DSPs allow changes, upgrades, etc., to be downloaded to the user device. From the user device, the upgrade can then be loaded onto the DSP.

TYPICAL LINK LAYOUT

Figure 6–2 shows a typical layout for a data communications link. Several of the prominent physical layer (L_1) standards do not specify the complete physical interface between two user devices (called data terminal equipment (DTE) in the ITU-T specifications). Specifically, the span between the modems may not be defined. Prominent examples are the EIA-232 and V.24 standards. Fortunately, this part of the physical inter-

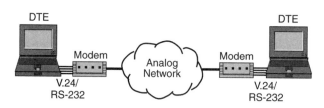

Figure 6–2   Analog configuration

---

[1]For more information on V Series recommendations, see [BLAC95].

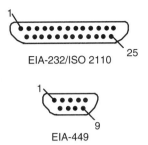

Figure 6–3   Physical connector examples

face is standardized through the ITU-T V Series modem specifications. Figure 6–2 shows the relationship of these specifications to the physical layer interface.

The cables and wires between the DTE ports and the modems are joined to connectors that take the shape of small metal pins. The pins serve as "plugs" into the computers and modems. These connectors are called *interchange circuits*. Figure 6–3 shows two choices for the physical interchange circuits, as well as the International Standards Organization (ISO) mechanical connectors. The connectors' interchange circuits are identified by numbers, by alphabetic identifiers (AB, AC, etc.), or by functional descriptions (transmit data circuit, request-to-send circuit, etc.). You may not see these connectors on your PC or workstation. Some manufacturers use a proprietary connector, and many have migrated to a conventional telephone jack.

THE V.24 INTERFACE STANDARD

V.24 is used on the vast majority of modems to describe the functions of the interchange circuits ("pins" or circuits) on the interface. Many products use this standard, principally in modems, line drivers, multiplexers, and digital service units. The V.24 interchange circuits are listed in Table 6–1, with a brief description of their functions.

THE EIA-232 INTERFACE

The RS-232/EIA-232 standards have been widely used throughout the world and are functionally aligned with the ITU-T V.24 recommendations. During the last two revisions, RS-232-C was redesignated as

Table 6–1   V.24 interchange circuits

Interchange Circuit Number	Interchange Circuit Name
102	Signal ground or common return
102a	DTE common return
102b	DCE common return
102c	Common return
103	Transmitted data
104	Received data
105	Request to send
106	Ready for sending
107	Data set ready
108/1	Connect data set to line
108/2	Data terminal ready
109	Data channel received line signal detector
110	Data signal quality detector
111	Data signal rate selector (DTE)
112	Data signal rate selector (DCE)
113	Transmitter signal element timing (DTE)
114	Transmitter signal element timing (DCE)
115	Receiver signal element timing (DCE)
116	Select standby
117	Standby indicator
118	Transmitted backward channel data
119	Received backward channel data
120	Transmit backward channel line signal
121	Backward channel ready
122	Backward channel received line signal detector
123	Backward channel signal quality detector
124	Select frequency groups
125	Calling indicator
126	Select transmit frequency
127	Select receive frequency
128	Receiver signal element timing (DTE)
129	Request to receive
130	Transmit backward tone
131	Received character timing

(continued)

Table 6–1   V.24 interchange circuits (*continued*)

Interchange Circuit Number	Interchange Circuit Name
132	Return to nondata mode
133	Ready for receiving
134	Received data present
136	New signal
140	Loopback/maintenance test
141	Local loopback
142	Test indicator
191	Transmitted voice answer
192	Received voice answer

EIA-232-D, then EIA-232-E. One revision includes the definition of three testing circuits, a redefinition of ground, and some other minor changes. Another revision made other changes to align EIA-232 with V.24. Table 6–2 summarizes the EIA-232 standard and its relationship to the ITU-T V.24 circuits.

Figure 6–4 summarizes several key points about the point-to-point physical layer and provides an example of how the EIA-232/V.24 interchange circuits are employed for the transfer of the data packet across the interface between the DTE and the modem. Be aware that the packets noted in Figure 6–4 may occupy the full duplex channel at the same time.

The following interchange circuits are on, thus permitting a handshake to take place between the modems: (a) DTE ready, (b) Data set ready, (c) Request to send, (d) Clear to send. The activation of these circuits means the modem and the user terminal are powered up, have completed several diagnostic checks, and are ready to engage in a full duplex connection. The signal-detect interchange circuits are turned on only after the modems have completed their handshakes. As explained later, the handshake entails an analysis of the quality of the link between the modems and the associated decision as to the appropriate bit rate to be used. Other parts of the handshake include the possible use of LAPM and data compression.

You may have noticed that it takes few seconds for you to get a connection to your ISP after you have clicked the "Sign On" button; the

Table 6–2   EIA-232 and ITU-T V.24 interchange circuits

EIA Interchange Circuit	V.24 ITU-T Equivalent	Description
AB	102	Signal ground/common return
BA	103	Transmitted data
BB	104	Received data
CA	105	Request to send
CB	106	Clear to send
CC	107	DCE ready
CD	108.2	DTE ready
CE	125	Ring indicator
CF	109	Received line signal detector
CG	110	Signal quality detector
CH	111	Data signal rate selector (DTE)
CI	112	Data signal rate selector (DCE)
DA	113	Transmitter signal element timing (DTE)
DB	114	Transmitter signal element timing (DCE)
DD	115	Receiver signal element timing (DCE)
LL	141	Local loopback
RL	140	Remote loopback
SBA	118	Secondary transmitted data
SBB	119	Secondary received data
SCA	120	Secondary request to send
SCB	121	Secondary clear to send
SCF	122	Secondary received line signal detector
TM	142	Test mode

modems are going through a rather elaborate ceremony to set up a good connection for your traffic.

After all these preliminary operations are complete, packets are exchanged between the DTEs. Notice that the modems are providing clocking information to the DTEs, through the V.24 114/115 interchange circuits. The clocking keeps the bits aligned in time and phase between the modem and the user device.

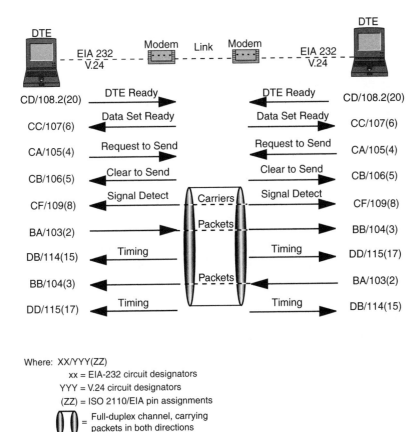

Figure 6–4   Conventional analog signaling

TYPICAL MODEM LAYOUT

Figure 6–5 shows a typical layout for a V Series modem [STEVb98]. The architecture is divided into the controller and the data pump. The controller is responsible for compression/decompression operations as well as for handling the AT command set.[2] It is also responsible for the V.42 operations, also known as Link Access Procedure for Modems (LAPM). LAPM is a conventional data link protocol. In some situations, Link Ac-

---

[2]The AT (attention) commands are based on the old Hayes modems. The commands "adjust" the operations of the modem and DTE. The commands control registers and buffers within the personal computer port and the modem. For more information see [BLAC96].

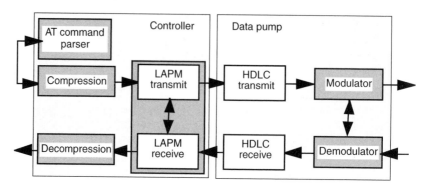

Figure 6–5   Typical modem layout [STEVb98]

cess Procedure, Balanced (LAPB) can be used instead of LAPM. They are quite similar to each other and are responsible for the following operations:

- They perform the layer-2 handshake after the layer-1 handshake is completed.
- They use the HDLC error check to acknowledge the receipt of traffic.
- They ensure the proper sequencing of the traffic.
- If frames arrive out of order or are missing, they notify the sending modem to correct the problem by resending the problem frames.

The data pump contains the HDLC flag/framing, error calculations, and bit stuffing/unstuffing operations for both transmit and receive, as well as the V Series modulation and demodulation operations.[3] LAPM uses the HDLC operations. As a whole, LAPM and HDLC form the layer-2 link protocol. The DSP operates at this part of the modem.

ROLE OF THE POINT-TO-POINT PROTOCOL

The Point-to-Point protocol (PPP) is also classified as a layer-2 protocol, but it relies on HDLC for the basic L_2 framing, error-checking, and bit-stuffing operations. It may also rest on top of LAPM or LAPB if error correction and retransmission operations are to be used. As depicted in

---

[3]For more details on the operations of HDLC, see [BLAC93].

Figure 6–1, an Internet session may entail the execution of three L_2 protocols: (a) HDLC, (b) LAPM or LAPB, and (c) PPP.

PPP was implemented to solve a problem that evolved in the industry during the last decade. With the rapid growth of internetworking, several vendors and standards organizations developed a number of network-layer (L_3) protocols. The Internet Protocol (IP) is the most widely used of these protocols. However, machines (such as routers) typically run more than one network-layer protocol. Although IP is a given on most machines, routers also support network-layer protocols developed by companies such as Xerox, 3Com, and Novell. Machines communicating with each other did not readily know which network-layer protocols were available during a session.

In addition, until the advent of PPP, the industry did not have a standard means to define a point-to-point encapsulation protocol. Encapsulation means that a protocol carries or encapsulates a network layer packet in its I field and uses another field in the frame to identify which network-layer packet resides in the I field. The PPP standard solves these two problems. Moreover, until PPP was developed, the industry relied on older, less efficient protocols, such as SLIP (Serial Link IP).

PPP encapsulates network-layer datagrams over a serial communications link. The protocol allows two machines on a point-to-point communications channel to negotiate the particular types of network-layer protocols (such as IP) that are to be used during a session. If a user is using dial-up access to an ISP, PPP is also used by the ISP to assign the user an IP address for the Internet session.

PPP also allows the two machines to negotiate other types of operations, such as the use of compression and authentication procedures. After this negotiation occurs, PPP is used to carry the network-layer packets in the I field of an HDLC type of frame.

This protocol supports either bit-oriented synchronous transmission, byte-oriented transmission, or asynchronous (start/stop) transmission. It can be used on switched or dial-up links. It requires a full-duplex capability.

THE PROTOCOL DATA UNIT ON THE LINK BETWEEN THE USER AND THE ISP

The traffic that is sent between the user and the ISP is known by various names. The most general term is protocol data unit (PDU). Most people in the industry call an L_2 PDU a frame. Figure 6–6 shows the format of this frame. The frame can contain three L_2 headers and the HDLC

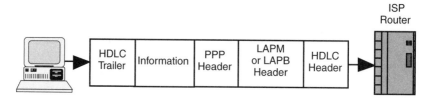

Figure 6–6   The layer-2 frame

trailer. If this implementation is used, the headers and the trailer perform these functions:

- *HDLC header:* Contains a specific set of bits (the flag) that are used at the receiver to detect the beginning of the frame.
- *LAPM or LAPB header:* Contains sequence numbers, flow-control bits, ACK and NAK bits, and bits that identify the type of frame (user data, control frame, etc.).
- *PPP header:* Contains information to negotiate a variety of services, as well as an encapsulation field that identifies the L_3 protocol residing in the information field of the frame.
- *HDLC trailer:* Contains an error check field, called the frame check sequence (FCS).

V SERIES MODEMS

The V Series recommendations (also called standards by many people) have become some of the most widely used specifications in the world for defining how data is exchanged between computers and communications equipment such as modems and multiplexers. In the past, the V Series recommendations were used principally in Europe because of the influence of the Postal, Telephone, and Telegraph (PTT) administrations in each European country. However, with the growing recognition of the need for international communications standards, the V Series recommendations have found their way into most countries of the world and into practically all vendors' modem products. Their use has paved the way for easier, more efficient, and less costly communications between users' computers, terminals, and other data processing machines.

The V.34 Operations

In the continuing quest to gain more bandwidth from the local subscriber loop, the ITU-T has been publishing specifications for high-speed modems for many years. A prominent entry is V.34, which forms the architecture for current modems (V.90 and V.92). V.34 retains some of the features of other modems, such as V.17, V.29, V.32, V.32 bis, and V.33, and at the same time adds many of its own unique characteristics. Below are listed some of the major attributes of V.34.

- Operates on two-wire, point-to-point telephone circuits (or circuits that meet telco specifications)
- Operates on dial-up (switched) or leased circuits
- Operates in half-duplex or duplex modes
- Achieves channel separation by echo cancellation
- Utilizes QAM on each channel
- Operates in synchronous mode
- Employs trellis coding
- Provides for an optional 200-bit/s asynchronous secondary channel
- Provides adaptive signaling (in bit/s) through line probing by adjusting to channel quality/capacity
- Uses conventional V.24 interchange circuits
- Supports the following signaling rates (bit/s):

2400	12000	21600
4800	14400	24000
7200	16800	26400
9600	19200	28800

Unlike the previous high-speed V Series modems, V.34 uses symbol rates other than 2400.[4] The following symbol rates are supported: 2400, 2743, 2800, 3000, 3200, 3429, with symbol rates of 2400, 3000, and 3200 mandatory. Furthermore, the carrier frequencies can also vary, ranging from 1600 to 2000 Hz.

Both the symbol rate and the carrier frequency are selected during the modem startup and handshaking procedure. During this procedure,

---

[4]You may be more familiar with the term baud, instead of symbol rate. They describe the same function, but the term baud is falling into disrepute, since many people incorrectly use baud to mean bit rate. Bit rate and baud are not the same.

the modems can select one or two carrier frequencies for each symbol rate.

For the reader who wishes to know the details of how modern modems operate, I have prepared Appendix C. I place this information in an appendix because although it is tangential to the subject of VoIP, I know that some of the readers will find this information useful. However, to keep with the main theme of this book, we now turn our attention to the principal modem used today, the 56 kbit/s modem, published by the ITU-T as V.90.

The 56-kbit/s V.90 Modem

The 56-kbit/s V.90 modem is the next step up from the V.34 modem. My description of this technology is based on the ITU-T V.90 Recommendation, [WEXL98] and a paper by P. Michael Henderson [HEND96]. I recommend Mr. Henderson's work to those readers who wish to delve into the details of 56-kbit/s modems.

The 56-kbit/s modem is really an evolution from the V.32 and V.34 quadrature amplitude modulation (QAM) concepts of placing more bits onto the voice-grade local loop. But there is one big difference. Modified digital pulse code modulation (PCM) techniques are used from the service provider, such as the telco or ISP (downstream), and QAM is used from the user to the service provider (upstream). The configuration is shown in Figure 6–7.

There are several reasons why the 56-kbit/s modem operates at this rate. First of all, Shannon's theorem is not being violated. The technology works with the assumption that the signal-to-noise ratio on the line must not exceed 45 dB in order to support 56 kbit/s. This ratio can be achieved on local loop lines.

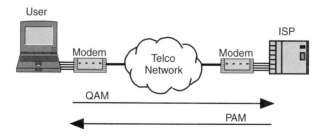

Figure 6–7   Setup for the 56-kbit/s modem

In the United States, the FCC limits the transmit power on local links. Consequently, some quantization points are not available. The circuit may also experience nonlinear distortion, which also cuts down the possible data rate. Another problem deals with the T1 technology. Certain T1 samples have bits robbed from them for signaling purposes. This means the full eight bits per sample may not be available. Remember that PCM operations rely on quantization, and some of these levels are given up because the customer's modem is unable to detect all possible quantization levels.

In effect, the downstream transmission does not use all of the conventional PCM steps. All these factors join together to limit the data rate to 56 kbit/s.

For the 56-kbit/s modem to operate successfully, both modems on the link must use the same technology. In addition, the modem pool at the service provider must have a digital connection to the network. Furthermore, no intermittent conversions can be performed on the traffic. These requirements do not create serious problems since most Internet access involves the connection to a local telco, so the telco bearer services can be invoked.

V.90: Consolidates the Technologies   Before the V.90 agreement, two proprietary specifications (which were incompatible) were deployed in the marketplace: (a) X2, developed by the U.S. Robotics Inc. (acquired by 3Com Corp.), and (b) k56flex, developed by Lucent Technologies and Rockwell Semiconductor Systems. V.90 offers a standardized compromise between the two. Appendix C provides more information on V.90.

V.100, V.110, AND V.120 RECOMMENDATIONS FOR ISDN INTERFACES

Several of the ITU-T V Series recommendations contain specifications on how certain signals are exchanged (and changed) between different types of networks. These standards have become increasingly important in the past few years as networks, carriers, and telephone administrations have implemented the ISDN and other digital-based systems, and as the ISDN standards require the use of the specifications described here. On a conventional analog-based link (see Figure 6–2), V.110 and V.120 define how certain V.24-interchange signals are carried on the modulated analog signal. Both user data and modem control signals are carried across the link.

Control signals are also applicable for systems in which modem signals must be tunneled through a packet data network, such as an inter-

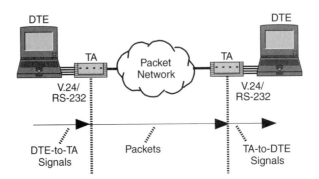

Figure 6–8   Transporting the signals through the packet network

net. Figure 6–8 shows this situation.[5] A machine called a terminal adapter (TA) maps the incoming V.24 signals to the appropriate bits in a packet and sends this packet to the receiving TA.[6] At the receiving TA, the process is reversed.

A modem modulates an analog carrier signal to convey information to another modem. This information can be user data, or it can be modem control signals. The user data is relatively straightforward: the TA maps between the analog signals and the digital bits. Control signals are more complicated. The TA must be intelligent enough to know which signals on the V.24/EIA-232 interface are to be mapped and transmitted in the packets to the receiving TA, and of course, the receiving TA must be able to perform the reverse operation.

The ITU-T defines the following specifications to perform these operations. We concentrate on V.110 in this part of the book but briefly describe V.100 and V.120.

- *V.100:* Interconnection between public data networks (PDNs) and the public-switched telephone network
- *V.110:* Support by an ISDN of data terminal equipment with the V Series types of interfaces

---

[5]The V Series recommendations discussed in this text are offered in some vendor products, but not in all of them. If they are not available, other operations are used to perform the same types of functions.

[6]The term *terminal adapter* is used by the ITU-T. In the Internet VoIP specifications, the term *gateway* is used. Both machines are responsible for mapping and syntax conversion operations between analog and digital systems. The TA is ISDN oriented and designed to use the ISDN B and D channels. The internet gateway can be ISDN oriented, but it need not be, and it can be configured to interface with IP, SS7, and conventional telephony signals, such as on-hook and off-hook.

- *V.120:* Support by an ISDN of DTEs with the V Series types of interfaces with provision for statistical multiplexing
- *V.230:* General data communications interface layer-1 specifications

The V.100 Recommendation

The connection of user workstations to data networks through the public telephone network is quite common today. To ensure that the dial-and-answer telephone procedures are consistent across different manufacturers' equipment, the ITU-T has published V.100. This recommendation describes the procedures for physical-layer handshaking between answering and calling modems. The recommendation defines procedures for both half- and full-duplex procedures.

V.100 requires that the dial-and-answer procedures of V.25 or V.25 bis be used to perform the initial handshaking between the modems. Among other requirements, the receiving modem must send an answer tone back to the transmitting modem. Once the transmitting modem has transmitted this tone to the receiving modem, it enters the operations defined in V.100.

Once the modems have exchanged the dial and answer tones, the answering modem transmits what is known as the S1 signal. This signal is of a certain frequency, depending upon the type of modem used.

Upon sending signal S1, the modem remains silent until it detects a signal S2. Based on its response to S2, it either disconnects or conditions itself to the selected mode as indicated in S2. To continue the example, the originating modem sends an S1 signal to verify that it is the modem type and the receiving modem sends back an S2 signal to complete the handshake.

The V.110 Recommendation

The V.110 recommendation has received considerable attention in the industry because it defines procedures that have been incorporated into several vendors' ISDN terminal adapters (TAs). Among other features, V.110 establishes the conventions for adapting a V Series data rate to the ISDN 64-kbit/s rate. Figure 6–9 illustrates the scheme used by V.110.

The V.110 terminal adapter consists of two major functions: rate adapter 1 (RA1) and rate adapter 2 (RA2). The RA1 produces an intermediate rate (IR), which is then input into RA2. RA1 accepts standard V Series interface data rates, ranging from 600 bit/s to 38,400 bit/s.[7] The k

---

[7]The standards always lag behind the commercial industry. Obviously, 38.4 kbit/s is cited in this standard, but commercial products have higher rates.

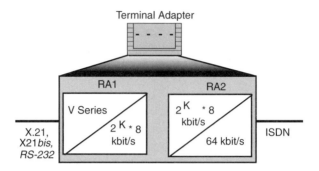

Figure 6–9   The terminal adapter

The B-Channel Problem

As an aside, it is the 64-kbit/s, channelized architecture that makes the V.100–V.110 series (and ISDN) rather inefficient and inflexible with regard to the transport of VoIP traffic. We have learned that VoIP is based on low-bit-rate coders whose signals are not aligned on the B channel (or a DS0) boundary. Nonetheless, ISDN is a big factor in many point-to-point, dial-up links, at least for the next few years, so ISDN is a pertinent subject for this book. Anyway, let us continue the analysis.

---

value is 0, 1, 2, or 3. The output of RA2 is always 64 kbit/s, in conformance with the ISDN B-channel rate.

RA Frame

Figure 6–10 illustrates the output of RA1, which is an 80-bit frame. The user data is placed into this frame, and some of the bits in the frame are also used for a variety of control functions:

- Seventeen bits are used for synchronization to provide frame alignment patterns.
- Several bits are used to convey information about the status of V.24 circuits 105, 106, 107, 108, and 109.
- Several bits are used for network-independent clocking information.

A maximum of 48 user bits can be sent in each frame. Therefore, up to 19.2 kbit/s can be placed in the intermediate frame, which has a maximum rate of 32 kbit/s. This value can be derived from a simple calcula-

Bit Position								Octet
1	2	3	4	5	6	7	8	Number
0	0	0	0	0	0	0	0	0
1	D1	D2	D3	D4	D5	D6	S1	1
1	D7	D8	D9	D10	D11	D12	X	2
1	D13	D14	D15	D16	D17	D18	S3	3
1	D19	D20	D21	D22	D23	D24	S4	4
1	E1	E2	E3	E4	E5	E6	E7	5
1	D25	D26	D27	D28	D29	D30	S6	6
1	D31	D32	D33	D34	D35	D36	X	7
1	D37	D38	D39	D40	D41	D42	S8	8
1	D43	D44	D45	D46	D47	D48	S9	9

Figure 6–10   The frame structure

tion: A 32-kbit/s channel allows 400 frames to be transmitted per second (32,000 divided by 80 equals 400). A maximum of 48 bits can be placed in each frame; therefore, 400 times 48 equals 19,200.

If a smaller data signaling rate is used, some of the positions in the frame are not relevant, and they are simply padded out with redundant data bits. For higher bit rates, RA2 creates a frame structure to handle rates of up to 64 kbit/s, for example, the user rate of 38.4 kbit/s.

We now examine how the bits in the frame are used. First, the synchronization bits are used to synchronize the machines' transmissions. The first octet serves as the initial synchronization signal and is set to all 0's. Thereafter, bit 1 of each of the following nine octets (set to 1) completes the synchronization pattern.

The S and X bits are called status bits, and they provide mapping functions of several of the V.24 interchange circuits that exist at the user device (DTE) and the TA. The state of these interchange circuits is mapped into the S and X bits, sent across the channel to the remote TA-DTE interface, and then used to operate the V.24 interchange circuits on the other side of the interface. With this approach, the system operates with digital bits in the frame, and no modems are required for the traffic inside the ISDN or packet network. The mapping scheme is as follows:

Circuit	Bit Map	Circuit
108	S1,S3,S6,S8 = SA	107
105	S4,S9 = SB	109
106	X	106

This mapping table is extracted from V.110 and becomes clearer with a few more explanations. The two circuit columns in the table represent the

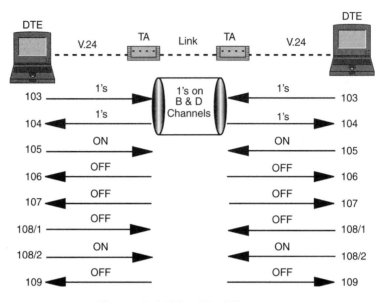

Figure 6–11(a)   The idle state

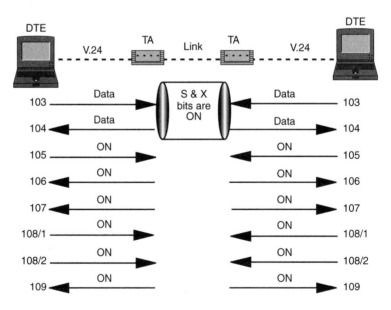

Figure 6–11(b)   The data transfer state

V.24 circuits at the two DTE-TA interfaces. The middle bit map column represents how the V.24 circuits are mapped into the bits in the frame. The state of the circuits (ON or OFF) is mapped to binary 0's and 1's, respectively. Several of the bits are used together and are called SA and SB.

The E bits provide several functions. Some of them identify the intermediate rate that is being used in the frame. Some optional E bits carry network-independent clock-phase information. As an example, a modem on a public telephone network may not be synchronized to the ISDN. These bits can be used to develop phase measurements for signaling synchronization.

V.110 Handshaking

Next we discuss the operations for V.110 handshaking. Figure 6–2 is shown in two parts. Figure 6–11(a) shows the interfaces during an idle state, and Figure 6–11(b) shows the interfaces during a data transfer state. This example assumes that the B channel has been established between the TAs and that they are awaiting the user DTEs to send traffic. Thus, they are in an idle state.

During the idle state, the DTEs are transmitting and receiving binary 1's on circuits 103 and 104. The TAs in turn send these 1's to each other in the B and D channels. The other pertinent circuits at the DTE-TA interfaces are ON or OFF, as depicted in the figure.

For data to be sent, circuit 108/1 must be placed in the ON state, as shown in Figure 6–11(b). This change on circuit 108/1 will cause the TAs to send the frame synchronization pattern. When this pattern is recognized, then the S and X bits are sent in the ON condition. The receipt of these bits at the TAs will cause the circuits that were OFF previously to be placed in the ON condition. Other rules (and timers) are associated with these operations, but the end result is the use of circuits 103 and 104 to pass packets between the user devices.

The interface is torn down by a DTE turning to OFF circuit 108/1. The TA will then send the frame with S = OFF. The result will be turning circuits 106, 107, and 109 to the OFF condition, and the disconnection is complete.

THE V.120 RECOMMENDATION

V.110 is the main subject for this part of the chapter, but a few words on V.120 are in order for those readers using ISDN interfaces. In recognition that the V Series will be in existence for a considerable period and in view of the need for ISDN devices (terminal equipment type 1 or TE1) to interwork with non-ISDN devices (TE2), the ITU-T has published the V.120 recommendation. V.120 supports an ISDN interface with a DTE and its associated physical layer interface. The DTE must operate with the V Series interfaces. V.120 also supports the multiplexing of multiple-user data links onto the ISDN S/T interface. V.120 uses a link-level protocol based on the modification of Link Access Procedure for the D Channel (LAPD) published as Q.921. LAPD is similar to LAPM and LAPB, discussed earlier in this chapter.

V.120 describes the use of a TA for the ISDN-to-V Series DTE interworking. However, this TA performs more functions than the TA we examined with V.110. It must perform the following services:

- Electrical and mechanical interfaces conversions
- Adaptation of bit transfer rate (as in V.110)
- End-to-end synchronization of traffic
- Call management between the two end users

Three modes of operations are supported with the V.120 terminal adapter: asynchronous, synchronous, and transparent. You are probably aware that asynchronous mode terminals (async TE2s) use start/stop bits and parity checks. The TA accepts the asynchronous stream from the user device and removes the start/stop bits. As an option, parity may be checked by the TA. In either case, the user data characters are placed in a frame for transmission to a peer entity. The peer entity is another TA or a TE1.

SUMMARY

Modems are designed to transport data over analog links. Since VoIP often is transported over these same links, modems must be employed for VoIP traffic as well. The prevalent modem architecture is based on the ITU-T V.34 Recommendation, which is the basis for the 56-kbit/s V.90 modem.

Higher speed lines do not use V.90 but rely on technologies such as DSL, ISDN, and other technologies that offer more bandwidth to the user.

7

Connecting to Service Providers Through the Local Loop

$\mathbf{T}$ his chapter explains how the VoIP user is connected to the Internet or an internet through the telco local loop. We look at the role of the telephone network, and we examine ISP configurations, as well as the network access point (NAP). We then analyze how the user's modem analog signal is terminated.

Since a major problem of the local loop is its limited capacity, the chapter also provides an overview of the Integrated Services Digital Network (ISDN), the emerging X digital subscriber line (xDSL), and the hybrid fiber coax (HFC) technologies, as well as a proprietary high-speed modem from Nortel Networks. All these schemes are designed to give the Internet user more bandwidth on the local loop to and from the service provider.

We conclude the chapter by showing how the telco facilities (and the telco circuit switch) can be bypassed.

PATH BETWEEN AN INTERNET USER AND THE INTERNET

Figure 7–1 shows a typical configuration employed between the user customer premises equipment and an internet. The user employs a conventional V Series modem to modulate the analog signals on the local loop to

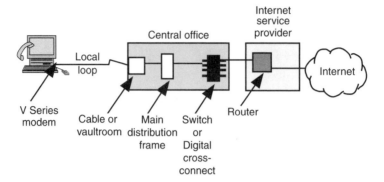

Figure 7–1   Connecting to the Internet Service Provider

the local telephone office. At the telephone office, the analog signals are digitized in some type of T1 frame (T1, T3, etc.) and are sent through the telephone digital backbone to a designated ISP. The telephone company performs the analog-to-digital (A-D) and digital-to-analog (D-A) conversion operations. The interface between the telephone system and the Internet service provider (ISP) node is therefore digital if the telco backbone is used.

The ISPs connect to each other through network access points (NAPs); see Figure 7–2. The NAP's job is to exchange traffic between ISPs and other networks. NAPs must operate at link speeds of 100 Mbit/s, and thus their local networks have been implemented with FDDI

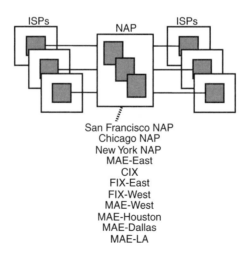

Figure 7–2   Network access point (NAP)

(the fiber distributed data interface), 100BASE-T (Fast Ethernet at 100 Mbit/s, or 1000Base-T) (Gigabit Ethernet at 1 Gbit/s). Many of them have ATM switches and SONET links to other NAPs and the larger ISPs.

Figure 7–2 lists 11 NAPs currently running in the United States. Some of them are called Metropolitan Area Exchanges (MAEs). Some base their names on the Federal Internet Exchange (FIX); others, on the Commercial Internet Exchange (CIX). FIXs were set up by the NSF to support federal regional networks. The CIX was set up by the public Internet service providers.

The NAP concept was established by the National Science Foundation (NSF) when it was managing the Internet. Originally, there were four NAPs (NSF-awarded NAPs), but due to the growth of the Internet, additional NAPs have been created, as shown in Figure 7–2.

For more information on NAPs and MAEs, as well as topology maps of the Internet, check www.boardwatch.com.

The ISP or NAP node can range from a simple configuration (for a small ISP) to one that has scores of routers, servers, LANs, and ATM/Frame Relay switches (for larger ISPs and NAPs). A typical ISP site will have high-speed LANs, multiple servers and high-speed access to the wide area networks, as shown in Figure 7–3. This site is where the bottlenecks can often occur. If LANs such as FDDI or Fast Ethernet inside the ISP site are not fast enough or if the routers become overloaded, then bottlenecks can occur. If the server farm is not large enough, then the servers may be buffering the data too long. Regardless of the type of equipment, the overall ISP system must be tuned frequently to deliver

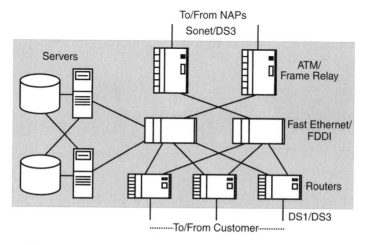

Figure 7–3   Typical NAP or large ISP configuration

steady streams of traffic into and out of the site. If this tuning does not happen, then congestion will occur [BATE99].

THE BANDWIDTH PROBLEM AT THE LOCAL LOOP

If I had to cite the biggest problem in deploying high-quality VoIP applications, data, and video to the masses (the general consumer), it would be the limited bandwidth on the local loop. Because of this problem, we spend time on the subject in this chapter.

For today's analog voice transport systems, the present structure on the local loop provides adequate capacity, but that capacity is insufficient for other applications, such as data and video. Voice has a modest bandwidth requirement, about 3.5 kHz of the frequency spectrum. The local loop (the distribution plant) is designed to support voice bandwidths.

The problem is that many applications that are now in the marketplace or that are being developed are significantly handicapped by local loop bottlenecks. As one example, file transfer and database accesses take too long with current technology. As another, Internet access and browsing is often a chore because of the limited bandwidth of the local loop. One of the reasons that so much research and development has been expended on low-bit-rate coders (Chapter 5) is because of the limited capacity of the local loop.

The present structure is not conducive to building multiapplication (multimedia) networks because voice, video, and data are difficult to run concurrently on the local loop.

In addition, the present digital systems retain the T1 legacy of using 64 kbit/s DS0 slots that are allocated with fixed, symmetrical bandwidth. This approach is not in line with today's applications that need dynamic, asymmetrical bandwidth.

Help is on the way. It is taking a long time, but it is surely coming. Let us now examine some of the new technologies purported to relieve the local loop bottleneck. The next discussion will not help the local loop problem, but it will help remove bottlenecks at the telco nodes and the telco backbone network.

TERMINATION OF THE MODEM ANALOG SIGNAL

As a general rule, voice and data service providers attempt to terminate the modem analog signal and convert it to a digital signal as soon as practicable. Figure 7–4 shows three scenarios for handling the analog

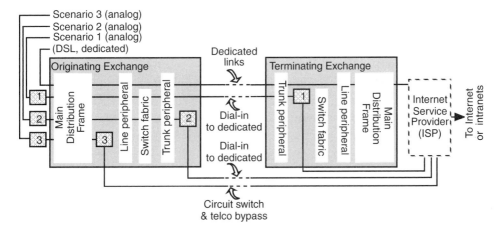

Figure 7–4   Possible modem terminations

modem termination.[1] The goal is to provide this termination as close to the subscriber as possible to allow more efficient techniques to be used on the remainder of the link to the Internet or corporate node. The shadowed boxes in the figure that are numbered 1, 2, or 3 symbolize the demarcation point at which the modem signals (modem connection) are terminated. Thereafter, digital signaling is employed at the physical layer, with Frame Relay or ATM operating over the physical layer and IP then operating over Frame Relay or ATM.

In scenario 1, the modem termination occurs at the trunk side of the terminating Central Office (CO) that is servicing the ISP. A data access switch is installed as a trunk-side peripheral at this CO. This configuration bypasses the line side of the remote CO, but this configuration is not a conventional method to terminate the modem interfaces because it entails sending the analog signal through the telco backbone, which is usually digital-based. Nonetheless, if parts of the telephone network are still analog oriented, this configuration is used.

In scenario 2, the modem termination occurs at the trunk side of the originating CO. The benefit of this approach is that it reduces or eliminates the need to upgrade the network's trunks to handle data traffic. The traffic is diverted to data networks before it hits the voice network. The data networks are designed to handle asynchronous data traffic. However, with this approach, the CO voice switch is still involved in the

---

[1]Additional information on these operations is available from *Telesis,* Issue 102, published by Nortel Networks, telesis@barcam.com.

processing of the data call, which results in tying up a port and resources on the local circuit switch.

Scenario 3 is the best approach. It terminates the analog connection before it enters the local voice switch. This example uses a front-end processor to intercept the user signal (this processor is not shown here but is explained later in this chapter). If the called party is an ISP customer, the call is diverted away from the CO facilities and sent directly to the ISP.

ALTERNATIVES TO THE MODEM-BASED LOCAL LOOP ACCESS

The conventional modem access to the Internet is the most popular way of getting a connection to a service provider. It is also one of the most inefficient ways. The high-speed modems (discussed in Chapter 6) cannot operate at speeds greater than 56 kbit/s. While this bit rate may seem adequate, it is not of sufficient capacity for large data transfers.

Several alternatives to modem access are emerging in several countries. The ISDN alternative has been around for a few years, but it does not solve the bandwidth problem because most commercial implementations are set for 64 kbit/s or (for a steep price) 128 kbit/s. The next section explains ISDN, but the emphasis in discussing alternatives in this chapter is on the digital subscriber line (DSL) and hybrid fiber coax (HFC) technologies.

THE INTEGRATED SERVICES DIGITAL NETWORK (ISDN)

In the 1960s and 1970s, as digital technology began to find its way into the telephone providers' networks and as the costs of digital technology declined, the telephone industry began to look for ways to move this technology into the local loop. The telephone service providers' view was that the superior characteristics of digital technology (over analog) would make it attractive to the customer.

Additionally, the use of analog signaling over the local loop was quite limited with regard to data rates (in bit/s). In fact, when ISDN was first introduced in 1984, the V.22 bis modem was just introduced, operating at only 2400 bit/s! So a 64 kbit/s rate sounded very attractive to the data user.

Then there was the recognition that the digital T1 technology was proving to be effective within the telephone carriers' backbone network—

so why not use some version of T1 at the local loop? This "version" is ISDN.

These factors lead to the deployment of ISDN in the local loop in the mid-1980s, especially in Europe. ISDN was not deployed much in North America until recently.

In the early 1990s, the Regional Bell Operating Companies (RBOCs) launched what is called National ISDN. It is a U.S. plan for a nation-wide, standardized implementation of ISDN technology. It places strict requirements on the vendors, manufacturers who build the ISDN equipment, and ISDN service providers.

As part of the plan, each Bell Operating Company set up deployment goals for (a) number of access lines that support ISDN, (b) number of wire centers to have ISDN presence, (c) total number of switches to have ISDN capabilities, and (d) total number of switches to have SS7 capabilities. These goals were tracked each year, with each RBOC publishing its progress report.

The telcos did a good job in meeting the deadlines. For more information on the National ISDN services, Bellcore document SR-3476 summarizes all the National ISDN features and capabilities that had to be available by 1996.

ISDN Bearer Services

The ISDN device connects to the ISDN through a twisted pair four-wire digital link; see Figure 7–5. This link uses time-division multiplexing (TDM) to provide three channels, designated as the B, B, and D channels (or 2B+D). The B channels operate at a speed of 64 kbit/s; the D channel operates at 16 kbit/s. The 2B+D is designated as the basic rate interface (BRI). ISDN also allows up to eight user devices to share one 2B+D link. The B channels carry the user payload in the form of voice, compressed video, and data. The D channel acts as an out-of-band control channel for setting up, managing, and clearing the B channel sessions.

For higher bandwidth needs, the interface can be a primary rate interface (PRI), which operates at the T1 rate of 1.544 Mbit/s or the E1 rate of 2.048 Mbit/s.

In other scenarios, the user device may not have ISDN installed. If this is the situation, a terminal adapter (TA) is used. The TA allows non-ISDN terminals to operate over ISDN lines. The user side of the TA typically uses a conventional physical-layer interface such as EIA-232 or the V Series specifications. It is packaged like an external modem or as a board that plugs into an expansion slot on the user devices.

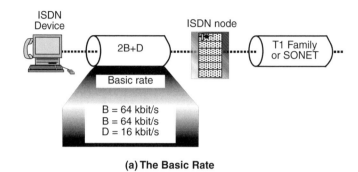

(a) The Basic Rate

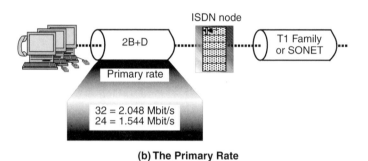

(b) The Primary Rate

Figure 7–5   ISDN services

Does ISDN Solve the Local Loop Bottleneck Problem?   I am not a big proponent of ISDN. I was a supporter until the V.34, and (later) the V.90, modems made it possible to pump 28.8 to 56 kbit/s (maybe) across the local loop to my ISP—at no additional charge. The ISDN B channel gives me 64 kbit/s, at an additional price of $20 to $60 dollars a month, depending on my location in the United States. The marginal increase in the data rate may not be worth the additional fee, but I recommend you investigate your local ISDN service provider before you decide.

Nonetheless, ISDN is here. If the 128 kbit/s rates are reduced, the technology will be more attractive. Moreover, since 1997, ISDN line installations (BRI and PRI) have been growing at an annual rate of over 25 percent.

So, what technology solves the local loop bandwidth problem? And it is a big problem. Two technologies solve the problem, or at least ameliorate it (it is too soon to know if they are complete solutions). They are discussed next.

ROLE OF DIGITAL SUBSCRIBER LINE (DSL) TECHNOLOGIES

The point was made earlier of the need to terminate the inefficient (and older) modem signals and convert them to digital signals or to more efficient analog signals. Part of the motivation for this transition is to take advantage of the higher bandwidths that are available with newer technologies. The technologies are known collectively as the digital subscriber line (DSL).

DSL distribution systems refer to a variety of systems that provide more capacity on the current embedded telephone-based copper loop plant. The asymmetric digital subscriber line (ADSL), very high bit-rate DSL (VDSL), and high bit-rate DSL (HDSL) are examples of DSL technologies. They are often grouped under the term "xDSL." Table 7–1 summarizes the xDSL technologies, including their bandwidth capacities and their intended deployment.

The installation of ADSL on the local loop does not disturb the existing cable in the distribution plant, nor does it necessitate taking down the customer's phone service for a long time. As shown Figure 7–6, the

Table 7–1   Digital Subscriber Line (DSL) technologies

xDSL Technology	Capacity	Deployment
Symmetrical digital subscriber line (SDSL)	Ranges from 64 kbit/s to 2,048 Mbit/s	Conventional T1/E1 symmetrical systems
High bit-rate digital subscriber line (HDSL)	1/2 of T1/E1 in each direction	T1 lines, with ISDN line coding
ISDN digital subscriber line (IDSL)	128 kbit/s in each direction	Proprietary xDSL
Asymmetrical digital subscriber line (ADSL)	*Downstream:* 6.144 Mbit/s, 384 kbit/s, 160 kbit/s, 64 kbit/s *Upstream:* 384 kbit/s, 160 kbit/s, 64 kbit/s	QAM techniques on twisted-pair
Rate adaptive ADSL (RADSL, or RDSL)	As above, and adapts to conditions on link	ADSL
Very high-rate digital subscriber line (VDSL)	Variation of ADSL	Variation of ADSL

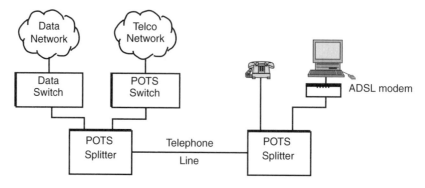

Figure 7–6   ADSL setup

customer's location is outfitted with a plain old telephone service (POTS) splitter and an ADSL remote unit. These interfaces allow the existing copper wire to be split into multiple channels: (a) Forward: Central Office to customer (upstream to downstream), and (b) Return: customer to central office (downstream to upstream).

The Evolving ADSL Technology

Figure 7–7 shows the reference model for ADSL. The interfaces are noted with dashed lines. This model is just that, a model. Some of the interfaces may not exist in a commercial product. For example, the T-SM interface might not exist, or might be the same as the T interface. The T interface might not exist if the terminal equipment (TE) is part of the ADSL transmission unit, remote side (ATU-R). The U interfaces might not exist if the splitter (S) is part of the ATUs or if the splitter is eliminated, which is the inclination in the industry.

First, the return channel (to the customer) operates at much lower frequency than the forward channel(s) (an asymmetrical configuration). Consequently, crosstalk is not so great a problem in comparison to conventional symmetrical configurations. The POTS voice signals are isolated from the ADSL signals by the lowpass voiceband splitter filter. The filter can be packaged with the interface card at the Central Office or CPE, or it can be packaged separately.

Be aware that some ADSL equipment manufacturers are building systems that eliminate the splitter.

Below is a list of names for the interfaces and other ADSL components and their functions shown in Figure 7–7 [GORA98]:

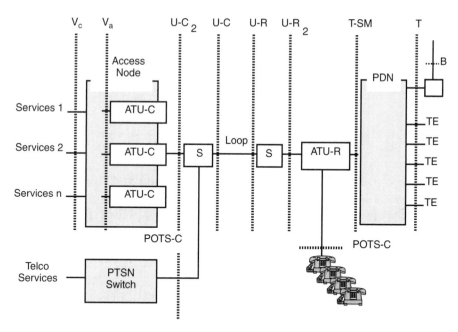

Figure 7–7   ADSL reference model [GORA98]

ATU-C	ADSL transmission unit, CO side
ATU-R	ADSL transmission unit, remote side
B	Auxiliary data input (set top box)
PDN	Premises distribution network
POTS-C	Interface between PSTN and splitter, CO side
POTS-R	Interface between PSTN and splitter, remote side
S	Splitter
T	Interface between terminal equipment and PDN
TE	Terminal equipment (user device)
T-SM	T interface for service module
U-C	U interface, CO side
U-C$_2$	U interface, CO side from splitter to ATU-C
U-R	U interface, remote side
U-R$_2$	U interface, remote side from splitter to ATU-R
V$_A$	V interface, access node side from ATU-C to access node
V$_C$	V interface, CO side from access node to network service

Unfortunately, there are not many DSL offerings at this time. They are beginning to emerge, but it remains to be seen how far the technologies will penetrate into the residential neighborhood. Estimates vary, with some studies predicting a penetration rate of 40% to 50% by 2002, and others predicting only 5% to 30%.

THE HYBRID FIBER COAX (HFC) APPROACH

Hybrid fiber coax (HFC) systems have been deployed in some suburban neighborhoods in several countries, and they are now slowly finding their way into the North American market. The supporters of this approach believe that ADSL technology (over the conventional twisted pair) does not provide enough bandwidth in relation to its costs. The HFC technology exploits the bandwidth capacity of fiber and coax.

As shown in Figure 7–8, the HFC network has an optical fiber facility running from the Central Office (the head end) to a neighborhood node. The fiber has forward and return paths. At the node, users are connected by coaxial cable.

Figure 7–9 shows a typical hybrid fiber coax system that uses the telco-based GR-303 and TR-08 standards. At the residence is a wall-mounted unit that typically supports two connections. This unit is labeled in the figure as coax/twisted pair node. This node connects the coaxial cable to the fiber/coax node in the distribution plant, which in turn connects the fiber to the Central Office. At the Central Office is a digital terminal that is composed of an access bandwidth manager, cable modems, and a spectrum manager.

On the downstream path (network-to-user), the cable modems are capable of receiving DS0 signals from the access bandwidth manager and converting them into RF signals suitable for transmission on a 2 MHz

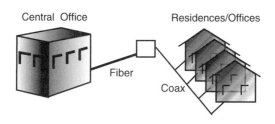

Figure 7–8   HFC configuration

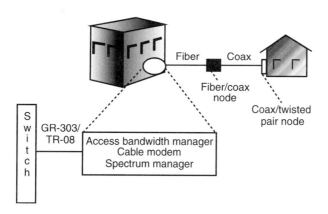

Figure 7–9   HFC interfaces

carrier path to the subscriber over the hybrid fiber coax network. The modems also receive RF signals from the subscriber (upstream path) via the fiber coax network and convert them into DS0 signals. The access bandwidth manager maps these DS0 signals to DS1 signals for communicating with the digital switch at the Central Office.

The cable modem shelf also has a maintenance and control interface that relays OAM information between the access bandwidth manager and the voice ports. As an example, this interface relays provisioning information to the line cards and sends and receives alarms, as well as performance data, to and from the access bandwidth manager. This system typically also maintains inventory information about equipment and facilities between the cable modem shelf and the outside wall of the subscriber locations.

The access bandwidth manager contains several circuit packs that perform the following functions:

- Transmitting 2–28 DS1 signals to and from the digital switch
- Mapping the DS0 signals from the cable modem to DS1 signals for transmission to the digital switch, and vice versa
- Gathering and distributing performance and alarm data
- Providing an interface for diagnosticians to review this information
- Performing typical call control functions such as call processing and digital switching communications

The spectrum manager is a passive monitoring and information-gathering device.

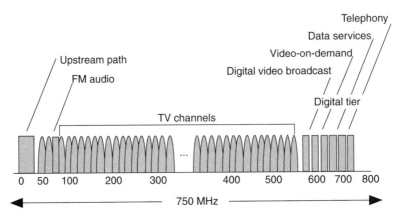

Figure 7–10   HFC spectrum

Figure 7–10 shows one view of how the 750 MHz bandwidth can be allocated. In addition to the analog signals just discussed, HFC can carry digital transmissions such as DS0 at 64 kbit/s or video-telephony at 384 kbit/s (6 DS0s), with quadrature phase-shift keyed (QPSK) digital signals. Digital video transmissions can be carried with a 64-state QAM scheme (64-QAM) at rates of 30 Mbit/s.

The deployment of HFC has also been slow because of the need to reconfigure the CATV one-way (half-duplex) architecture and because of other technical problems. However, as of this writing, it has a larger growth rate than its principal competitor, ADSL.

A HIGH-SPEED PROPRIETARY SOLUTION

Not everyone is waiting for the ADSL and HFC standards to evolve and for the resulting deployment of these standards. Some companies are developing two product lines: one based on the standards and one based on a proprietary design. Nortel Networks is an example of one of these companies.

Nortel Networks has introduced a high-speed modem to be deployed on the local loop. Known as the 1-Meg Modem™, it offers a high-speed data over voice over existing telephone lines. In addition, it does not require the rewiring of any customer site, and a POTS splitter is not needed. Although it does require some equipment changes in the Central Office, these changes can be done with only two plug-in circuit packs. Figure 7–11 shows the 1-Meg Modem configuration.

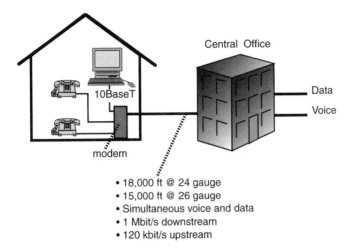

Central Office

Data

Voice

10BaseT

modem

- 18,000 ft @ 24 gauge
- 15,000 ft @ 26 gauge
- Simultaneous voice and data
- 1 Mbit/s downstream
- 120 kbit/s upstream

Figure 7–11   Nortel's 1-meg modem

The initial release of the 1-Meg Modem supports 1 Mbit/s downstream, 120 kbit/s upstream, and the simultaneous use of voice and data over any existing telephone jack at the customer location. Data connections are supported through the use of a standard 10BaseT Ethernet support on the modem. In addition, a pass through an RJ-11 jack on the unit permits a fax and analog modem or telephone to coexist with the unit.

The phones remain network powered, and if the modem loses power, the ongoing residential service continues to be supported. Current local loops are supported with a distance of 18 kilofeet on 24-gauge wire and 15 kilofeet on 26-gauge wire.

The service is available on Nortel's DMS-100, DMS-500, and MSL-100 equipment. With the eventual use of Nortel's AccessNode Express™, the modem services can be deployed on non-DMS switches. A 1.3-Mbit/s downstream service will be available, as well as a 320-kbit/s upstream service. As part of this upgrade, ATM is used to support the system.

BYPASSING THE CIRCUIT-SWITCHED TECHNOLOGY TO REACH THE INTERNET

For several years, the telephone network will continue to operate with circuit-switched technologies, as explained in Chapter 1. To relieve the load on the telephone facilities, a number of vendors have built systems that are installed in the telephone local exchanges. These systems use a

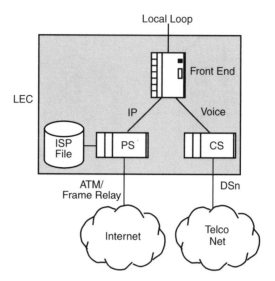

Figure 7–12   The circuit switch bypass

"front end" machine to intercept calls destined for Internet or intranet users and divert the calls to data facilities, thus avoiding the telco network and switches altogether. Figure 7–12 shows the general idea of circuit-switch bypass (CSB).

SUMMARY

The only wires out of most residences and businesses are the telephone company's wires. Those wires go to the telephone office. Consequently, it is necessary to use the telephone system to transport VoIP traffic to and from the Internet. The Internet and the ISP are connected to most VoIP users through the telephone's local loop facilities.

A substantial number of people have opted to use the cable TV network for their Internet connections. Indeed, cable modems are becoming quite popular.

Whatever the method used to connect to the Internet service provider, it must provide sufficient bandwidth to support the real time requirements for VoIP.

8

Performance Considerations and Traffic Engineering

This chapter examines the issues pertaining to the performance of VoIP networks and explains how traffic engineering (TE) is used to meet performance goals. The first part of the chapter examines the trade-offs of packet size, queue size, packet loss, and packet latency. The next part of the chapter describes queuing methods to assist the network operator in traffic engineering operations. That part of the chapter highlights Cisco's approach [CISC99a] and [CISC00c].[1] The last part of the chapter explains policy-based routing, constrained routing, and guaranteed service.

TRAFFIC ENGINEERING DEFINED

Traffic engineering (TE) deals with the performance of a network in supporting the network customers' QOS needs. The focus of TE is (a) the measurement of traffic and (b) the control of traffic. The latter operation focuses on operations to ensure the network has the resources to support

---

[1][CISC99a] The discussions on Cisco's queuing procedures are based on *Cisco IOS 12.0 Quality of Service,* Cisco Press, ISBN 1-57870-161-9. In addition, [CISC00c] provides information on how Cisco routers can be configured for VoIP operations.

the users' QOS requirements. Many TE operations consist of methods to *shape* traffic; that is, to determine how much traffic is released to the network from the edge node of the network. Other TE operations pertain to route determination, sometimes resulting in the constraining of the route to specific parts of the network. TE is an important operation for any application that needs some assurance of bandwidth and delay, notably VoIP applications.

Earlier discussions dealt with network congestion; let's revisit the issue briefly. Recall that congestion of users' traffic is influenced by the contention for resources in a network with limited resources. Therefore, traffic may become congested while waiting for a resource (such as an outgoing communications link) to be freed to service the traffic.

The end result of congestion is the reduction in user traffic throughput and increased delays in the delivery of the traffic to the receiver. The problems of congestion are such an ingrained part of data networks (and especially the Internet), that most of us take them for granted. Indeed, *best-effort* (doing one's best, with no guarantees on a congestion-free delivery) is the only method of handling users' traffic in most private internets and the public Internet. We also learned that congestion leads to delay and jitter and the deterioration of voice traffic quality.

With this review behind us, let us examine some methods to combat delay and jitter and to improve the performance of the network's support of voice traffic.

PACKET SIZE, QUEUE SIZE, LOSS, AND LATENCY

The VoIP network designer must pay attention to queue sizes, packet sizes, and the packet loss rate. These statements hold for VoIP traffic:

- Packet loss decreases the quality of the VoIP session.
- Large packet sizes increase the delay in the VoIP packets' one-way delay, resulting in poorer quality of the VoIP session.
- Large queues increase the delay of the VoIP packets' one-way delay, resulting in poorer quality of the VoIP session.
- Larger queues decrease packet loss, aiding the quality of the VoIP session.

To understand these statements, let us examine a G.711 64-kbit/s voice signal. First, consider the loss of user traffic. The size of the packet is quite important for speech because of the concept of packet length (the duration of the packet on the channel). Packet length is a function of the number of user bits in the packet and the coding rate of the signal (for example, 64 kbit/s). Studies reveal that losing traffic that is around 32–64 ms (for G.711 traffic) in duration is disruptive, because it means the loss of speech phonemes. On the other hand, cell loss of a duration of some 4–16 ms is not noticeable or disturbing to the listener. Therefore, as shown below, a payload size of anywhere around 32 to 64 bytes would be acceptable to an audio listener. The actual perception of audio loss is a function of other factors, for example, the compression algorithms used. But for this general example, the following examples show loss for G.711 traffic. It can be seen that the longer packets suffer more loss. The examples are for packets with 32, 48, and 64 bytes of user voice traffic.[2]

32 bytes × 8 bits per byte = 256 bits
256 ÷ 64,000 = .004

48 bytes × 8 bits per byte = 384 bits
384 ÷ 64,000 = .006

64 bytes × 8 bits per byte = 512 bits
512 ÷ 64,000 = .008

Next, consider queue size. A larger queue will increase delay (it takes more time to service large queues) and decrease the loss rate (the larger queue allows more flexibility in play-out, and the machine does not have to discard as many packets). But the continued decrease of the queue size, while decreasing delay, means more packets will be discarded. In effect, as the queue size approaches 0, the machine operates at wire speed but will experience more loss of traffic. Figure 8–1 shows the relationships between packet loss and unidirectional delay for G.729 traffic [COX98].

---

[2]These examples are from studies performed on ATM cells. After extensive deliberations in the ATM standards working groups, it was agreed that a cell payload size between 32 and 64 bytes would perform satisfactorily in that it (a) worked with ongoing equipment (did not require echo cancellers), (b) provided acceptable transmission efficiency, and (c) was not overly complex to implement. Japan and the United States favored a cell size with 64 bytes of user payload; Europe favored a size of 32 bytes. Eventually, a consensus was reached on 48 bytes. A 5-byte header was added to yield the standard 53-byte cell.

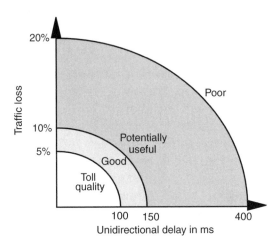

Figure 8–1   Traffic loss vs. traffic delay [COX98]

The figure might show some surprises. It is known that although most high-quality networks keep one-way delay to no more than 150 ms (keep in mind that it does vary), some people are tolerant of greater delays. Also, traffic loss can indeed occur. The loss of one or two successive samples is not perceptible to the listener. In the event of loss, the receiving codec usually employs *concealment* operations; this practice entails the reuse (the replay) of the previous packet. With this approach, an approximate 5% loss is tolerable if averaged across the call. However, losses of multiple, contiguous samples will definitely be detected by the listener.

As mentioned, the voice packet should be small in order to reduce latency and improve quality. That is, because of packet processing delays, large packet sizes are inversely proportional to interactive voice quality. One could take this idea to the extreme and postulate a packet of, say, one byte (or even one bit!). Obviously, there is a point of diminishing returns where the overhead of headers to the miniscule user packet is so high that it militates against building an efficient network.

Another consideration is to attempt to build the packet size in consonance with the output of the codec. But this approach may not be possible. For example, if these voice packets are placed inside a fixed-length frame, they may not fit exactly in the fixed payload of the frame. If this is the situation and the payload size of the frame cannot be altered, the system should be able to break the sample into even-byte boundaries and place it into successive frames to make the best use of the payload bandwidth. This approach is common today, and some examples are provided in Chapter 12.

Guidance on Fragmentation It is not possible to control the size of the VoIP sample because the codec dictates the sample size. However, Cisco supports (in some of its routers) the ability to establish the number of samples per packet. As with most implementations, Cisco supports default packet sizes in relation to the G.xxx codec sample sizes. For example, with G.729, two 10-ms samples are multiplexed into one packet. Therefore, with proper queuing configurations, it is possible to send a VoIP packet every 20 ms.

Table 8–1 provides guidance from [CISC00c] on the relationships of link speeds, packet sizes, and the transmit time for different sample sizes.

Compressing the Headers Another effective tool to reduce the size of the VoIP packet is a commonly used procedure called header compression. Most systems support the compression of the IP, UDP, and RTP headers. The gain in bandwidth utilization is significant. For example, an uncompressed VoIP packet (L_1 and L_2 headers are excluded) is:

IP header = 20 bytes, UDP header = 8 bytes, RTP header = 12 bytes

Using conventional compression routines, one can reduce this 40-byte header to 2 to 4 bytes. Cisco's compression technique, called cRTP, uses the techniques employed in TCP header compression. The compressed header is 2 bytes if UDP checksums are not used, and 4 bytes if they are used.

It can be seen that the amount of VoIP traffic over a given link can be increased with the use of compression. For example, a G.729 two-

Table 8–1   Delay and sample size [CISC00c]

	1 Byte	64 Bytes	128 Bytes	256 Bytes	512 Bytes	1024 Bytes	1500 Bytes
56 kbit/s	143 µs	9 ms	18 ms	36 ms	72 ms	144 ms	214 ms
64 kbit/s	125 µs	8 ms	16 ms	32 ms	64 ms	128 ms	187 ms
128 kbit/s	62.5 ms	4 ms	8 ms	16 ms	32 ms	64 ms	93 ms
256 kbit/s	31 ms	2 ms	4 ms	8 ms	16 ms	32 ms	46 ms
512 kbit/s	15.5 ms	1 ms	2 ms	4 ms	8 ms	16 ms	23 ms
768 kbit/s	10 µs	640 µs	1.28 ms	2.56 ms	5.12 ms	10.24 ms	15 ms
1536 kbit/s	5 µs	320 µs	640 µs	1.28 ms	2.56 ms	5.12 ms	7.5 ms

Table 8–2   Header compression with cRTP [(CISC00c) and (RUDK97)]

	Bit Rate	Sample Size	Bandwidth without cRTP	Bandwidth with cRTP	Sample Latency
G.729-one sample	8 kbit/s	10 ms	40 kbit/s	9.6 kbit/s	15 ms
G.729-two samples	8 kbit/s	10 ms	24 kbit/s	11.2 kbit/s	25 ms

sample packet requires 24 kbit/s of bandwidth for an uncompressed transmission and only 11.2 kbit/s for a compressed transmission. Table 8–2 provides information on Cisco's cRTP algorithm in relation to G.729 [CISC00c] and [RUDK97].

Interarrival Jitter

As defined in Chapter 1, interarrival jitter is the difference in relative transit time for two successive packets belonging to the same voice channel. It is the difference between the packet's RTP timestamp and the receiver's clock at the time of arrival of the packet. Even though traffic may be sent into the network with no jitter, say, a sample every 20 ms, the queuing delays encountered in the network will introduce jitter during the transmission.

Jitter is calculated continuously as each data packet is received from the source, using this difference for that packet and the previous packet in order of arrival.

An effective tool to combat interarrival jitter is to set up jitter queues at the receiver. Some systems allow the queues to operate as dynamic queues that can grow or shrink depending on the interarrival time of the packets. The interarrival delay variation of the last few arriving packets causes the queue to increase or decrease, thereby effectively reducing loss and minimizing jitter.

GOALS OF TRAFFIC ENGINEERING

We introduced traffic engineering (TE) at the beginning of this chapter. Let's take another look at it. In its simplest form, TE attempts to optimize users' QOS needs by making the best use of network resources to support those needs. The limitation, of course, is the network resources.

Therefore, if a network does not have sufficient bandwidth (link speeds and node processing power) to support all users' QOS require-

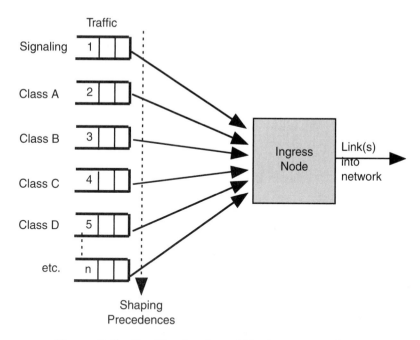

Figure 8–2   Traffic shaping at the ingress node

ments every moment of the day, then traffic engineering operations must *shape* the users' traffic. This statement means mechanisms must be in place to determine (shape) how the network supports the different classes of user traffic.

As depicted in Figure 8–2, the shaping can occur at the ingress node (some networks shape traffic at the egress node) and entails setting up queues and acting on priorities assigned to a traffic class (giving precedence to one class of traffic over another). In this example, each traffic class is assigned to a different queue, and signaling traffic is given precedence over the other traffic classes (a common practice). Thus, shaping entails the granting of more or less bandwidth to the network user, based on the user's traffic class and priority.

THE COMMITTED ACCESS RATE

Cisco supports a service, called the committed access rate (CAR), on many of its routers. The purpose of CAR is to limit the input or output transmission rate on an interface. CAR is often configured on interfaces at the edge (ingress) router to control the amount of traffic sent to and received from a network.

CAR can be set up based on the router performing a match on (a) all IP traffic, (b) traffic based on Ethernet MAC addresses, (c) traffic based on the IP precedence field, or (d) an IP access list.

Each interface can have multiple CAR policies. For example, it is possible to limit the bandwidth given for low-priority traffic and give more bandwidth to high-priority traffic. If multiple rate policies are used, the router examines each policy in the order it is entered in the configuration tables until a match is found.

CAR deals with bursts of traffic, so that aspect of CAR is important because a router sends bursts of traffic. Additionally, CAR does not smooth or shape traffic. This operation is performed by queuing mechanisms, discussed shortly.

Another technique, called distributed CAR (DCAR), classifies packets into a group to allow the network manager to set up multiple priority levels for classes of service. The main difference between CAR and DCAR is that DCAR can be configured with a weighted random early detection (WRED) service (discussed later in this chapter).

For a CAR setup, an interface is configured with an *interface* command and *a rate-limit* command. The interface command simply specifies the interface on the router. The rate-limit command establishes the access rate on the interface, for both input and output traffic, as shown in Figure 8–3. The parameters shown in Figure 8–3 are explained in the next section.

CAR Data Rates

The network operator defines and configures three parameters pertaining to CAR data rates. The first parameter is the *long-term average rate*. It is a long-term average of the transmission rate, determined by internal Cisco procedures. It must be equal to or less than the link bandwidth rate, such as 45 Mbit/s for a DS3 link. The second parameter is the *normal burst size*. It determines how large the traffic burst can be (in bytes) and still be considered to conform to a required traffic profile. The third parameter is the *excess burst size*. It determines how large a traffic burst can be (in bytes) before the traffic is considered to exceed a rate limit.

Figure 8–3 shows two other parameters that are configured by the network operator. The *conform action* directs the actions of the router if the traffic is in conformance with the CAR data rates, and the *exceed action* does the same if the traffic is not in conformance.

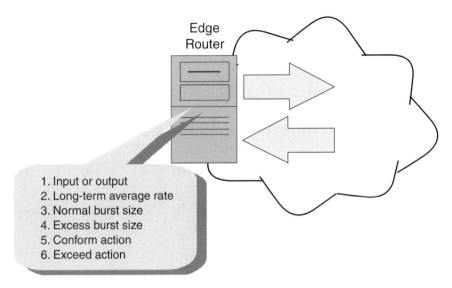

Figure 8–3   Committed access rate (CAR)

Let's clarify the excess burst size. If traffic that falls between the normal and excess burst sizes exceeds the rate limit *and* if the burst actually exceeds the excess burst size, the following actions can be established:

- Drop the packet.
- Transmit the packet.
- Set the IP precedence packet and transmit the packet. This action has the effect of *re-marking* the packet. The term re-marking means changing parameters in the user's packet; the result is usually to reduce the user's consumption of bandwidth.

Therefore, if the interface is so configured, a traffic burst over the normal burst size but not exceeding the excess burst size is permitted.

Setting Up CAR Subrate Services

Figure 8–4 shows an example of how CAR works. The configuration list in the figure is a general depiction of the parameters the network operator enters to configure the interface (the communications link).

For this example, we assume a network operator supports a DS3 (T3) link (with an IP address of 10.1.0.9) to the customer, and offers the customer a 20 Mbit/s subrate service. The customer only pays for the

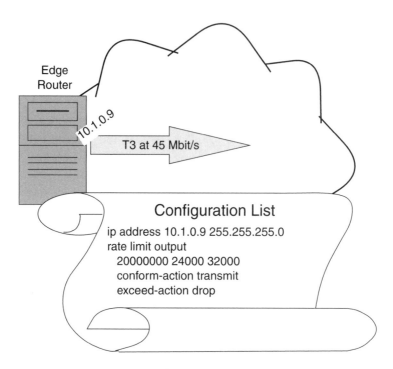

Figure 8–4   Setting up a subrate service

subrate. The operator limits the rate of bytes that the customer can deliver to the network. The customer is allowed to send a burst of 24,000 bytes, with the excess rate set at 32,000 bytes. If the traffic is in conformance, it is sent; if it is not in conformance, it is dropped.

Figure 8–5 represents another example of a CAR configuration. The customer is connected to an ISP by a DS3 (T3) link with address 200.200.14.250. The ISP limits the customer's traffic (both to and from the customer) to 20 Mbit/s, with a burst of 24,000 bytes. Any packets that exceed this rate are dropped; that is, excess rates are not permitted.

Routers allow the network operator to view the results of the configuration by examining some statistics. For a Cisco router, by entering the *show interfaces rate-limit* command, and specifying the interface, the operator receives information on how many packets and bytes were sent and received during a time period.

Access Lists

Access lists can be used to limit the rate at which a specific application uses network resources. This capability ensures that certain user

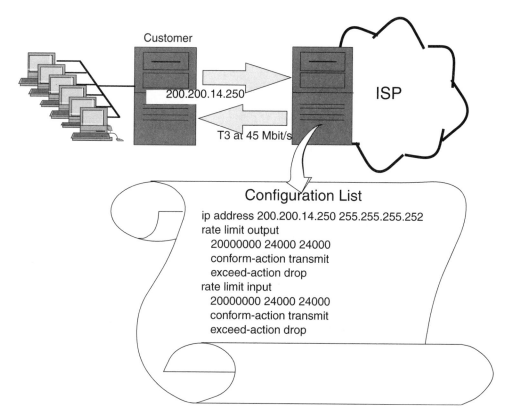

Figure 8–5   The ISP controls customer traffic

traffic (say, traffic that is mission critical) can be given the bandwidth capacity to meet their requirements. Figure 8–6 shows an example of the
use of access lists (other list values can be coded, but they are not germane to this discussion).

Two access lists are set up for interface 200.200.14.250, one for
WWW traffic (access list 101), and the other for FTP traffic (access list
102). The access lists stipulate the protocol source to be TCP.

For the Web traffic, an average rate of 20 Mbit/s is established, with
a normal burst of 24,000 bytes and an excess burst size of 32,000 bytes. If
the traffic is conforming, the IP precedence bits are set to 5. For nonconforming traffic, the precedence bits are re-marked and set to 0.

For the FTP traffic, an average rate of 10 Mbit/s is established, with
a normal burst of 24,000 bytes, and an excess burst size of 32,000 bytes.

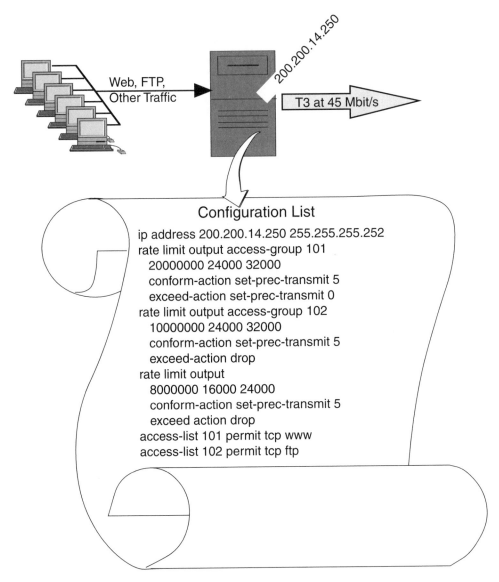

Figure 8–6   Rate limiting by access lists

If the traffic is conforming, the IP precedence bits are set to 5. For non-conforming traffic, the packets are dropped.

The remaining traffic is limited to 8 Mbit/s, with a normal burst size of 16,000 bytes and an excess burst size of 24,000 bytes. Conforming traffic is sent with an IP precedence of 5. Nonconforming traffic is dropped.

SUPPORTING TRAFFIC ENGINEERING WITH QUEUING

Many networks support traffic engineering with queuing operations. Queues allow the network operator to shape the customer's traffic in accordance with the service level agreement (SLA)[3] and the capabilities of the network. The prevalent types of queues are the following:

- *First-in, first-out queuing (FIFO):* Packets are transmitted in the order of their arrival.
- *Weighted fair queuing (WFQ):* The available bandwidth across queues of traffic is divided on the basis of weights. Given its weight, a traffic class is treated fairly. This approach is often used when the overall traffic is mix of multiple traffic classes. For example, class A traffic is accorded a heavier weight than class D traffic and receives more bandwidth on an interface.
- *Custom queuing (CQ):* Bandwidth is allotted proportionally for each traffic class. CQ guarantees some level of service to all traffic classes. It allows the stipulation of how many bytes or packets are withdrawn from the queue.
- *Priority queuing (PQ):* All packets belong to a higher priority class are transmitted before any lower priority class. Therefore, some traffic is transmitted at the expense of other traffic. In this situation, it is possible that a low-priority queue will never be serviced, so PQ does not guarantee a level of service to all traffic classes.

EXAMPLES OF QUEUING METHODS

This part of the chapter provides examples of how WFQ, CQ, and PQ can be used to allocate bandwidth among different flows. We start with WFQ.

Weighted Fair Queuing

Recall that WFQ assigns a weight to each flow; it is "precedence" aware and determines the transmit order for queued packets, based on the IP precedence field. Before showing some examples, let's find out more about how the WFQ method operates.

---

[3]The service level agreement is a contract between the network operator and the network customers. It sets forth the obligations of both parties about using the network.

WFQ is an automated scheduling method in Cisco routers. Figure 8–7 depicts its operations. WRQ does not require any configuration (as do the CQ and PQ techniques). WFQ applies a priority (a weight) to identified traffic and determines how much bandwidth to give to the traffic relative to other traffic that is vying for the bandwidth. WFQ also gives equal bandwidth to concurrent applications of the same weight. For example, two FTP flows are accorded the same level of service.

WFQ is quite flexible in accommodating different flows. As the number of flows increase or decrease, the amount of bandwidth given to a flow will also increase or decrease. WFQ dynamically adjusts to changing conditions and traffic flows. Thus, the WFQ method may not be appropriate for traffic that needs an absolute assurance of a specific amount of bandwidth. For this type of traffic, CQ and PQ should be considered.

Before transmission, WFQ places the classified traffic into fair queues. The order of the removal from the queues is determined by the time the last bit in the arriving packet is received.

On occasion, the incoming traffic may be more than the output link(s) can support. If this situation occurs, the router executes a *congestive-messages threshold* value to discard excess traffic. Nonetheless, high-priority traffic (such as small packets containing voice traffic and certain signaling traffic such as RSVP messages) will be queued for as long as possible.

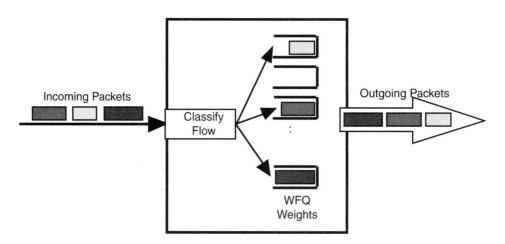

Figure 8–7   Weighted fair queuing (WFQ)

Comparison of Use and Nonuse of WFQ

Figure 8–8 compares the use (and nonuse) of a weighted fair queuing procedure [McCU99]. This study tested two G.723 voice transmissions running across a 64 kbit/s link. In addition, traffic from a TCP file

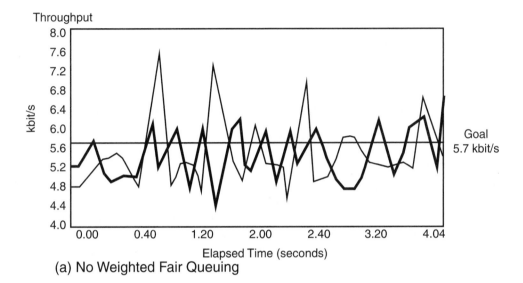

(a) No Weighted Fair Queuing

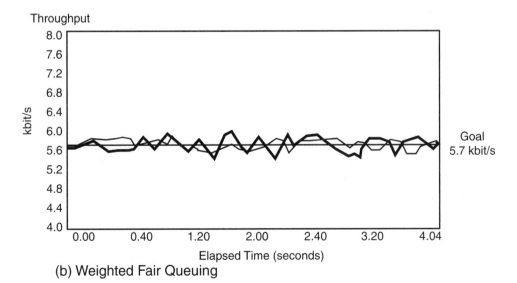

(b) Weighted Fair Queuing

Figure 8–8   Comparison of no weighted fair queuing and weighted fair queuing [McCU99]

transfer application was placed on the link, sharing bandwidth with the two voice transmissions. These figures compare the use and nonuse of the procedure and reinforce the idea of reducing interarrival jitter, the subject of an earlier discussion in this chapter.

For ease of study, the figures are drawn so that one voice session is represented with a thin line, and the other voice session with a thicker line. The voice sessions run on UDP in both directions. The figures do not show two other lines representing the flow of the two voice calls in the other direction.

Figure 8–8(a) shows the performance of the two voice sessions (the TCP session is not shown) without the use of weighted fair queuing. The goal was to achieve an average throughput of 5.7 kbit/s. This goal was met, but the variation in throughput (and resulting jitter) varied by large amounts. The authors of the paper state that the two conversations experienced almost 50% throughput variation during a 4-minute measurement period.

Figure 8–8(b) shows the results of the same traffic mix. There were no changes to the flows, except the enabling of a weighted fair queuing procedure. No other protocols were involved (no RSVP, for example). For this test, the authors report that there was a throughput variation of less than 10%.

The test was between two user computers, with two routers in between these user devices. While the test does validate the efficacy of weighted queues, keep in mind that in a larger network with more router hops (and thus more variable delay), these results will not be this good. There may still be a need for a reservation protocol or some form of constrained routing, subjects discussed later in this chapter and in Chapter 9.

WFQ Example   To learn how WFQ is used to traffic-engineer a link, we assume that a SONET OC-3 link with a 155.52 Mbit/s capacity can accept an absolute maximum of 353,207 ATM cells per second. Given the assumption that the system is consuming the OC-3 bandwidth perfectly (which depends on the efficiency of the node), the following holds: 155,520,000 (less the overhead of the 155.52 Mbit/s OC-3 frame yields a rate of 149.760 Mbit/s) / 424 bits in a 53-byte cell = 353,207 cells per second.

For this example, eight levels of priority are permitted. The reason for eight levels is that (a) the IP TOS precedence field is three bits and could be used by the user application to signal to the network the user's precedence needs, (b) an MPLS shim header Exp field is also three bits and can carry the TOS precedence bits. In addition, Cisco routers use this approach for native-mode IP packets.

For this example, all eight queues are to be serviced every second. Based on the weights assigned to the eight queues, n number of cells will be extracted from each queue and sent onto the SONET link. The limit is 353,207 cells during the one-second service cycle.

A single flow is in each queue, and each flow receives part of the bandwidth according to this simple scheme:

Total Weights: $8 + 7 + 6 + 5 + 4 + 3 + 2 + 1 = 36$

The traffic flow in the highest precedence queue is accorded 8/36th of the bandwidth. The traffic flow in the lowest precedent queue is accorded 1/36th of the bandwidth. Translating these ratios to percentages:

$8/36 = .222$, and $1/36 = .027$

Consequently, flow A gets 78,411 cells extracted from its queue during the service cycle, almost 1/4 of the total capacity of the link ($353,207 \times .222 = 78,411$). The lowest precedence flow has 9,536 cells serviced ($353,207 \times .027 = 9,536$). Keep in mind that each flow likely consists of traffic flow from more than one end user. This aspect of WFQ is determined by how the routers are configured.

VIP Distributed WFQ   A variation of WFQ is VIP-distributed WFQ, shown in Figure 8–9. This technique also uses the WFQ methods just described. It classifies into the same flow packets in which these values are the same:

- Source and destination IP addresses
- Source and destination port numbers
- Protocol ID
- TOS field

Each flow corresponds to a separate queue. For example, one flow might be associated with one set of IP addresses, and another flow with a different set of IP addresses, and so on.

Multiple Flows With the Same Weight   WFQ is more flexible than the operations shown in the previous example. Let's assume that more than eight flows are associated with the traffic classes and that it is still desirable to allocate bandwidth fairly among all flows. For this example,

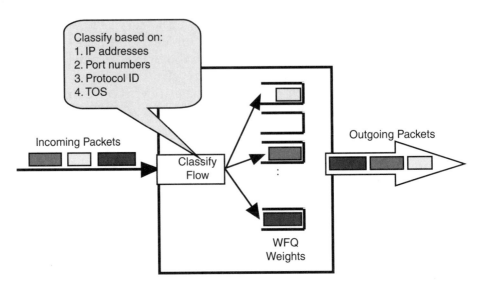

Figure 8–9   VIP distributed WFQ

the flow class (and associated flow) is inferred from the VIP distributed WFQ parameters. Therefore, many flows can be identified. Assume four flows are associated with precedence 5, two flows with precedence 4, and one flow with the others:

$$8 + 7 + 6 + 5\,(4) + 4\,(2) + 3 + 2 + 1 = 55$$

With this set of flows, each flow in precedence 5 gets 5/55th of the bandwidth (32,109 cells per second for each flow), and each flow in precedence 4 gets 4/55th (25,687 cells per second for each flow).

With Cisco routers, the network operator can configure the number of queues for WFQ. Each queue corresponds to a different flow. Thus, the four flows with a weight of 5 would be placed into different queues. But each queue within the flow would still receive the same level of service.

Custom Queuing

Custom queuing (CQ), shown in Figure 8–10, allows bandwidth to be allotted proportionally for each traffic class. It guarantees some level of service to all traffic classes. It allows the network operator to stipulate how many bytes or packets are withdrawn from the queue.

CQ cycles through the queues in a round-robin fashion and extracts the packets in accordance with the portion of allocated bandwidth set up

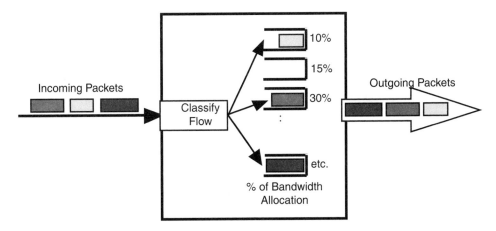

Figure 8–10   Custom queuing (CQ)

for each queue. If a queue is empty, CQ goes to the next queue. It ensures that no flow will given more than a predetermined amount of bandwidth. It does not adapt to changing network conditions.

The router sends packets from a queue until the byte count for the queue is exceeded. However, it will not cease the byte extraction from a queue if bytes that make up a complete packet remain. It will send out a full packet.

To configure CQ, the network operator must specify the number of queues, their length, and the number of bytes that are to be extracted during each service cycle. In addition, access lists are used to assign flows to specific queues.

Priority Queuing

As noted earlier, with priority queuing (PQ) all packets that belong to a higher priority class are transmitted before any lower priority class. Therefore, some traffic is transmitted at the expense of other traffic. Thus, during the transmission process, PQ gives higher priority queues absolute preferential treatment over the lower priority queues. The idea is shown in Figure 8–11.

In a Cisco router, packets are classified on user-specified criteria (IP, IPX, source interface, etc.), and placed into one of four output queues: (a) high, (b) medium, (c) normal, or (d) low.

When a packet is to be sent out onto a link, the queues for that link are examined in descending order of priority. Each time a packet is scheduled for transmission, this process is repeated. Consequently, if

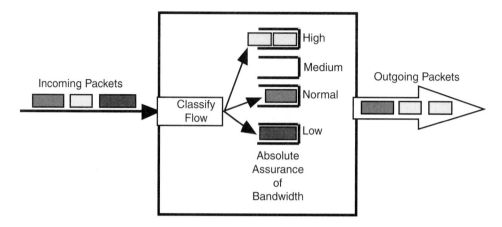

Figure 8–11   Priority queuing (PQ)

packets arrive at the router and are classified as high priority and thus moved to the high-priority queue, the lower priority queues will not be serviced. If packets come into the queue to the point that they exceed a queue length limit (a configurable parameter), these packets are dropped.

As stated earlier, it is possible that lower priority traffic may not be granted any bandwidth. This situation is a severe way to handle a user's traffic. To mitigate this effect, the router can be configured with CAR to rate limit the higher priority traffic. Of course, this configuration might lead to a Catch-22 situation in which the rate limit defeats the purpose of according absolute bandwidth to mission-critical applications.

CONGESTION-AVOIDANCE PROCEDURES

Tail Drop, RED, and WRED

In the first part of this chapter, the subject of congestion avoidance was introduced, and the mechanisms of queuing were explained as one tool to manage user traffic. Certainly, the use of rate limits and various queuing methods can help avoid congestion. But other tools are available, and they are known specifically as *congestion avoidance* procedures. This part of the chapter discusses three congestion avoidance features: (a) Tail Drop, (b) Random Early Detection (RED), and (c) Weighted Random Early Detection (WRED).

Tail Drop   Tail drop is quite straightforward. Traffic is not classified or differentiated; everything is treated the same. When a queue starts to fill, any *arriving* packets are dropped until potential congestion is eliminated.

RED   Work was done on TCP in the early 1990s to address the problem of congestion. The idea is to be proactive to the potential problem rather than merely reactive, as is the tail drop procedure. The proactive stance requires that the TCP sender slow down its transmission rate when packets are lost en route to the receiver. This idea is called RED. Even though VoIP does not use TCP, it will be helpful to show how TCP/RED operates as a precusor to the discussion on WRED.

RED informs a sending host that (a) received traffic is correct, (b) some traffic is missing (or in error), (c) no additional data has been received but the receiving host is "alive," and (d) perhaps the host should slow down or speed up its transmissions.

TCP Retransmission Scheme   TCP has a unique way of accounting for traffic on each connection. Unlike many other protocols, it does not have an explicit *negative acknowledgment (NAK)*. Rather, it relies on the transmitting entity to retransmit data for which it has not received a *positive acknowledgment (ACK)*. This concept is illustrated in Figure 8–12, which shows eight operations labeled with numbers 1 through 8. Each of these operations will be described in order. Note that this example assumes the receiver is sending its ACKs back to the sender with a credit window that permits the sender to continue sending segments.

Event 1: TCP A sends a segment to TCP B. This example assumes a window of 900 bytes and a segment size of 300 bytes. The sequence (SEQ) number contains the value of 3. As indicated in this event, 300 bytes are sent to TCP B.

Event 2: TCP B checks the traffic for errors and sends back an acknowledgment with the value of 303. This value is an inclusive acknowledgment that acknowledges all traffic up to and including 302: SEQ number 3 through 302. As depicted by the arrow in event 2, the traffic segment has not yet arrived at TCP A when event 3 occurs. (The tip of the arrow is not at A's location.)

Event 3: Because TCP A still has its transmit window open, it sends another segment of data beginning with number 303. How-

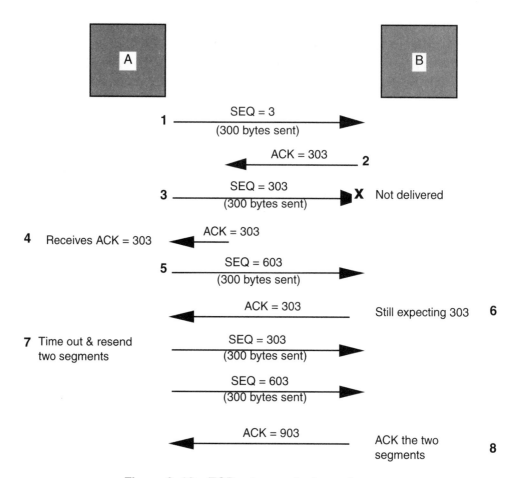

Figure 8–12 TCP retransmission schemes

ever, this traffic segment is not delivered to TCP B for some reason—bit errors, discarded traffic, etc.

Event 4: The acknowledgment segment transmitted in event 2 arrives at TCP A, stipulating that TCP B is expecting a segment beginning with number 303. At this point, TCP A cannot know if the traffic transmitted in event 3 was not delivered or simply has not yet arrived because of variable delays in an internet. Consequently, it proceeds with event 5.

Event 5: TCP A sends the next segment beginning with the number 603. It arrives without error at TCP B.

Event 6: TCP B successfully receives the segment number 603, which was transmitted in event 5. However, TCP B sends back a segment with ACK 303 because it is still expecting segment number 303. The frequency of sending ACKs varies, but a common practice is to send ACKs every 200 ms. The receiver interprets this message as a repeatedly sent ACK.

Event 7: Eventually, TCP A must time out and resend the segments for which it has not yet had an acknowledgment. In this example, it must resend to TCP B the segments beginning with numbers 303 and 603.

Of course, the idea depicted in event 7 has its advantages and disadvantages. It makes the protocol quite simple, because TCP simply goes back to the last unacknowledged segment number and retransmits all succeeding segments. On the other hand, it likely retransmits segments which were not in error, for example, the segment beginning with number 603 which had arrived error-free at TCP B. Nonetheless, TCP operates in this fashion at the risk of some degraded throughput for the sake of simplicity. Moreover, if TCP A receives three successive ACKs with the same sequence number, it is smart enough to resort to a "selective retransmission" and resend only one segment.

Event 8: All traffic is accounted for after TCP B receives and error checks segments 303 and 603 and returns an ACK value equal to 903.

Notes: Upon resending a packet, TCP adjusts its transmission rate to half of what it was before the drop was detected, resulting in a back-off of traffic into the network.

WRED is similar to these operations, but is more powerful and is explained shortly. (That is why TCP is explained.)

The Slow Start TCP implements an operation called the slow start. Slow start uses a variable called the congestion window (*cwnd*). The sending TCP module is allowed to increment *cwnd* when it receives acknowledgments of previously transmitted segments.

As Figure 8–13 shows, upon initialization or error recovery, TCP A sends one segment; and at this time *cwnd* = 1. In event 2, TCP B acknowledges TCP A's segment 1, which allows TCP A to increment *cwnd* = 2. In event 3, it sends two segments numbered 2 and 3.

Notice that slow start is really not a slow start but an exponential start, albeit starting with only one transmission. In event 4, TCP B acknowledges segments 2 and 3 which allows TCP A to increment *cwnd* to a value of 4 and sends the four segments shown in event 5.

This exponential increase in the transmission of segments from TCP A is constrained by its transmit window, which of course is governed by TCP B.

One point is noteworthy here. The variable *cwnd* will not continue to be increased exponentially if a timeout occurs and the TCP sending module must resend segments. In this situation, *cwnd* is set to one segment (or half the rate it was sending traffic before it received the notice that traffic is missing), which is in harmony with the slow start concept: take it easy and don't send traffic if the network is congested.

Jacobson has contributed much to the analysis and understanding of TCP operations, as well as contributing his ideas of how to use TCP to support the transport of data through networks and hosts that exhibit varying

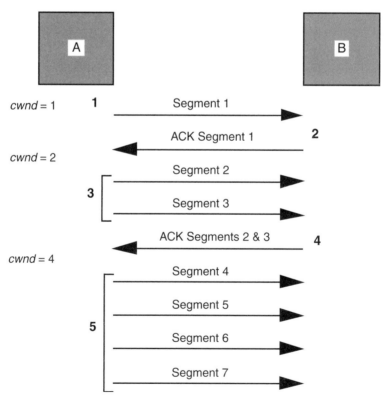

Figure 8–13 The slow start and the congestion window (*cwnd*)

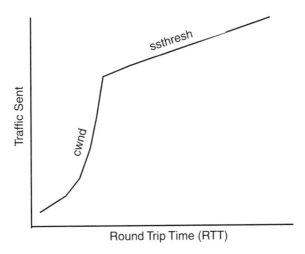

Figure 8–14   Congestion window (*cwnd*) and threshold size (*ssthresh*) [STEV94]

types of behavior in regard to delay and throughput. The example in Figure 8–14 is from Stevens [STEV94]. It shows that TCP supports the rule that the sending TCP module will not send traffic continuously at an exponential rate if the ACKs to the segments are delayed. In essence, a point is reached where the sending TCP refrains from sending of segments.

Two TCP variables are pertinent here: *cwnd* and *ssthresh*. The operation proceeds as follows. If the TCP module detects congestion either through a timeout or through the reception of duplicate acknowledgments, a value is saved in *ssthresh*. This value must be one-half of the current window size but can be at least two segments. Moreover, if a timeout occurs, *cwnd* is reset to the value of 1, which reinitializes the slow start operation.

Therefore, congestion avoidance requires that *cwnd* must be incremented by 1/*cwnd* each time an ACK is received. Consequently, for this situation, this behavior results in a linear increase in the traffic sent.

Congestion avoidance actually goes one step further, in addition to *cwnd* being increased by 1/*cwnd,* it has an added factor, which is the segment size/8. The use of segment size/8 allows the faster opening of windows for sessions that were initialized with large windows.

WRED   WRED uses the concepts of RED and the IP precedence field to support preferential treatment of high-priority traffic. It can selectively discard lower priority traffic during periods of high traffic loads. Thus, it performs different services for different classes of traffic.

During congestion, WRED will drop flows other than RSVP flows, assuming it has sufficient available queue depth to handle the RSVP traffic (which it should have). WRED goes a step further; it attempts to anticipate and avoid congestion rather than simply trying to control it once it occurs. Figure 8–15 shows the general idea of WRED. After traffic has been classified, it is examined for possible discard, based on the amount of traffic in the queues. The subsequent output onto the outgoing link is simple FIFO.

Why is WRED more effective than a tail drop? It is smarter, and its use is likely to avoid a condition on the Internet called *global synchronization*. For example, consider a high-end router operating at a major transit or peering point in the Internet. The router handles multiple concurrent TCP sessions, and when a lot of traffic is coming into the router, the total traffic volume may exceed the queue limit. If the router simply tail-drops a bunch of packets, that course will affect many TCP sessions, which must then execute their slow-start procedures. Tail-drop operations have the result of creating giant peaks and valleys in the Internet traffic. WRED can direct selected sessions to slow down and in that way it smooths out these peaks and valleys.

Additionally, since WRED can use the IP precedence field, the network operator can set up VoIP packets with a high precedence value, thus providing this traffic better service.

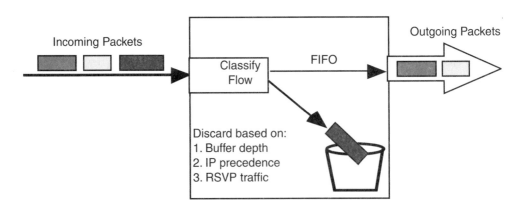

Figure 8–15   WRED: general concepts

POLICY-BASED ROUTING

This part of the chapter changes pace and discusses methods to route traffic through different parts of a network. The idea is to use "parts" of the network that have more resources than other parts. The first topic is policy-based routing (PBR), which is often associated with label switching protocols, such as Frame Relay, ATM, or MPLS. It can also be implemented with IP by using the precedence field as well as port numbers, the IP Protocol ID, or the size of the packets, as shown in Figure 8–16.

Using these fields, PBR enables the network operator to classify different types of traffic, preferably at the edge of the network. The core routers can then use the precedence field to decide how to handle the incoming traffic. This "handling" can entail the use of the different queues and different queuing methods previously discussed.

IP policy-based routing also allows the network manager to execute a form of constraint-based routing. Based on the packet's meeting or not meeting the criteria just discussed, the network manager can execute policies that enable a router to do the following:

Set the precedence value in the IP header.

Set the next hop to route the packet.

Set the output interface for the packet.

Set the next hop only if there is no route in the routing table.

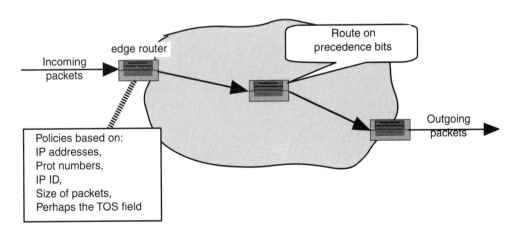

Figure 8–16   Policy-based routing

CONSTRAINED ROUTING WITH MPLS AND OSPF

Policy-based routing goes by another name when used with MPLS. It is called constrained routing, or constraint-based routing (CR). It is a mechanism used to meet traffic engineering requirements for MPLS networks.

CR can be set up as an end-to-end operation; that is, from the ingress node to the egress node. The idea is for the ingress node to initiate CR and for all affected nodes to be able to reserve resources.

The term constraint implies that in a network and for each set of nodes (the nodes are called label-switching routers, or LSRs) there exists a set of constraints that must be satisfied for the link or links between the two nodes. An example of a constraint is a path that has a minimum amount of bandwidth. Another example is a path that is secure. The protocol that finds such paths (such as a modified OSPF) is constrained to advertise (and find) paths in the routing domain that satisfy these kinds of constraints.

In addition, constraint-based routing attempts to meet a set of constraints and at the same time optimize some scalar metric [DAVI00]. One important scalar metric is hop count for delay-sensitive traffic, such as VoIP. We have learned in earlier chapters that extra hops create jitter, especially if the Internet is busy and the routers are processing a lot of traffic.

Explicit Routing

Explicit routing is integral to constraint-based routing. This route is set up at the edge of the network and is based on QOS criteria and routing information. Figure 8–17 shows an example of explicit routing.

The explicit route starts at ingress router A, traverses B and then D, and exits at egress router F. The path is known as the *label-switching path* (LSP). The explicit route is not allowed to traverse LSRs C and E. The allowed route can be established by means of special signaling messages [JAMO99] and the explicit route is coded in a label request message. The message contains a list of nodes (or group of nodes) that define the CR route.

The capability to specify groups of nodes, of which a subset will be traversed by the CR-LSP, allows the system a significant amount of local flexibility in fulfilling a request for a constraint-based route. Moreover, with constraint-based routing, the path can be calculated by the source of the LSP traffic (LSR A in Figure 8–17).

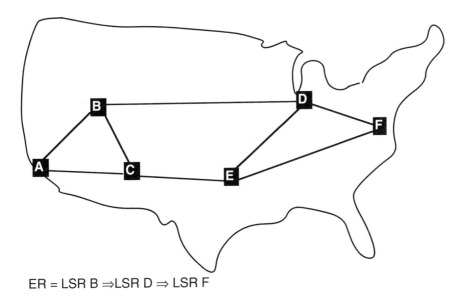

ER = LSR B ⇒LSR D ⇒ LSR F

Figure 8–17   Explicit routing

LDP and Constraint-Based Routing

If the Label Distribution Protocol (LDP)[4] is used for constraint-based routing, the constraint-based route is encoded as a series of explicit route (ER) hops contained in a special field in the LDP messages. Each ER hop can identify a group of nodes in the constraint-based route, and fields in the message are available to describe traffic parameters, such a peak burst and an excess burst. A constraint-based route is then a path including all of the identified groups of nodes in the order in which they appear in the message.

Preemption

CR-LDP conveys the resources required by a path on each hop of the route. If a route with sufficient resources cannot be found, existing paths can be rerouted to reallocate resources to the new path. For example, in Figure 8–17, if node B is down or has insufficient resources to meet the QOS requirements of the network customer, node C can be selected instead.

---

[4]LDP is a protocol designed to operate on label switching networks, such as MPLS. It associates (binds) IP address prefixes to bindings. It can also be used as tool to set up constrained routes in the network.

This idea is called path preemption. Setup and holding priorities are used to rank existing paths (holding priority) and the new path (setup priority) to determine if the new path can preempt an existing path.

The setup priority of a new CR-LSP and the holding priority attributes of the existing CR-LSP are used to specify priorities. Signaling a higher holding priority expresses that the path, once it has been established, should have a lower chance of being preempted. Signaling a higher setup priority expresses the expectation that, in the case that resources are unavailable, the path is more likely to preempt other paths. The setup and holding priority values range from 0 to 7. The value 0 is the priority assigned to the most important path. It is referred to as the highest priority. Seven (7) is the priority for the least important path.[5]

Example of Constrained Routing to Support VoIP

MPLS supports the concept of constrained routing as well as protection switching and backup routes. An MPLS network can be set up to (a) constrain traffic through a specific part of the network and (b) ensure that a link for a node failure will not create a situation wherein the user traffic is not delivered. Figure 8–18 shows these operations.

In Figure 8–18(a), the traffic is forwarded across the primary LSP from LSR A to the final destination node F, through LSRs B and D. This route has been defined and constrained for a certain type of traffic, say, VoIP packets. The notation of 44 means that the VoIP packet sent by LSR A contains a label header with the value of 44 in the label. LSRs A and B are configured to know that VoIP traffic for an IP address destined for node F has been assigned label 44 and that LSR A is to send this packet on to its interface to LSR B (and not LSR C). In addition, LSR A knows that label 44 is to be afforded more bandwidth on the link than other traffic (perhaps label 44 is given a large weight in the WFQ queues).

When LSR B receives this packet, it consults a preconfigured routing table and determines that label 44 is to be routed to LSR D, given precedence in the WFQ queues, and furthermore, that label 44 is to change to label 67 (a process called label swapping).

---

[5]Be careful when using a three-bit precedence/priority field. In some implementations, the highest level of "importance" of traffic starts at 0, with the lowest level of importance at 7. In contrast, other systems (Cisco—see [CISC00a, page 200]) use the opposite approach, with 7 being the highest level of importance and 0 being the least important.

(a) Label use on primary route

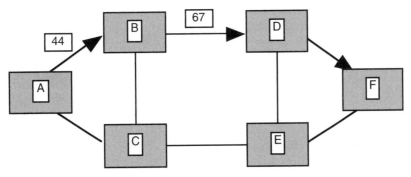

(b) Primary route (arrows); secondary route (no arrows)

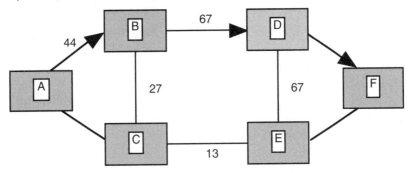

(c) Label use on secondary route

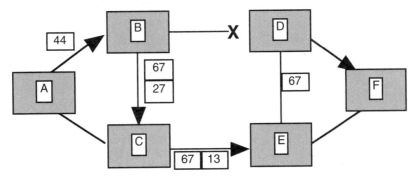

Figure 8–18   Constrained routing with protection switching and backup routes

When LSR D receives the packet labeled 67, it consults a preconfig-ured routing table and determines that label 67 is a local label: the packet has reached its final LSR, and the destination IP address is on a node attached to LSR D (that is, node F). Therefore, LSD can strip away the label header and present the native VoIP packet to node F.

The other labels show that the other parts of the network in Figure 8–18(b) of 27, 13, 67 have also been configured for the label-switched path from LSR A to LSR D, except that the backup LSP is also through LSRs C and E. LSRs C and E are used for a constrained backup route in case of a failure to the primary LSP.

In Figure 8–18(c), the link between LSR B and D fails. (LSR B de-tects this failure by not receiving an acknowledgment to its keep-alive messages from LSR D.) By prior arrangement, LSR B knows the backup path for this LSP is to LSR C and that the label for this part of the path is 27. LSR B is configured to place label 67 into the label header behind label 27. Recall that label 67 was to be used at LSR D. Therefore, label 67 has not been removed but has simply been placed (pushed) behind label 27 in the label header

A label swap occurs at LSR C (27 for 13). Label 67 is not examined, since it is not at the top of the stack. At LSR E, label 13 is removed (popped), leaving label 67 as the only label that arrives at LSR D. LSR D is configured to know that this label is associated with the same path as the one with the same label number of 67 emanating from LSR B.

It is noteworthy that the backup path has also been configured with WFQ to ensure that the VoIP traffic is given sufficient resources through the path to meet delay and jitter requirements.

Furthermore, several potentially vexing problems pertaining to the traffic engineering of the network for VoIP packets have been (at least partially) solved:

- A constrained route ensures that the best path has been found for the delay-sensitive traffic.
- Label switching is very fast and should lead to faster processing at congested routers.[6]

---

[6]One of my colleagues informed me he saw some statistics that prove conventional IP switching (using special cache and/or ASIC) can process IP traffic more quickly than can a native-mode MPLS label switch. I am still waiting to receive those statistics. If you have this information, please forward it me. In other words, I don't believe it! ... espe-cially for very large routing domains.

- Backup routes with the protection switching provide for a very robust service to the VoIP session.

A GUARANTEED RATE FOR VOICE TRAFFIC

Chapter 9 discusses the operations of DiffServ (DS). We need to explain one aspect of this Internet standard in relation to TE: DS Guaranteed Rate (GR).

An Internet Networking Group has been working on specifications to define a DiffServ (DS) guaranteed rate per-hop behavior (PHB) [WORS98]; see Figure 8–19. The concepts revolve around non-real-time traffic with a guaranteed rate (GR). This rate is also defined in ATM as part of the available bit rate (ABR) service. One difference between the ATM and DS approaches is that ATM is constrained to defining a successful delivery as one in which all the bits in the user frame are delivered successfully, which may entail more than one successfully delivered cell. This distinction is avoided in DS because the DS operations are defined at the L_3 IP level. The following is an overview of the DS GR, as defined in [WORS98].

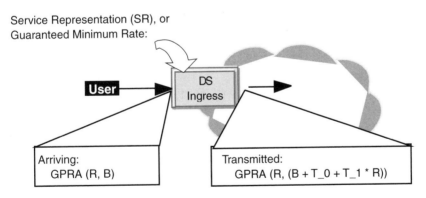

- **GR given if user:**
        Sends bursts < maximum burst limit
- And:
        User can send in excess of limit…
        With service within available resources

Figure 8–19   DiffServ guaranteed rate (GR)

The GR service provides transport of IP data with a minimum bit rate guarantee under the assumption of a given burst limit.

GR implies that if the user sends bursts of packets that in total do not exceed the maximum burst limit, then the user should expect to see all of these packets delivered with minimal loss. GR also allows the user to send in excess of the committed rate and the associated burst limit, but the excess traffic will only be delivered within the limits of available resources. You may recognize these ideas; they are fundamental to the committed access rate (CAR) discussed earlier in this chapter, as implemented in Cisco routers.

For excess traffic, each user should have access to a fair share of available resources, in the spirit of WFQ. The DS GR uses the term service representation (SR) to describe a guaranteed minimum rate and the packet characteristics to which the DS GR service commitment applies. The guaranteed minimum rate uses the generic packet rate algorithm (GPRA) with the rate and credit parameter as follows: GPRA (x, y), where x is the rate parameter in bytes per second and y is the credit limit parameter in bytes.

The SR is defined by (S, CR, BL), where S is the set of characteristics of the packet stream to which the service is being committed. The guaranteed minimum rate specification is defined as GPRA (CR, BL), where CR is the committed rate in bit/s and BL is the burst limit in bytes.

The interpretation of the SR is this: The network commits to transporting with minimal loss at least those packets belonging to the stream specified by S that pass a hypothetical implementation of the GPRA (CR, BL) located at the network's ingress interface.

The following theorem ensures a DS GR level of service that is always at least R as defined in the GR PHB. I quote directly from Worster [WORS98]:

Let a_j be the arrival time of the start of packet j, let t_j be the time when the start of packet j is transmitted, and let TL_j be the total length of packet j. Suppose the transmission times satisfy $s\_j < t\_j < s\_j + T\_2$, where $s\_{(j+1)} - s\_j <= (TL\_j/R)$, and also suppose that if a packet arrives when no other packets in the stream are awaiting transmission, then $a\_j + T\_0 <= s\_j < a\_j + T\_0 + T\_1$. T_0, T_1, and T_2 are, respectively, the fixed empty-queue packet latency, the maximum variation in the empty-queue packet latency, and the scheduling tolerance. Then, if the arriving packets all pass GPRA(R, B), the transmitted packets will all pass GPRA(R, (B + (T_0 + T_1)*R)).

The proof for this theorem is found in an ATM Forum paper by [WENT97].

> Though perhaps not all "guaranteed rate" nodes will schedule packets in a way that fits this form, the preceding theorem suggests that it is reasonable to expect that a significant class of such devices would have the ability to guarantee that if the input packet stream satisfies GPRA(R, B) then the output packet stream will satisfy GPRA(R, B + BTI) where BTI is the device's burst tolerance increment for the stream in question. This result allows us to consider several possible schemes by which an edge-to-edge guaranteed rate service commitment may be made. For example, if we know that each node has a BTI that does not exceed BTI_max, then we can establish GR service with parameters {S, CR, and BL} by provisioning a GR PHB with parameters {S, R = CR, and B = BL + BTI_max} along the stream's path though the network. We do not attempt to specify the rules by which a network operator should distribute appropriate GR PHB parameters. To some extent the appropriate scheme will depend on characteristics of the implementation of the GR PBH in network nodes. It may also depend on limitations of the protocol used to distribute the parameters. GR service can also be supported across concatenated GR diff-serv networks.

PERFORMANCE OF VoIP IN THE INTERNET

This part of the chapter examines a test conducted by 3Com on the performance of VoIP in the Internet. The source for this study is [COX98].

The study entailed sending and receiving traffic between three nodes: University of California, Davis (UCD); University of Illinois, Chicago (UIC); and DePaul University. See Figure 8–20. The tests were run for a six-month period. During these tests, a client would transmit once an hour to a server for three minutes. The transmissions involved a trace that allowed the analysts to judge round-trip transmission time (RTT) as well as packet loss. To control how routers handle conventional ping packets, the engineers designed their own "ping" program and did not rely on internet pings. Observations were made in the evenings as well as various times during the business day and on weekends.

In addition, different codecs were employed in the tests with the emphasis on G.723.1 and G.729A. Tests were done with PC-to-PC communications and VoIP gateways.

We can summarize several key aspects of the study with the examination of the three figures depicted in Figure 8–21.

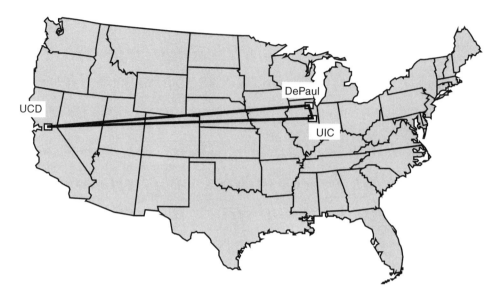

Figure 8–20   Topology for the study

Figure 8–21(a) compares the average round-trip delay (in ms) in relation to the hop count. The hop count represents the number of nodes traversed between the client and the server. This figure reveals some interesting facts. The first fact is that round-trip delay rarely exceeds 200 ms. This conclusion is borne out by other studies. The second fact is that the delay is highly variable. On one occasion a delay going through the same number of nodes is, say, 100 ms and on another occasion it may be 200 ms.

Keep in mind that these data represent RTT measured with a ping only and do not include analog-to-digital conversion, codec operations, or other factors that would increase RTT.

Figure 8–21(b) is the same figure as 8–21(a). The oval is placed on the figure to emphasize that despite the variability in the round-trip-delay in relation to hop count, increased hop counts do indeed contribute to delay.

Figure 8–21(c) has some numbers placed around several of the points in the graph. These numbers represent the geographical distances in miles between the sender and receiver of the trace. It is clear that geographical distance cannot be correlated to round-trip delay. Indeed, a short distance of only 477 miles with a hop count of 21 resulted in a 240 ms round-trip delay. To emphasize: Hop distance is a key factor in delay, and geographical distance is less a factor (unless geosynchronous satellites are used).

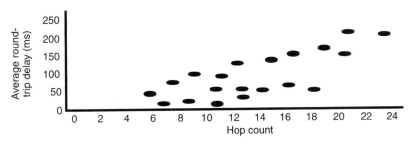

(a) Average delay and hop count

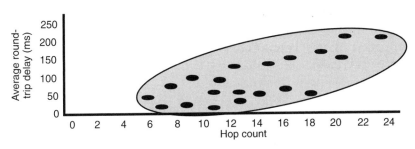

(b) Correlation of delay to distance

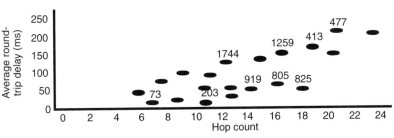

(c) Relationship of delay and geographical distance

(Note: numbers represent distance in miles)

Figure 8–21   Round-trip delay vs. hop count [COX98]

SUMMARY

In this chapter we examined several issues pertaining to the performance of VoIP networks and discovered how traffic engineering (TE) is used to meet performance goals. The first part of the chapter examined the trade-offs of packet size, queue size, packet loss, and packet latency. The next part of the chapter provided a description of queuing methods to assist the network operator in traffic engineering.

Even though TCP is not used to transport VoIP traffic, some of its concepts have been used in congestion control mechanisms for Internet traffic. We discussed these mechanisms, notably WRED.

We also learned how policy-based and constraint-based routing can be implemented to enhance the performance of networks to support VoIP applications. The emerging MPLS and LDP technologies should go a long way toward improving the delay and jitter problems in packet networks.

The Cox study, cited in the last part of the chapter, demonstrates that voice over IP is quite feasible in private networks with leased lines, but marginal in the public Internet.

It is a good idea to remember that packet voice is in its infancy. In a few years, it is reasonable to expect that the Internet will also deliver toll-quality speech—in a few years.

9

RSVP, DiffServ, and Other Supporting Procedures in VoIP Networks

$\mathbf{D}$uring the discussion on the VoIP Model in Chapter 3, I promised that several other protocols and technologies supporting VoIP would be explained in subsequent chapters. This is one of the chapters that contains this material. The emphasis in this chapter is on two Internet standards that provide QOS for user traffic: IntServ (as implemented with RSVP) and DiffServ. The chapter also includes discussions on RTP, NTP, and multicasting, and concludes with a look at the Session Description Protocol (SDP).

RESERVING RESOURCES FOR VOICE TRAFFIC

We learned in earlier chapters that voice traffic is characterized as *real-time* traffic. The term real time was coined in the 1960s to denote a situation in which events happen very fast. When a telephony speaker says hello, this greeting is passed through the telephone network to the listener almost instantaneously. The network is not allowed to delay traffic delivery; it must present the speech to the listener as soon as possible.

A well-designed voice network (be it circuit or packet switched) is engineered to make delay imperceptible between the two conversing parties, regardless of their locations. The people engaged in a telephone call may be located in distant parts of the planet; their conversations may traverse thousands of miles, and the voice traffic may be transported through scores of components (such as switches). Yet the network provides such fast response time that the conversationalists may think they are next door to each other.

For these operations to occur in a packet-switched data network (and specifically, an internet or the Internet), some means must exist to configure the network resources (links and nodes) to provide the required QOS for voice traffic. In many situations, this configuration entails the reservation of resources.

QOS MODELS: INTSERV AND DIFFSERV

The Internet Engineering Task Force has established two working groups to develop QOS standards. The first group deals with Integrated Services (IntServ). The focus is on long-lived unicast and multicast flows[1], and the Resource Reservation Protocol (RSVP) is used with this approach. This model guarantees each flow's QOS requirements through the complete path from the sender to the receiver. Each node in the path is aware of each flow's requirements and participates in the QOS support operation. The second group is working on Differentiated Services (DiffServ). This model does not work with individual flows. Rather, it combines flows with the same service requirements into a single aggregated flow. Whereas IntServ might discern each flow that belongs to (say) VoIP traffic, DiffServ would group all VoIP traffic together. This aggregated flow then receives levels of service based on the flow's priority.

However, nothing precludes DiffServ from operating with granular, individual flows. But as a matter of intent, DiffServ is not set up to be concerned with each individual flow; its premise is to aggregate flows.

These two approaches are different in how they approach providing QOS to the user, and we devote time to them shortly. For now, it is interesting to note that both IntServ and DiffServ specify QOS at layer 3 in contrast to Frame Relay and ATM, which define QOS at layer 2.[2]

---

[1]For this discussion, a flow is a stream of traffic associated with at least a destination address, and perhaps a destination port number and an IP Protocol ID. It could also be a stream of traffic associated with a label, such as an MPLS label.

[2]The supposedly layer 2 operations of Frame Relay and ATM are actually a combination of layer 2 and layer 3 operations. X.25 provides the model: Its virtual circuits are managed at its layer 3 in a separate layer 3 header. For Frame Relay and ATM, virtual circuit management has been "pushed down" to layer 2, and the layer 3 header has been eliminated.

Let's look at IntServ first. With this method, an application makes a request for QOS resources *before* sending traffic. This request entails explicit signaling; that is, the sending of messages to other nodes. The message contains parameters dealing with QOS requirements for the session.

Once the QOS is set up, the application is expected to adhere to its request, so it is considered to be self-policing. Furthermore, IntServ is expected to meet the QOS (proper queuing, etc.) on a per-flow basis. Once again, a flow can be assigned to each user in a voice call, a video session, etc.

With DiffServ, there is no signaling from the application. Therefore, DiffServ is not a protocol. That is, DiffServ operations in a node are not set up with messages, but with configuration operations that are established by the network operator. In addition, the application is not necessarily expected to police itself. DiffServ will perform the policing function, unless the network is engineered to provide a guaranteed rate (GR) for certain packets (see Chapter 8 for this aspect of DiffServ in relation to traffic engineering).

DiffServ does not work with a flow on an end-to-end basis. It operates on each packet on a hop-to-hop basis (DiffServ uses the term hop to mean a node) and is tasked with providing QOS for each individual packet in relation to each hop in the network. In contrast, IntServ is oriented toward providing QOS to all packets that belong to a flow, and a specific hop should provide the same behavior as any other hop, something like the telephone network.

In contrast, DiffServ is oriented toward per-hop behavior (PHB). Each node (hop) may react differently to the same flow, depending on the congestion state of the specific node. Of course, for a user session to be effective, DiffServ should provide consistent performance for all packets in a user session (that is, a flow). But the performance of DiffServ (guaranteed rate excluded) is not intended to be as consistent as the IntServ model.

RSVP

The Resource Reservation Protocol (RSVP), as its name implies, defines a *reservation* procedure for real-time multimedia sessions. It is an example of the IntServ model. RSVP is uniquely different from some other technologies, such as ATM, Frame Relay, and X.25, because it is the recipient of the traffic that places the reservation. In contrast, other technologies allow the sender of the traffic to establish the requirements. The rationale for the RSVP approach is that it is the recipient of the traffic that has the best knowledge of its capacity and limitations. For example, a video server may be sending traffic to its clients at a very high bit rate, perhaps 100 Mbit/s for high-quality video. However, the various recipients (clients) might vary in their ability to receive this high-quality transmission. Consequently, they can send their reservation resource request to the server, defining different types of throughput requirements. As an example, a device attached to an ATM network running a low-speed interface might be unable to support the full 100 Mbit/s bandwidth transmission, or a personal computer attached to a legacy Ethernet may only be able to support 10 Mbit/s of bandwidth. Therefore, these two devices can send to the server their reservation request describing their capacity (their bandwidth availability).

Recall that RSVP uses the concept of a flow for its reserved traffic. Flows are somewhat similar to connection-oriented virtual circuits found in Frame Relay and ATM. They identify the traffic streams from the sending application to the receivers. The idea of a flow is to differentiate between various kinds of traffic and to treat this traffic differently in the network depending on the timing and synchronization requirements of the traffic. The flows are placed in different queues at the intervening routers and the servers.

RSVP Operation Entities

This part of the chapter provides a summary of the major aspects of the RSVP standard, as published in RFC 2205.

RSVP requests resources for simplex flows; that is, resources in one direction. Therefore, RSVP treats a sender as logically distinct from a receiver, although the same application process may act as both a sender and a receiver at the same time.

RSVP does not transport application data but is rather an Internet control protocol, like ICMP, IGMP, or routing protocols, like OSPF. Some people call RSVP a signaling protocol. Like the implementations of routing and management protocols, an implementation of RSVP will typically execute in the background, not in the data forwarding path, as shown in Figure 9–1.

Quality of service is implemented for a particular data flow by mechanisms collectively called "traffic control." These mechanisms include (1) a classifier, (2) admission control, (3) a packet scheduler (or some other link-layer-dependent mechanism to determine when particular packets are forwarded), and (4) a policy control mechanism.

The classifier determines the QOS class (and perhaps the route) for each packet by examining the IP and Transport layer headers. For each

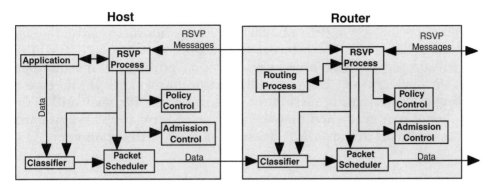

Figure 9–1   The RSVP operational entities

outgoing interface, the packet scheduler or other link-layer-dependent mechanism achieves the promised QOS. The packet scheduler implements QOS service models defined by the Integrated Services Working Group.

During reservation setup, an RSVP QOS request is passed to two local decision modules: admission control and policy control. Admission control determines whether the node has sufficient available resources to supply the requested QOS. Policy control determines if a flow is permitted by administrative rules, for example, certain IP addresses are or are not permitted to reserve bandwidth; certain protocol IDs are or are not permitted to reserve bandwidth, and so on.

Sessions

RSVP defines a session as a flow with a particular IP address destination and transport-layer protocol. Recall that RSVP treats each session independently.

An RSVP session is defined by IP destination address (DestAddress), IP protocol ID (ProtocolId), and destination port ID (DstPort). The IP destination address of the data packets can be a unicast or multicast address. The ProtocolId is the IP protocol ID. The optional DstPort parameter is a "generalized destination port." DstPort could be defined by a UDP/TCP destination port field, by an equivalent field in another transport protocol, or by some application-specific information.

It is not necessary to include DstPort in the session definition when DestAddress is multicast, since different sessions can always have different multicast addresses. However, DstPort is necessary if more than one unicast session is addressed to the same receiver host.

RSVP does not provide routing operations but uses IP as the forwarding mechanism in the same fashion as the Internet Control Message Protocol (ICMP) and the Internet Group Message Protocol (IGMP) use IP. RSVP operates with unicast or multicast procedures and interoperates with current and planned multicast protocols. Like IP, it relies on routing tables to determine routes for its messages. It uses IGMP to first join a multicast group and then executes procedures to reserve resources for the multicast group. IGMP is discussed later in this chapter.

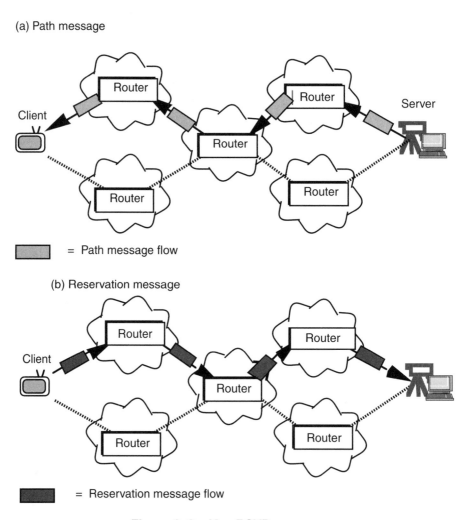

Figure 9–2   Key RSVP messages

The Key RSVP Messages

RSVP requires the receivers of the traffic to request QOS for the flow. The receiver host application must determine the QOS profile, which is then passed to RSVP. After the analysis of the request, RSVP sends request messages to all the nodes that participate in the data flow. As Figure 9–2(a) shows, the operations actually begin with the RSVP PATH message. It is used by a server (the flow sender) to set up a path for the session.

Figure 9–2(b) shows that the RSVP RESERVATION messages are sent by the receivers of the flow, and they allow sender and intermediate machines (such as routers) to learn the receivers' requirements. The route taken back to the server in the network by the RESERVATION message must be the same route taken by the PATH message.

Admission Control and Policy Control

As depicted in Figure 9–3, the RSVP process passes the request to admission control and policy control. If either test fails, the reservation is rejected and the RSVP process returns an error message to the appropriate receiver(s). If both succeed, the node sets the packet classifier to select the data packets defined by the *filterspec,* and it interacts with the

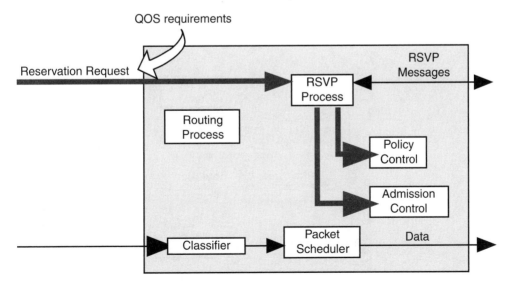

Figure 9–3 Processing the reservation request

appropriate link layer to obtain the desired QOS defined by the *flowspec*. Let's examine the flowspec and the filterspec.

The Flow Descriptor

A simple RSVP reservation request consists of a flowspec together with a filterspec; this pair is called a *flow descriptor*. See Figure 9–4. The flowspec specifies a desired QOS. The filterspec, together with a session specification, defines the set of data packets—the flow—to receive the QOS defined by the flowspec.

The flowspec sets parameters in the node's packet scheduler or other link layer mechanism, and the filterspec sets parameters in the packet classifier. Data packets that are addressed to a particular session but do not match any of the filterspecs for that session are handled as best-effort traffic.

The flowspec in a reservation request generally includes a service class and two sets of numeric parameters: (1) an *Rspec* (R for reserve) that defines the desired QOS and (2) a *Tspec* (T for traffic) that describes the data flow. The formats and contents of Tspecs and Rspecs are determined by the integrated service models (see RFC 2210).

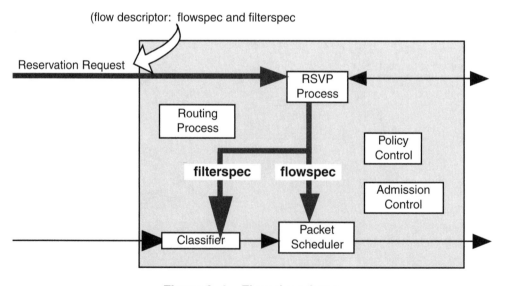

Figure 9–4   Flow descriptor

The Reservation Style

An RSVP reservation request includes a set of options that are collectively called the reservation style. One reservation option concerns the treatment of reservations for different senders within the same session: establish a distinct reservation for each upstream sender or else make a single reservation that is shared among all packets of selected senders.

Another reservation option controls the selection of senders; it may be an *explicit* list of all selected senders or a *wildcard* that implicitly selects all the senders to the session. In an explicit sender-selection reservation, each filterspec must match exactly one sender; in a wildcard sender-selection no filterspec is needed. The following styles are currently defined:

- *Wildcard-filter (WF) style:* The WF style implies the options shared reservation and wildcard sender selection, which means the WF-style reservation creates a single reservation shared by flows from all upstream senders. This reservation may be thought of as a shared "pipe," whose "size" is the largest of the resource requests from all receivers, independent of the number of senders using it. A WF-style reservation is propagated upstream toward all sender hosts, and it automatically extends to new senders as they appear.
- *Fixed-filter (FF) style:* The FF style implies the options distinct reservations and explicit sender selection. Thus, an elementary FF-style reservation request creates a distinct reservation for data packets from a particular sender, not sharing them.
- *Shared-explicit (SE) style:* The SE style implies the options "shared" reservation and "explicit" sender selection. Thus, an SE-style reservation creates a single reservation shared by selected upstream senders. Unlike the WF style, the SE style allows a receiver to explicitly specify the set of senders to be included.

Shared reservations, created by WF and SE styles, are appropriate for those multicast applications in which multiple data sources are unlikely to transmit simultaneously. Multiconference VoIP is an example of an application suitable for shared reservations. Since a limited number of people talk at once, each receiver might issue a WF or SE reservation request for twice the bandwidth required for one sender (to allow some overspeaking). On the other hand, the FF style, which creates distinct reservations for the flows of different senders, is appropriate for video signals.

RSVP does not permit the merging of shared reservations with distinct reservations, since these modes are fundamentally incompatible. RSVP also disallows merging explicit sender selection with wildcard sender selection, since this might produce an unexpected service for a receiver that specified explicit selection. As a result of these prohibitions, WF, SE, and FF styles are all mutually incompatible.

RSVP Set Up in the Router

Setting up RSVP on a router is a simple, straightforward process. With the configuration command of ip rsvp [interface kbps] [single-flow-kbps], the network operator can enable RSVP in an interface configuration command with the following parameters.

- *Interface kbit/s:* Amount of bandwidth in kbit/s that is to be reserved on the specified interface. The range for this parameter is 1–10,000,000. This parameter is optional.
- *Single-flow kbit/s:* Amount of bandwidth in kbit/s that is to be reserved for a single flow. The range is 1–10,000,000. This parameter is also optional.

If parameters are not coded, 75% of the bandwidth on the interface is reserved for RSVP flows.

RSVP Scaling

Most literature on RSVP states that RSVP will not scale well to a large user base. This statement is true if a large (say) audio conference sets up a session for each individual user. However, as noted earlier, shared reservations can be used for multicast applications in which multiple data sources are unlikely to transmit simultaneously. If the application can control who speaks (as in my VoIP multicast application explained in Chapter 1), the scaling problem of RSVP is diminished.

IP RTP Reserve

Cicso IOS software has an option that you might consider using in place of RSVP. It is called IP RTP Reserve, and its use can replace RSVP (and the use of the IP precedence field). The configuration command simply specifies a range of UDP port numbers (up to 100) that are to be given a maximum amount of bandwidth. The router will then prioritize the stated bandwidth for the VoIP packets with these port numbers in the UDP header. IP RTP Reserve uses Cisco's WFQ mechanisms defined in Chapter 8.

DIFFSERV

DiffServ provides a framework that enables service providers to offer each customer a range of services that are differentiated on the basis of performance (and perhaps an associated price). The customer and the service provider negotiate a service level agreement (SLA) describing the customer's traffic rate submittal and the provider's support of the customer's packet rate. If the customer submits traffic in excess of the SLA, that traffic need not be given the service established in the SLA.

DiffServ is designed to scale to large networks and a large customer base. It forces many of the QOS operations *out* of the network and into the nodes surrounding the network (edge nodes). These nodes do not affect the overall performance of the network core, and even though they themselves may experience problems, those problems affect only the customers at that node and not the customer universe inside the network.

The key ideas of DiffServ are to classify traffic at the boundaries of network and to possibly condition this traffic at the boundaries. The classification operation entails the assignment of the traffic to behavioral aggregates (BAs). These behavioral aggregates are a collection of packets with common characteristics—common insofar as how they are identified and treated by the network. They are called a DS behavior aggregate and are defined as a collection of packets with the same DS codepoint crossing a link in a particular direction.

The Codepoint and Per-Hop Behavior

The DiffServ traffic is assigned a value called the differentiated services (DS) codepoint. For IPv4, the codepoint is part of the TOS field (six bits); for IPv6, the codepoint is in the traffic class byte. Refer back to Figure 2–7 in Chapter 2 for a review of the TOS field. Therefore, for DiffServ, the IP TOS field is redefined, with the high-order six bits used for the codepoint.

After the packets have been classified at the boundary of the network, they are forwarded through the network on the basis of the DS codepoint. The forwarding is performed on a per-hop basis; that is, the

DS node alone decides how the forwarding is to be carried out. As noted earlier, this concept is called per-hop behavior (PHB).

To provide a controlled environment and prevent congestion, the traffic conditioning must enforce rules on the influx of traffic into and out of the DS domain. These rules are known collectively as the *traffic conditioning agreement* (TCA). They govern how the user packet stream is treated within a service level agreement (SLA).

The DS Domain

DiffServ uses the idea of a DS domain, as shown in Figure 9–5. It is a collection of networks operating under an administration with a common DiffServ provisioning policy, called the DS domain service provider. It is responsible for meeting a service level agreement between the user and the DS domain service provider.

The DS domain consists of a contiguous set of nodes that are DS compliant and that agree to a common set of service provisioning policies. The DS domain also operates with a common per-hop behavior definitions. Recall that the PHB defines how a collection of packets with the same DS codepoint is treated.

A common example of PHB behavior is how packets are forwarded by a DS node. If one behavioral aggregate is used on a link, the operation is simple: The loading of the link determines the PHB behavior. When more

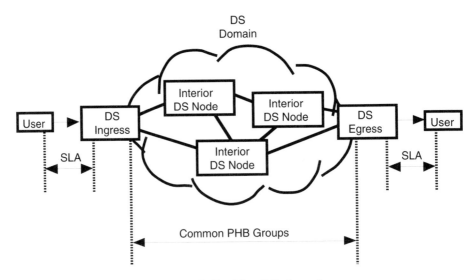

Figure 9–5   The DS domain

than one behavior aggregate competes for link resources, the PHB allocates resources to these behavior aggregates. Thus, the PHB provides a hop-by-hop resource allocation and enables the support of differentiated services, usually with the queuing mechanisms discussed in Chapter 8.

The manner in which PHBs are specified and implemented varies. They can be set up in terms of resource allocation of the QOS relative to other PHBs, for example.

A PHB group is a set of one or more PHBs. It allows a set of related forwarding behaviors to be specified together. For example, a PHB group can specify more than one dropping priority for user traffic.

The DS domain contains DS boundary nodes that are responsible for the classifying operations and the possible conditioning of ingress traffic. I have more to say about conditioning later; for this introduction, conditioning consists of controlling the traffic to make sure it "behaves" according to the rules of the DS domain (and, one hopes, the desires of the user).

Once past the ingress node and inside the DS domain, the internal nodes forward packets as determined by the DS codepoint. Their job is to map the DS codepoint value to a supported PHB. Thus, there are DS boundary nodes and DS interior nodes. The DS boundary nodes connect the DS domain to other DS domains or to noncompliant systems. There is no restriction on what type of machine executes the boundary or interior node operations. For instance, a host might play the role of a DS boundary node.

Here is a brief summary of the terms and concepts discussed thus far:

- Boundary link: A link connecting the edge nodes of two domains.
- DS boundary node: A DS node that connects a DS domain to a node.
- DS egress node: A DS boundary node in its role in handling traffic as it leaves a DS domain.
- DS ingress node: A DS boundary node in its role in handling traffic as it enters a DS domain.
- DS interior node: A DS node that is not a DS boundary node.

Multiple DS domains constitute a DS region. These regions are able to support differentiated services along paths in the domains that make up the DS region. One advantage to defining a DS region is that DiffServ allows the DS domains in the DS region to support different PHB groups. For example, a DS domain on a college campus may have different PHB groups than those of a DS domain in an ISP, such as AOL, yet these two "peering" domains must be able to interwork in a predictable and structured manner. They must define a peering SLA that establishes a TCA for the traffic that flows between them. Of course, it might happen that these domains set up common PHB groups and codepoint mappings. That being the case, there would be no need for traffic conditioning between the two DS domains.

Metering, Marking, Shaping, and Policing Operations

Regardless of what machine runs the DS boundary node functions, the DS node must act as an ingress node and egress node for traffic flowing into and out of the DS domain. It is responsible for supporting traffic conditioning agreements (TCAs) with other domains. Traffic conditioning means the enforcement of rules dealing with traffic management and includes four major operations: metering, marking, shaping, and policing.

Metering entails measuring the rate of a stream of traffic. Marking entails setting the DS codepoint. Shaping entails the emission of traffic (perhaps the delaying of it) to meet a defined traffic emission profile. Policing entails the discarding of packets (based on the state of the meter) to enforce a defined traffic profile.[3]

Traffic Classification and Conditioning

The DS node must provide traffic classification and traffic conditioning operations. The job of packet classification is to identify subsets of traffic that are to receive differentiated services by the DS domain. Classifiers operate in two modes: (a) the behavior aggregate classifier (BA) classifies packets only on the DS codepoint, and (b) the multifield classifier classifies packets by multiple fields in the packet, such as addresses, and port numbers.

The classifiers provide the mechanism to guide the packets to a traffic conditioner for more processing. The traffic stream selected by the classifier is based on a specific set of traffic profiles, such as variable or constant bit rates, jitter, delay, etc.

The packets presented to a specific traffic conditioner may be in-profile, or out-of-profile. In-profile packets are "conformant" to the user-network SLA. Out-of-profile packets are outside an SLA, or because of network behavior, arrive at the traffic conditioner at a rate that requires the conditioner to condition them (delay their delivery, drop them, etc.).

---

[3]The term policing has a limited definition in DiffServ. Some networks use the term to describe all four of the DiffServ functions.

As a general practice, classification and conditioning operations take place at the network boundaries, but nothing precludes the internal nodes from invoking these operations, and their classification and conditioning operations are more limited than those of the boundary nodes.

Relationships of the DS Functions

Figure 9–6 shows a logical view of the relationships of the key DS functions for DS packet classification and traffic conditioning operations. A traffic stream is selected by a classifier and sent to a traffic conditioner. If appropriate, a meter is used to measure the traffic against a traffic profile. The metering procedure may be used to mark, drop, or shape the traffic, based on the packet being "in profile" or "out of profile." The packets that exit the DS boundary node must have the DS codepoint set to an appropriate value, based on the classification and traffic conditioning operation.

The packet marking procedure sets the DS field of a packet to a codepoint and adds the marked packet to a specific DS behavior aggregate. The marker can be configured to mark all packets that are steered to it to a single codepoint. Alternatively, the marker can mark a packet to one of a set of codepoints. The idea of this configuration is to select a PHB in a PHB group, according to the state of a meter. The changing of the codepoint is called packet remarking.

The shaping procedure is used to bring the packet stream into compliance with a particular traffic profile and can use many of the queuing mechanisms discussed in Chapter 8. The packet stream is stored in the

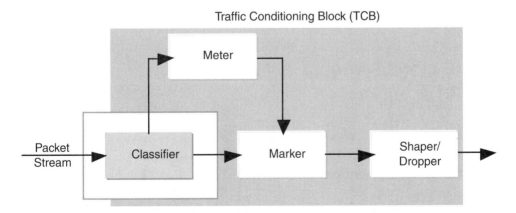

Figure 9–6   DS traffic classification and conditioning model

shaper's buffer, and a packet can be discarded if there is not enough buffer space to hold the packet. The dropping procedure polices the packet stream to bring it into conformance with a particular traffic profile. It can drop packets to adhere to the profile. Figure 9–6 shows the shaper and dropper as one entity because a dropper can be implemented as a special case of a shaper (by setting the shaper buffer size to 0 packets).

The originating node of the packet stream (the DS source domain) is allowed to perform classification and conditioning operations. This idea is called premarking and can be effective in supporting the end application's view of the required QOS for the packet stream. The source node may mark the codepoint to indicate high-priority traffic, such as VoIP packets. Next, a first-hop router may mark this traffic with another codepoint and condition the packet stream.

As stated earlier, the collective operations of metering, marking, shaping, and dropping are known as the traffic conditioning block (TCB). The classifier need not be a part of the TCB because it does not condition traffic. However, the classifiers and traffic conditioners can certainly be combined into the TCB. These options are shown in the Figure 9–6 by dashed lines.

DiffServ in the Router

Cisco states it supports DiffServ with several of the features described in Chapter 8 (as of this writing, the DS codepoint is not supported, and, therefore, neither is the formal Internet DiffServ standard):

- Committed access rate (CAR)
- WRED and WFQ
- WRED and VIP-Distributed WRQ

THE REAL-TIME PROTOCOL (RTP)

The Real-Time Protocol (RTP) is designed to support real-time traffic, that is, traffic that requires playback at the receiving application in a time-sensitive mode, such as for voice and video systems. RTP also operates with both unicast and multicast applications.

RTP provides services that include payload type identification, sequence numbering, timestamping, and delivery monitoring. Applications usually run RTP on top of UDP to make use of UDP's multiplexing and checksum services. RTP supports data transfer to multiple destinations, using multicast distribution if provided by the underlying network (an IP multicast implementation).

RTP does not provide any mechanism to ensure timely delivery, nor does it provide other quality-of-service guarantees; instead, it relies on lower layer services to provide these services. It does not guarantee delivery or prevent out-of-order delivery, nor does it assume that the underlying network is reliable and delivers packets in sequence. The sequence numbers included in RTP allow the receiver to reconstruct the sender's packet sequence, but sequence numbers might also be used to determine the proper location of a packet.

Figures 9–7 and 9–8 show two major features of RTP and illustrate how RTP can support the traffic between RTP session senders and receivers, using translation and mixing. These operations are not required of an RTP implementation. Rather, RTP is a good tool by which to implement them.

In Figure 9–7 the RTP system is acting as a translator. The RTP translator translates (encodes) from one payload syntax to a different syntax. This figure shows how the RTP translator operates. The user devices on the left side of the figure are set up to use a 512 kbit/s video stream for their video application. The user device on the right side of the figure uses a 384 kbit/s video stream. As another possibility, the transit network may not be able to support the 512 kbit/s rate. So, whether from

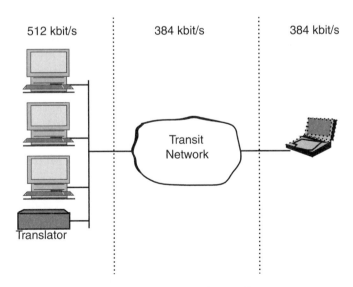

Figure 9–7   The RTP translator

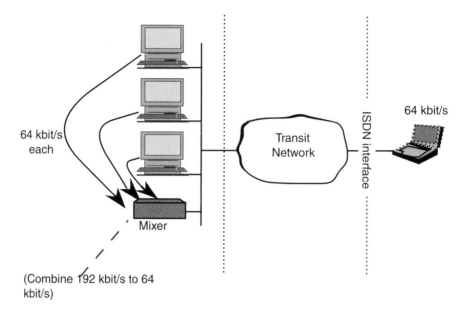

Figure 9–8   The RTP mixer

the user station on the right or the network in the middle, the users cannot communicate with each other.

The RTP translator allows these user stations to interact with each other. The job of the translator is to accept the traffic of the stations on the left side of the figure, translate (encode) that traffic into a format that is (a) in consonance with the bandwidth limitations of the transit network, or (b) in consonance with the bandwidth limitations of the user station on the right side of the figure. The user's RTP packet shows that the user is the synchronization source.

Figure 9–8 shows an RTP server performing a mixer operation. Mixers combine multiple sources into one stream. Typically, mixers participate in audio operations and do not decrease the quality of the signal to the recipients. They simply combine the signals into a consistent format.

RTP mixers do not translate each source payload into a different format. The original format is maintained, and the various source payloads are combined into one stream. The mixer is used for audio conferences, but not for video sessions, since mixing video streams is not yet a commercial reality. On the other hand, if the audio streams are uncomplicated pulse code modulation (PCM) traffic, it is possible to arithmetically sum the values of each source payload and combine them into a single stream.

CLOCKING PROTOCOLS WITH NETWORK TIME PROTOCOL (NTP)

The Network Time Protocol (NTP), published in Request for Comments (RFC) 1119, is used for timestamping operations.

Clocking information for a network is provided through the primary time server designated as a root. The time server obtains its clocking information from master sources. In the United States, this is usually one of three sources:

- *Fort Collins, Colorado:* Station WWV, operated by the National Institute of Standards and Technology (NIST), uses high-frequency (HF) frequencies.
- *Kauai, Hawaii:* Station WWVH, operated by NIST, also uses HF frequencies.
- *Boulder, Colorado:* Station WWVB uses low-frequency transmissions.

All timestamps are 64 bits in length with 32 bits reserved for a whole number and 32 bits for the fraction. Timestamps are benchmarked from 1 January 1900.

NTP can operate above UDP or TCP. Be aware that the information retrieved and displayed to the user on a terminal is not very readable. For example, the value gives the number of seconds since January 1, 1900, midnight (GMT). Consequently, the date of January 1, 1980 GMT at midnight would be retrieved and displayed as 2,524,521,600. Of course, a simple program can be written to translate this notation into a user-friendly format.

ROLE OF MULTICASTING

Multicasting concepts in the Internet have been around for over 25 years. They will play an increasing role in VoIP since they support multiparty calls and multiconference sessions. A wide variety of multicasting operations are defined for packet networks; the key ones are described below. You should refer to a companion book to this text, *Internet Telephony: Call Processing Protocols,* for a more thorough discussion on multicasting.

The first RFC on the subject was RFC 966. In this specification was information on IP class D addresses, showing the format for multicast addresses. RFC 988 followed; it described mechanisms for establishing multigroup memberships. RFC 988 was replaced by RFC 1054, which specified the procedures for the Internet Group Management Protocol (IGMPv0). This document built on RFC 988 and describes how hosts notify an IGMP router about joining or leaving a multicast group. RFC 1112 replaced RFC 1054 as IGMPv1 and is the prevalent multicasting standard in use today.

Another protocol, published as RFC 1075, documents multicasting routing. It is called the Distance Vector Multicast Routing Protocol (DVMRP). Still another standard, published in RFC 2352, deals with the Protocol-Independent Multicast (PIM) operations. The well-known Open Shortest Path First (OSPF) standard is enhanced for multicasting with Multicast OSPF (MOSPF), published in RFC 1584.

Basic Concepts

A few concepts should be discussed about multicasting's support of VoIP. The first one is the idea of a multicast group. It is an identified set of users that receive traffic from a common source (say, another user or a conference chairman in a multiconferencing VoIP session). The multicasting operations of the group are managed by a multicast manager, often located in a router or a server.

One of the main features of multicasting is the joining and leaving of a group. This aspect of multicasting is simple in concept. A user joins a group by sending messages to an multicast manager and leaves the group by a similar procedure.

For an example of these operations, please refer to Figure 1–8 in Chapter 1. For my lectures, my students join and leave my multicasting group by logging on or off to the VoIP multicast server. They can also leave the conference temporarily (say, to take a call), but they are still a member of my group. See Figure 9–9.

Numerous issues are involved in this activity. For example, there must be a means to associate a user's unicast address (an IP address) to another IP address that identifies the group; that is, a multicast address. In addition, there must be some way to associate a route with the multicast address so that traffic can flow back and forth among the group members. For some applications, it will be important that joining and leaving a multicast group occur quickly. For example, if an internet supports real-time TV, channel surfing may entail the quick joining and leaving of a program.

My students are registered to my VoIP server with an IP multicasting address, and this address is used to multicast my traffic (voice, slides, drawings, etc.) to each student.

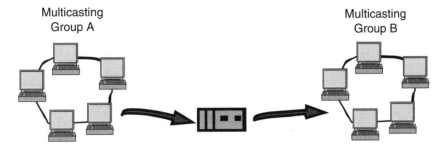

(a) Sending to a multicast group

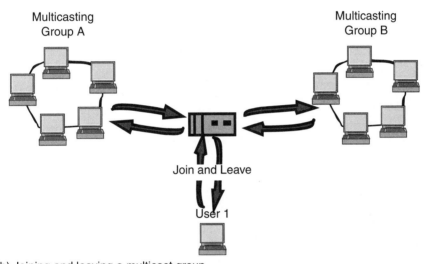

(b) Joining and leaving a multicast group

Figure 9–9　Multicasting groups

Multicast Trees

In addition to adding and joining a multicast group, pruning the distribution tree, or, simply pruning, is another aspect of multicasting. Pruning entails removing selected parties in the multicasting group. In Figure 9–10, parties A, B, and C are pruned from the distribution tree.

Pruning can occur in an multicast internet to improve the efficiency of the multicast operation. For example, a party (node) may be pruned because that node is being reached through another part of the distribution tree. It may be that node A and its lower entries (leaf entries) are in another part of the tree, perhaps at Node D. So, pruning would remove redundant entries.

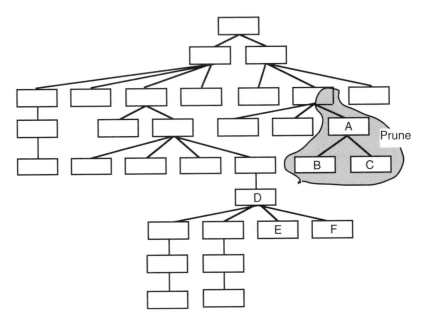

Figure 9–10   Pruning the distribution tree

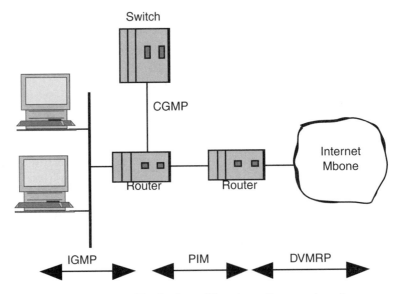

Figure 9–11   Typical multicast routing protocols

In earlier versions of a multicasting application in the Internet, called Mbone, the multicast traffic was actually broadcast throughout the backbone. Of course, this approach is very inefficient and isn't multicast at all. For the past few years, efforts have been made to move away from this approach and implement pruning capabilities in all Mbone nodes.

Key Protocols

Figure 9–11 shows the position of several multicasting protocols. One of the Cisco protocols is included in the figure because of Cisco's position in the industry. They are as follows:

- *CGMP—Cisco Group Management Protocol:* Used on routers that are connected to Cisco switches. The protocol performs functions similar to those of IGMP.
- *DVMRP—Distance Vector Multicast Routing Protocol (DVMRP):* Used on the Internet Mbone for multicast routing.
- *IGMP—Internet Group Management Protocol:* Used between hosts and routers to set up and leave multicasting groups. RSVP uses IGMP as part of its operations.
- *PIM—Protocol-Independent Multicast:* Used between routers to track which packets the routers are supposed to forward to each other and their respective (directly attached) LANs.

THE SESSION DESCRIPTION PROTOCOL (SDP)

SDP conveys session information to recipients, as well as media information that pertain to the session, and it allows more than one media stream to be associated with a session. For example, one media stream could be for audio, and another might be for a whiteboard media stream.

SDP is essentially a standard that specifies a format for a session description. It does not incorporate a transport protocol and is intended to use different transport protocols as appropriate, including the Session Initiation Protocol (SIP), Megaco, and the Hypertext Transfer Protocol (HTTP).

The conveyance of information about media streams (audio, video, etc.) in multimedia sessions allows the recipients of a session description to participate in the session if they can support these streams. This concept also supports the negotiation of media stream parameters, such as a sampling rate of the signal, the size of packets, and so on. For VoIP, SDP can be used to negotiate the use of specific codecs for a call.

Not only does SDP inform the receivers of its messages about the existence of a session, it also conveys sufficient information to enable the joining and participating in the session. The SDP information includes (a) the session name and its purpose, (b) the time the session is active, (c) the media pertaining to the session (video, audio, formats for the video/audio), and (d) the pertinent IP addresses and port numbers for the session.

For more information on the SDP, take a look at RFC 2327 and Chapter 5 of *IP Internet Telephony: Call Processing Protocols,* the companion book to the one you are reading.

SUMMARY

It is evident that the term VoIP means much more than simply running voice traffic over IP. This chapter has introduced several protocols and procedures that can play a key role in aiding VoIP in providing high-quality audio services between users.

RSVP and DiffServ provide a defined level of QOS for the VoIP traffic. They operate in conjunction with many of the performance operations (queuing, constrained routing) covered in Chapter 8.

Other protocols that come into play for VoIP support are the Real-Time Protocol, the Network Time Protocol, the Session Description Protocol, and a variety of multicasting protocols. And these are not exhaustive. Missing from this list are the IP Call Processing Protocols, the subject of the next chapter.

10

VoIP Gateways and IP Call Processing Protocols

The industry is migrating to several protocol suites and call processing protocols to support VoIP. They are the H.323 Recommendations, published by the ITU-T, and the Session Initiation Protocol (SIP), Megaco, and the Media Gateway Control Protocol (MGCP), published by the IETF.

These systems are not stand-alone specifications. They rely on many other supporting protocols to complete their operations. The approach taken in this chapter is to concentrate on the core operations of these systems.[1]

As a prelude to the examination of these protocols, we analyze a model that defines the interfaces and functional entities of VoIP Gateways and VoIP Gateway Controllers.

TASKS OF THE VoIP GATEWAY

The main task of a VoIP Gateway is to support the interworking of telephone conversations between two or more parties through a network or networks in which part of the path between the parties is an IP network; that is, a packet network. Its simplest form is shown in Figure 10–1.

---

[1]A companion book to this series is devoted to these subjects. It is titled *Internet Telephony: Call Processing Protocols*.

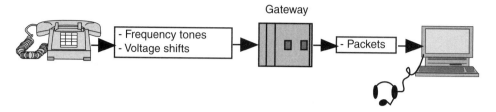

Figure 10–1   The VoIP Gateway

The Gateway accepts the telephone's signals, such as its dialed digits, off-hook indicator, etc., and converts these signals into binary bits. This information is then encapsulated into the IP datagram (packet) and forwarded to the other party or parties who participate in the telephone call.

The binary representation of the telephone signals can take one of two forms: (a) a reserved name assigned for each tone (for example, a name for the digit 5), or (b) a description of the acoustical property of the signal (for example, 770/1336 DTMF Hz for digit 5). For the audio conversation, the analog signals emanating from the telephone are converted into digital samples of the speech pattern, and these samples are then transported to the other party in IP datagrams.

These binary representations must then be converted back to native tones at the called telephone. However as shown in Figure 10–1, if the called party is using a computer, then the PC is designed to handle the packets, and translate them to operations in the computer to simulate a telephone. The person using the computer for the telephone conversation is unaware of this conversion process. Of course, the process works in the reverse order for traffic emanating from the computer.

THE GATEWAY/GATEKEEPER MODEL

Several terms are used to describe the placement of the VoIP functions in the VoIP physical entities, and we have explained some of them in this book. This aspect of packet telephony can be confusing because the various specifications use different terms to describe the same or similar functions. For example, H.323 uses the term Gatekeeper to describe a similar entity residing in the MGCP as a Call Agent.

To help clarify these terms and concepts, [VAND98] has published a model of the Media Gateway Controller and the Media Gateway, which also includes the Gatekeeper, the H.323 terminal, and the Signaling

Gateway. This model is shown in Figure 10–2. The model is not yet finished; that is, the references (A, B, C, etc.) have not been fully defined.

In this model, the *Gateway* (a generic term at this point in the discussion) is made up of the Media Gateway Controller (MGC), the Media Gateway (MG), and the Signaling Gateway (SG). This generic Gateway is the node in the network that interfaces an IP-based network and the telephony network (local loops or trunks). It must provide two-way, real-time communications interfaces between the IP-based network and the telephony network.

Note that the H.323 Gatekeeper is not part of the Gateway. The reason is that this model is based on work done in the IETF, and H.323 is part of the ITU-T efforts. Notwithstanding, the Internet Gateway components are able to interwork with the H.323 Gatekeeper because of other IETF specifications (see Chapter 11).

The three components that make up the Gateway are described next. Keep in mind that these three components can be housed in one machine, such as a PBX, a VoIP server, a router, and so on. The reason they are defined as separate entities is to permit options and provide flexibility in how they are implemented. For example, one component might be housed in vendor A's machine and another in vendor B's ma-

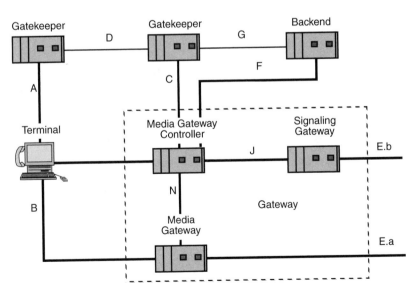

Figure 10–2 The VoIP Gateway/Gatekeeper reference model [VAND98]

chine. They should still be able to communicate with each other because of the IP call processing standards that are established as to how the components send, receive, and act on call processing messages.

- The *Media Gateway* provides the mapping and translation functions of the user traffic between the IP/telephony networks. For example, it might translate G.711 64 kbit/s speech into G.723.1 6.3 kbit/s speech, and vice versa. These operations are referred to as stream conditioning and may also include echo cancellation if necessary. For traffic emanating from the IP network, the IP VoIP packets do not operate on the telephony side. Therefore, these packets must be mapped into telephony user bearer channels (DS0s, ISDN B channels). The opposite operations occur when traffic emanates from the telephony network.

    The Media Gateway can also be responsible for support services such as announcements and tone generation as necessary. It can keep track of traffic and statistics on network usage.

- The *Signaling Gateway* is responsible for the signaling operations of the system. It provides the interworking of the IP call processing messages sent from the packet-switched network with SS7 ISUP signaling operations sent from the circuit-switched network. For example, it might translate an H.323 SETUP message coming from an H.323 Gatekeeper into an SS7 ISUP initial address message (IAM) that is to go to a telephony exchange.

- The *Media Gateway Controller* is the overall controller of the system. That is, it controls the Media Gateway and the Signaling Gateway. In many implementations, it must interwork with the H.323 Gatekeeper so that it can process H.323 messages. It monitors the resources of the overall system and maintains control of all connections.

The H.323 *Gatekeeper* is also a controller and has some of the same responsibilities as the Media Gateway Controller, except it need not control the Signaling Gateway or the Media Gateway. Its job is to control the H.323 activities on the IP-based network.

The *backend* may be used by the Gateways and Gatekeepers to provide support functions such as billing, database management, routing and address resolution.

The reference interfaces labeled E have the following functions: (a) E.a is the interface for telephony user links (lines and trunks) to support the interworking of user bearer channels (for example, VoIP packets with DS0 channels) and (b) E.b is the interface for the SS7 and/or ISDN signaling links to interface with the IP Call Processing Protocols.

IP CALL PROCESSING PROTOCOLS

As introduced in Chapter 3, several protocols provide the control and management of telephony sessions in an internet. They are known as signaling or call processing protocols. The principal job of these protocols is to set up and clear calls in an IP network. Their counterparts in conventional circuit-switched networks are Q.931 (in ISDN networks) and ISUP (in SS7 networks). These protocols are:

- H.323
- Megaco
- MGCP
- SIP

I have grouped these systems in to the category of call processing for purposes of this general explanation. But keep in mind that their many operations do vary. For example, SIP defines procedures to locate parties that are to be part of a call. The other protocols shown here do not have this type of service, at least not to the extent that SIP provides.

For another example, H.323, SIP, MGCP, and Megaco have operations that define how to set up and clear down a voice call across an IP network, but their individual rules for this service are different.

As noted earlier, one can wonder why multiple protocols have been published that exhibit considerable redundancy in their operations. The answer is that some of these procedures are developed by the ITU-T and others by the IETF, two different standards bodies with their own views on VoIP standards. Another answer is that there are often honest differences of opinion from network operators, vendors, and users about how to design a protocol to meet a stated set of objectives, and these differences may lead to multiple efforts.

Considerable coordination has occurred between some of these working groups and task forces. This situation sometimes results in the dovetailing of one standard into another. For example, Megaco is now published as part of the ITU-T H Series (H.248).

Nonetheless, the proliferation of multiple protocols that have over-lapping operations can be confusing to an outsider, but one hopes this "competitive" approach will lead to better specifications.

Let's now take a look at these four protocols. The next four sections of this chapter examine them, using the following organization:

- General description of the protocol (including a comparison chart)
- Architecture of the protocol
- Major operations of the protocol

H.323 GENERAL DESCRIPTION

The H.323 protocol is now being deployed in many voice over packet net-works. It defines in considerable detail the operations of user devices, gateways, and other nodes. The H.323 user terminal can provide real-time, two-way audio, video, or data communications with another H.323 user terminal. The terminal can also communicate with an H.323 Gate-way or a Multipoint Control Unit (MCU). While I cite the ability to sup-port voice, video, and data, the terminal need not be configured for all those services, and H.323 does not require the terminal to be capable of multiservice operations.

Table 10–1 summarizes the major aspects of H.323. The table is self-descriptive, but a few comments may prove helpful. The ITU-T developed

Table 10–1   H.323 comparison chart

What? A call processing system for voice/video/data

Where does it fit? Handsets, PCs, PBXs, conference bridges, gateways

What does it do? Finds resources, registers users, allocates bandwidth, negotiates capabilities, sets up logical channels for media flows (voice, fax, etc.), defines messages and their formats, sets up and clears calls

Applications? Regular voice calls, multiparty conferencing, seminars, chalk talks for working sessions, fax and data support for unicast and multicast sessions

Unique aspects? Defines in detail the functions of multiconferencing units, uses several on-going ITU-T standards for managing a user session

Pros/Cons?

+ quite prevalent; + powerful, especially for conferencing
– complex (expensive to implement); – built on ITU-T OSI Layer 6

Future? Relative to market, deeply entrenched, but not a favorite with Internet implementers

H.323 by borrowing from some other standards published by this standards body. As such, H.323 is a patchwork of procedures. Additionally, it was not designed to interwork with Web architecture, such as HTTP, URLs, and text-oriented transfer syntaxes. Indeed, its data structures and transfer syntaxes are based on the OSI Presentation Layer (layer 6 of the OSI Model). That stated, it is the most prevalent VoIP-oriented call processing system in the industry at this time. As examples, Microsoft and IBM use it in many of their VoIP products.

Architecture of H.323

As depicted in Figure 10–3, the H.323 Gateway is a node on a packet network (a LAN for example) that communicates with the H.323 terminal or other ITU-T terminals attached to other networks. If one of the terminals is not an H.323 terminal, the Gateway translates the transmission formats between the terminals.

One H.323 Gateway can interwork with another H.323 Gateway. In addition, the Gateway can operate with other ITU-T switched-circuit networks (SCNs): (a) the general switched telephone network (GSTN); (b) the narrowband-ISDN (N-ISDN); and (c) the broadband-ISDN (B-ISDN, an ATM-based network). Also, the Gateway can operate as an H.323 Multipoint Control Unit (MCU), as we see next.

The Multipoint Control Unit (MCU) supports multiconferencing between three or more terminals and Gateways. A two-terminal, point-to-

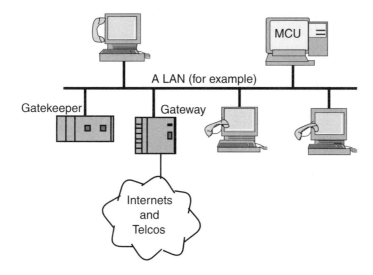

Figure 10–3   The H.323 architecture

point conference can be expanded to a multipoint conference. The example in Chapter 1 (Figure 1–8) of the VoIP multicast server is a good example of an MCU.

Major Operations of H.323

H.323 invokes several operations (and protocols) to support end-user communications with other terminals, Gateways, and MCU (all these devices are called endpoints). These operations are called phases in some parts of the H.323 literature. Figure 10–4 shows the major phases, and others can be invoked, depending upon specific implementations.

Event 1: The discovery phase entails an endpoint, such as a user workstation, finding a Gatekeeper with which it can register. This procedure allows the network operator to control who uses the H.323 network. For example, certain users may or may not be allowed to discover a Gatekeeper. During this phase, the endpoint

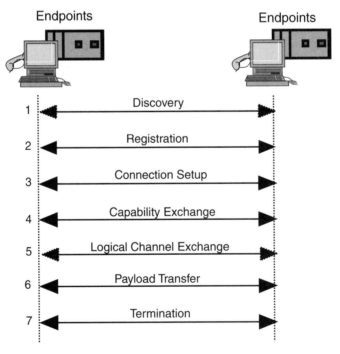

Figure 10–4   Major operations of H.323

and the Gatekeeper exchange addresses. IP multicast address 224.0.1.41 is reserved for Gatekeeper discovery.

Event 2: The registration operations define how an endpoint registers with a Gatekeeper. The addresses established during the discovery process are used during this phase, as are some optional addresses. The terminal type is identified, for example, an end-user terminal, a Gateway, or an MCU. The basic idea of the register operation is to allow H.323 nodes to join a calling *zone;* the zone is that part of a network controlled by the Gatekeeper. Ports 1718 and 1719 are reserved for UDP discovery and UDP registration, respectively.

Event 3: In the connection setup phase, a connection is set up between two endpoints for the end-to-end call.

Event 4: The capability exchange is executed. Its purpose is to ensure that any multimedia traffic sent by one endpoint can be received correctly by the receiving endpoint. Information about the session, such as bit rates, and codec types are exchanged during this event. This operation allows the endpoints and the Gatekeeper to negotiate their capabilities.

Event 5: H.323 permits the transmittal of different types of media streams over logical channels. This phase is used to open one or more logical channels to carry the traffic. For example, one logical channel could be set up for a chalk talk, another for a chat room, and still another for a spreadsheet.

Events 6 and 7: After all these procedures have been completed, user traffic can be exchanged. Eventually, after the user session is complete, termination operations take place. Termination entails the release of the logical channels and other resources (bandwidth) that were set up during the earlier phases.

Figure 10–5 provides another example of H.323 operations: the messages exchanged for the Gatekeeper discovery operation. In event 1, endpoint 1 sends a Gatekeeper Request (GRQ) message. This message is examined by the Gatekeeper, which may (or may not, depending on the implementation) respond with a Gatekeeper Confirmation (GCF) message.

The endpoint starts a timer upon issuing the GRQ message. If no response is received, the timer expires and another GRQ can be issued. If the problem continues, the network administrator must troubleshoot to deter-

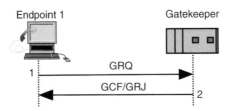

Figure 10–5   Gatekeeper discovery operations

mine the problem. Alternatively, the Gatekeeper may return a Gatekeeper Reject (GRJ) message if it chooses not to be the endpoint's Gatekeeper.

Once the discovery process has taken place, registration procedures are undertaken. These operations define how an endpoint joins a zone and provides the Gatekeeper with its port numbers and address(es). Figure 10–6 shows the message exchange, with an endpoint 1 sending the Registration Request (RRQ) message to the Gatekeeper. In event 2, the Gatekeeper responds with the Registration Confirmation (RCF) message or the Registration Reject (RRJ) message.

Either the endpoint or the Gateway can cancel the registration and end the association between the two entities. The operations in events 3 and 4 show the registration cancellation emanating from the endpoint with the Unregister Request (URQ) message. The Gatekeeper can respond with the Unregister Confirm (UCF) message or the Unregister Reject (URJ) message. As shown in events 5 and 6, the Gatekeeper starts the registration cancellation process with the URQ message and the endpoint must respond with the UCF message.

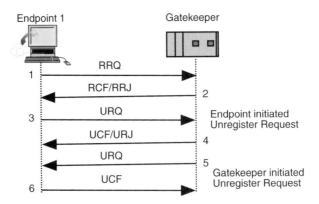

Figure 10–6   Registration procedures

H.323 defines the use of a modified Q.931 signaling protocol. An example of how Q.931 is used with the other H.323 messages is shown in Figure 10–7 to support the Admission procedures. Notice that the basic H.323 messages are used between the terminals (endpoint 1 and endpoint 2) and the Gatekeeper. The Q.931 messages are exchanged between the H.323 terminals, shown as events 3 and 4 and 7 and 8 in Figure 10–7.

In events 1 and 2 and 5 and 6, the terminals and the Gatekeeper exchange these messages:

- *ARQ:* The Admission Request message
- *ACF:* The Admission Confirmation message
- *ARJ:* The Admission Reject message (perhaps)

The information in these messages allows the endpoints to learn the details about each other. The key parts to these messages are as follows:

- A number unique to the sender. It is returned by the receiver in any response associated with this specific message.
- A parameter in the message used by the Gatekeeper to determine the nature of the call, such as multipoint or point-to-point connections.

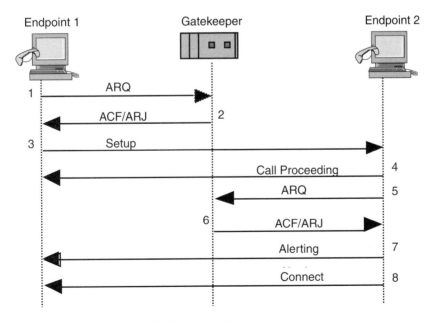

Figure 10–7   Admission procedures

- An endpoint identifier, used as a security measure to help ensure that the endpoint is a registered terminal within its zone.
- Addresses for the source and destination terminals, such as E.164 addresses or H323 IDs, as well as any needed port numbers.
- Bandwidth needed for the bidirectional call.
- Reason the bandwidth request was denied (if it is).
- Information on support of optional Q-Series protocols (to make H.323 more compatible with ISDN operations, which vary from country to country).
- Unique conference identifier (for a multiconference call).

MEGACO GENERAL DESCRIPTION

Megaco is yet another call processing protocol. It exhibits some of the features of H.323, but it is also different as suggested by the summary profile shown in Table 10–2. We take a more detailed look at these features in this part of the chapter.

Architecture of Megaco

Figure 10–8 shows a topology for a Megaco IP call processing system. Megaco's architecture is somewhat similar to H.323 in that both systems use the concept of a Gateway Controller. In H.323, this controller is called a Gatekeeper. In Megaco, it is called a Media Gateway

Table 10–2 Megaco comparison chart

What? A call processing system for voice/video/data

Where does it fit? Operates in a Gateway Controller

What does it do? Negotiates capabilities, defines syntaxes for traffic, sets up and clears calls

Applications? Regular voice calls, conferencing

Unique aspects? Now part of the H.323 suite, and the IETF is defining Megaco-based telephones with a Megaco Media Gateway

Pros / Cons? + Web-based; + Relatively simple

Future? An RFC standard (RFC 3015), market predictions show a high growth rate in the future

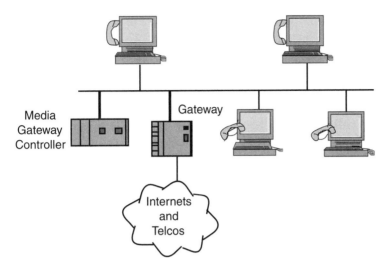

Figure 10–8   The Megaco architecture

Controller (MGC). Also, in both systems, these controllers oversee the operations of their respective gateways. And of course, both support call processing.

The similarity of H.323 and Megaco does not go much farther. Megaco is Web-based and uses different schemes for its operations. The most notable are two concepts, called *abstractions*. It is necessary to examine abstractions in order to understand the fundamentals of Megaco. For the reader who has studied the behavior of PBXs, these concepts will look familiar. These two abstractions are known as *Terminations* and *Contexts*.

First, Terminations (T) represent entities such as a DS1 trunk, a DS0 channel on the D1 trunk, an individual party in a telephone call, etc. Terminations can also take other forms such as an RTP traffic flow and VoIP streams. Therefore, Terminations are not just physical terminations, such as DS1 link, but logical terminations as well, such as the voice traffic in an RTP packet that flows over a DS1 link. The idea is that a Termination sources or sinks one or more media streams.

Second, Contexts (C) are collections of Terminations. For example, audio connections can be modeled by viewing the Context as a mixing bridge. Another example is a Gateway that interfaces a telco DS1 trunk and DS0 voice channels to a VoIP network. A Context can contain multiple Terminations, one for the DS0 Termination, and one for the VoIP RTP stream.

Megaco defines how to add and subtract Terminations to a Context and how to move Terminations between two Contexts. It defines how Terminations can be programmed to detect events, as well as how to add or subtract events from those Terminations. Terminations can also be modified, such as changing a Termination from an "idle" state to a "send/receive" state. Gateways can send notification messages to Media Gateway Controllers about the status of Terminations or about events that occur at Terminations.

Example of Contexts and Terminations   An example of a Context is a telephone call between two parties. Two Terminations could be in this Context (say, Context 1), one each for the conversations between the parties. We call them Termination A and Termination B for party A and party B, respectively. Let's say party A receives another call from party C. Megaco could handle the incoming call by creating a new Termination (say, Termination C) and placing Termination C into another Context (Context 2). It could then move party B's Termination B out of Context 1 (perhaps into yet another Context), and move party C's Termination C into Context 1. These operations have the effect of placing party B into a "call hold" state.

Those readers who have written software can see the attraction of these two abstract concepts. They are used by software to manage the calls. Megaco operates with Terminations and Contexts to define the state of a call, similarly to what happens in PBX call processing systems.

Moreover, Terminations give the network designer a powerful tool for configuring a VoIP system, as well as a means to allow Megaco user agents to negotiate a wide variety of options. For example, the service status of a Termination may have the properties of test, in-service, and out-of-service. It may have a property that sets rules on how traffic flows into and out of it, such as send only, receive only, send and receive, or loop-back the traffic. Termination properties can describe a type of modem, a version of IP, response/execution timers, the size of a jitter buffer, even the maximum number of Terminations that may be associated with a Context.

An Example of Using Megaco in Multiconferencing   Again, let's use Figure 1–8 in Chapter 1 as an example of a Megaco operation (my example extends the Megaco RFC a bit, but it is technically feasible). My multiconferencing system could (but does not at this time) use Megaco's Context to associate my students with my lecture. I could then create a Termination for each student in my lecture (the lecture is my Context).

To make the lecture more flexible, I would likely create multiple Terminations for each student: (a) one for the student's chat room with me, (b) one for the student's microphone with her or his audio channel to me, (c) one for my audio channel to all students, (d) one for their interactions such as clapping, booing (yes I do permit this procedure), raising their hands, and so on. I would place all the student's microphone Terminations in a *do not send mode,* because I do not want them to use these Terminations to interrupt my talk.

However, I would place the Termination dealing with the raised hand in *send mode,* so any student could query me at any time. Upon receiving a query (the raised hand), I would then use Megaco to modify the student's microphone Termination to a *send* mode. This action would result in the students' screen showing an icon meaning that the student can talk. The student could then ask the question.

For the (admittedly rare) student who becomes disruptive to the conference, I would place that person's raised hand Termination in the do not send mode. (Certain aspects of Megaco's multicasting possibilities are quite attractive.)

Well, we could go on, and redesign my multiconferencing system, but I hope you get the idea of how the seemingly abstract ideas of Contexts and Terminations are powerful tools for the network designer.

Major Operations

Figure 10–9 shows the major operations of Megaco, based on [CUER99] and amplified by me. The term "local" denotes the calling party. The "remote" Gateway supports the called party. In this example, one MGC controls both Gateways.

To keep this example relatively simple, I don't show the full contents of the Megaco messages. The intent is to show how the three nodes set up a Context and a Termination. A notation in parenthesis represents my tutorial explanation of the protocol exchange. For example, "(Ack)" indicates that the gateway or the MGC has responded with an acknowledgment of a previous command. It comes in the form of the same message that precipitated it; for example, a Notify command precipitates a Notify ACK. This ACK often contains additional information, such as the result of setting up a new RTP port, naming a null Context, etc.

Also, the MGC uses local (LocalDesc) and remote descriptors (RemoteDesc) to reserve and commit MG resources for media decoding and encoding for the given media stream(s) and the Termination to which

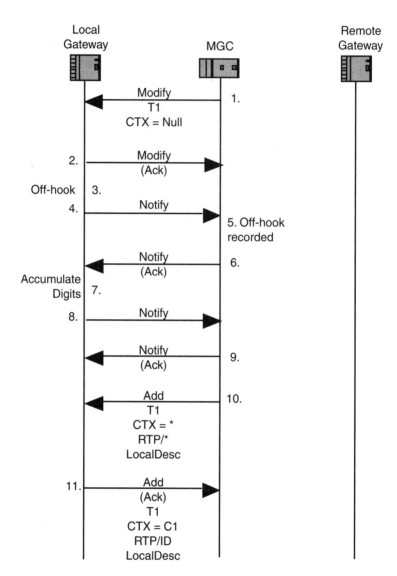

Figure 10–9(a)   Megaco protocol flow: Events 1–11

they apply. The gateway includes these descriptors in its response to indicate what it is actually prepared to support.

Event 1: The MGC sends a Modify message to the local gateway to request that Termination 1 (T1) detect for off-hook. When off-hook is detected, the local gateway is to collect digits. The Context is

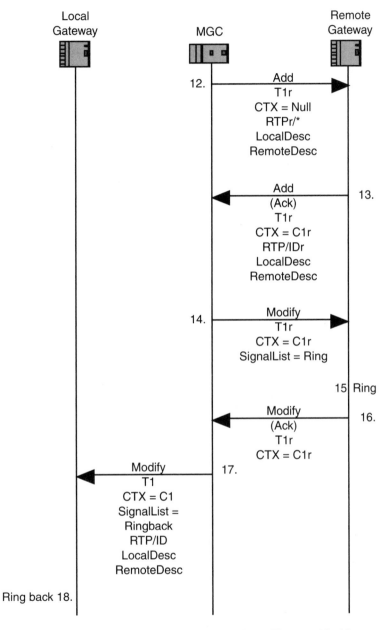

Figure 10–9(b)   Megaco protocol flow: Events 12–18

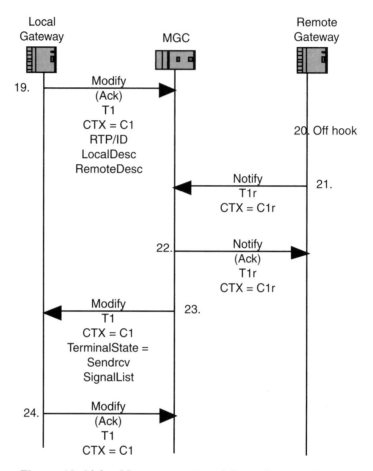

Figure 10–9(c)   Megaco protocol flow: Events 19–24

null (CTX = Null) for the time being, since it is not associated with a connection.

Event 2: The command is acknowledged.

Event 3: The local gateway detects an off-hook condition.

Event 4: It notifies the MGC.

Event 5: The MGC records this event.

Event 6: The MGC acknowledges the Notify message.

Event 7: The local gateway accumulates the digits dialed from the user in accordance with the digit plan that was downloaded from the MGC earlier, usually in a Modify command. A digit plan is simply a map sent to the Gateway to inform it how to interpret the dialed digits.

Event 8: The collected digits are sent to the MGC in a Notify command.

Event 9: The MGC acknowledges the receipt of this information.

Event 10: The MGC determines that the digit string is correct and sufficient to make a call. It sends an Add command to the local gateway to create a Context that includes T1. The notation of "CTX=*" means the Context name has not yet been given. The local gateway will provide a name for the Context in its response in event 11. This message also specifies an unnamed packet Termination of RTP/*. Again, the local gateway will fill this in with the response message. The LocalDesc, which is another field in the Add message, can specify a choice of codecs for the call.

Event 11: The local gateway responds to the MGC with an ACK and a Context named C1. It also sends back an RTP Termination identifier (RTP/ID). Its LocalDesc specifies the supported codecs on the receiving RTP port.

Event 12: Based on the information received from the local gateway, the MGC now can inform the remote gateway to add the Termination (T1r) that corresponds to the dialed digit string the MGC had received from the local gateway. It is the job of the MGC to map T1 and T1r into a Context. It also sends an unnamed RTP port field in this message. The information in T1's LocalDesc is passed to the remote gateway in the RemoteDesc field, which specifies the codecs for T1r from the perspective of the local gateway. The LocalDesc field in this message could be blank, or it could contain parameters that the MGC expects the remote gateway to use for this call, such as the packet size for the VoIP samples.

Event 13: The remote gateway responds to the Add command with a named Context of C1r, a named RTP Termination of RTP/IDr, and its LocalDesc specifying the supported codec(s) on its receiving RTP port. Notice that the LocalDesc values sent to this gateway by the MGC in event 12 might be changed by the gateway in this event.

Event 14: The MGC now uses a Modify command to request that ringing be applied on T1r. The message also requests the gateway to look for off-hook.

Event 15: The remote gateway applies ringing to the called party line.

Event 16: It so indicates to the MGC with a Modify response.

Event 17: The MGC sends a Modify command to the calling local gateway. The command requests that ring-back be applied to T1 and identifies the remote receiving RTP port in the RemoteDesc field in the message.

Event 18: Ring-back is applied.

Event 19: A reply acknowledges that ring-back is being applied and that the RTP settings have been updated.

Event 20: The called party answers the call by going off-hook.

Event 21: The remote gateway sends a Notify to convey this information to the MGC, and of course, ringing is canceled.

Event 22: The MGC acknowledges the Notify.

Event 23: The MGC issues a Modify command to cancel ring-back on T1 and to set the two-way talk path (TerminalState = Sendrcv). The information in SignalList is used to cancel ring-back.

Event 24: The local gateway acknowledges the modify, removes ring-back, and the call setup is now completed.

Several observations can be made about this example. First, the MGC initially set up the Termination in the Null Context, which contains all Terminations that are not associated with any Context. In this (typical) example, idle lines are associated with the Null Context. Second, all three nodes use IP addresses to identify who sent the MGC message. This sending IP address is placed in the message (of course, it is also in the IP header). Third, the messages contain a variety of parameters, not shown in this general example, such as Termination IDs, event descriptors, the send-receive mode and in some messages, SDP coding (see Chapter 9) to describe the profile for the session.

MGCP GENERAL DESCRIPTION

We now focus on the Media Gateway Control Protocol (MGCP). It is published as RFC 2705 and integrates the Simple Gateway Control Protocol (SGMP) and the Internet Protocol Device Control (IPDC) specification. It is quite similar to SGMP but provides several features beyond that offered by SGMP. The pertinent aspects of SGMP and IPDC are included in our discussion of MGCP. Table 10–3 summarizes the major aspects of MGCP. We examine these aspects in more detail in the following material.

MGCP describes an application programming interface and a complementary protocol. MGCP's purpose is to define the operations of telephony Gateways. Call control comes from external call control elements, known as *Call Agents*. The telephony Gateway provides conversion and internetworking operations between the audio signals used on telephone circuits and data packets used by the Internet or other packet-oriented networks. The Call Agent directs the operations of the Gateway.

Architecture of MGCP

Figure 10–10 shows a topology for the MGCP IP call processing system. MGCP's external architecture is similar to that of Megaco in that both systems use the concept of a Gateway Controller. In MGCP, that controller is called a Call Agent. Also, in both systems, these controllers oversee the operations of their respective gateways. And of course, both support call processing. Both are Web-based. However, MGCP does not use the Termination and Context concepts that are employed in Megaco.

Major Operations

Figures 10–11(a) and (b) present an example of MGCP in action. For those readers who want more detail on the MGCP and these examples, I refer you to [ARAN98], [ARAN98a], and [TAYL98]. Figure 10–11(a) shows events 1–24, and Figure 10–11(b) shows events 25–37. Two Gateways are involved, a residential Gateway and a trunking Gateway. In addition, a common database and an accounting Gateway are shown. These two entities are added for clarification of the operations, although

Table 10–3   MGCP comparison chart

What? A call processing system for voice/video/data

Where does it fit? Operates in a Gateway Controller, called the Call Agent

What does it do? Negotiates capabilities, defines syntaxes for traffic, sets up and clears calls

Applications? Regular telco calls, conferencing

Unique Aspects? RFC 2705 is an informational document, not a standard

Pros / Cons?

+ Web-based; Relatively simple

− Lots of redundancy relative to Megaco; − not an Internet standard

Future? Unclear; will probably fade away, as Megaco becomes more prevalent

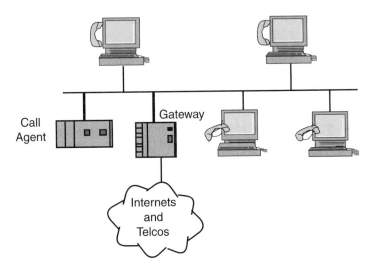

Figure 10–10   MGCP architecture

they are not required in an MGCP procedure. Here is a description of each event:

> *Event 1:* The NotificationRequest message must be sent to the res-idential Gateway before the Gateway can handle a connection. This message is not a crafting (configuration) command. The Call Agents and Gateways must be preconfigured. Let us assume that this message is directing the Gateway to monitor for an off-hook condition on a specific endpoint connection, similar to the example of Megaco in the previous section.
>
> *Event 2:* The Gateway acknowledges the message. It uses the same transaction number that was in the message in event 1 to correlate the two messages.
>
> *Event 3:* Thereafter, the Gateway monitors for this transition, and eventually the user goes off-hook to make a call.
>
> *Event 4:* The Gateway sends a Notify message to the Call Agent, with the message coded to show the off-hook event for the moni-tored endpoint.
>
> *Event 5:* The Call Agent must acknowledge the Gateway's trans-mission.

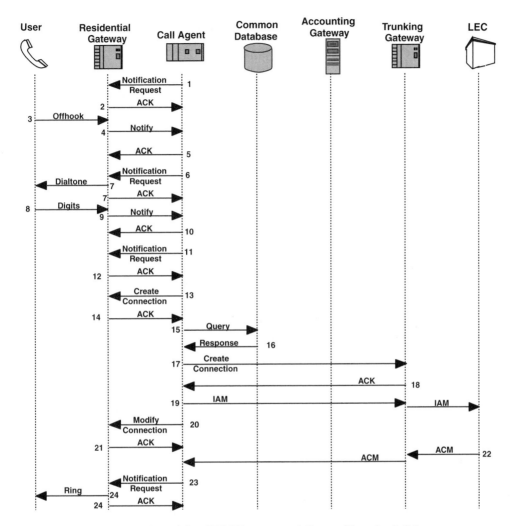

Figure 10–11(a)   MGCP protocol flows: Events 1–24

Event 6: The Call Agent's decisions on what to tell the Gateway next will depend on the type of line being monitored. Assuming it is a conventional dialup (nondirect) line, the Call Agent sends a NotificationRequest message directing the Gateway to play a dial tone and to collect digits.

Event 7: The Gateway responds with an ACK, and gives the dial tone to the user. The exact sequence of these two events varies, depending on the specific implementation.

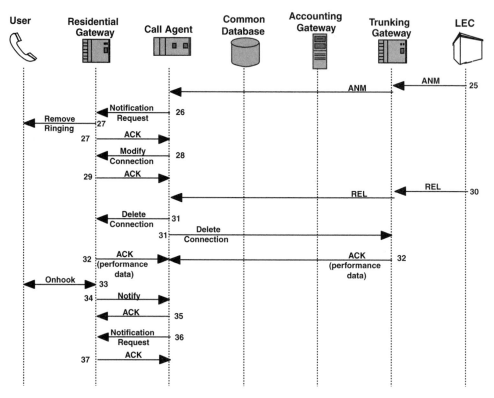

Figure 10–11(b)   MGCP protocol flows: Events 25–37

Event 8: Based on the digit map sent to it (perhaps in event 1), the Gateway accumulates digits.

Event 9: Based on this digit map, the Gateway notifies the Call Agent with a Notify message containing an ObservedEvent parameter. This parameter contains the collected digits.

Event 10: The Call Agent acknowledges the message.

Event 11: Next, the Call Agent sends a NotificationRequest message to direct the Gateway to stop collecting digits and to monitor for an on-hook transition.

Event 12: The Gateway acknowledges the message.

Event 13: The CreateConnection message is sent by the Call Agent to seize the incoming circuit. This message contains information such as (a) packetization period in milliseconds, which allows the Gateway to make decisions on how to multiplex the voice samples in to the VoIP packets, (b) compression algorithm (G.723, G.729, etc.), (c) bandwidth for the connection, and (d) use or nonuse of echo cancellation.

Event 14: The Gateway acknowledges the message. In this message is the identification of the new connection (ConnectionId) and the session description (an SDP an- nouncement) that is used to describe the audio traffic and other aspects of the session. This description may contain the IP address at which the Gateway is ready to receive the audio data, the protocol used to transport the packets (RTP), the RTP port (3456), the audio-video profile (AVP, in accordance with RFC 1890). The AVP defines the payload type, such as G.711. This message can also be used to inform the Call Agent that the Gateway is ready to use other audio profiles. For example, G.726 for 32 kbit/s ADPCM might also be stipulated.

Event 15: The Call Agent now must determine where to route the call and to which egress Gateway the connection should be established. It sends a query to the common database to obtain this information. This database typically contains enough information to establish a route for the call. In its simplest form, it is an IP routing table.

Event 16: The needed information is returned to the Call Agent.

Event 17: The Call Agent has sufficient information to send a CreateConnection message to the egress Gateway, in this example, a trunking Gateway. The parameters in this message mirror (with minor differences) the parameters exchanged in events 13 and 14 between the residential Gateway and the Call Agent, and the SDP session description in this message is the same as the description given to the Call Agent by the residential Gateway.

Event 18: The trunking Gateway responds with an ACK. In this message is this Gateway's SDP session description such as its IP address, its port number, and its RTP profile.

Event 19: Based on the information obtained in event 18, the Call Agent now builds an SS7 ISUP initial address message (IAM) and sends it to the trunking Gateway, which relays it to a designated local exchange carrier (LEC). Some of the information gathered in events 1–18 are used to help build the IAM. For example, calling and called party numbers, echo cancellation, international call, ISUP used end-to-end, and other fields are placed in this message.

Event 20: The information obtained in event 18 is used to create the ModifyConnection message that is sent to the residential Gateway. Therefore, the parameters in this command reflect the parameters in the ACK in event 18.

Event 21: The Gateway acknowledges the command.

Event 22: The LEC returns an SS7 ISUP address complete message (ACM) to the Call Agent. This message contains fields (backward call indicators) to aid the Call Agent in directing the actions of the residential Gateway, as explained in the next event.

Event 23: The receipt of the ACM at the Call Agent precipitates the sending of a NotificationRequest command to the residential Gateway. This message directs the Gateway to place ringing tones on the line.

Event 24: The Gateway acknowledges the commands and places ringing tones on the line to the user telephone.

Event 25: When the called party answers the call at the remote end, the off-hook condition will result in an ISUP answer message (ANM) being returned to the Call Agent.

Event 26: The Call Agent sends a NotificationRequest message to the residential Gateway to instruct it to remove the ring tone from the line.

Event 27: The Gateway removes the ring tone and acknowledges the command.

Event 28: To this point, the connection at the local end has been in a receive-only mode. To change the connection to full-duplex mode, the Call Agent sends a ModifyConnection message to the Gateway.

Event 29: The Gateway responds and sends back an ACK. The connection is now established.

Event 30: After the parties have finished their telephone conversation, the called party hangs up, and the off-hook condition precipitates the ISUP Release message (REL), which is conveyed to the Call Agent.

Event 31: The Call Agent sends a DeleteConnection message to both Gateways. Each message contains sufficient identifiers for the Gateways to know which connection is to be dropped.

Event 32: The Gateways respond with the performance data fields in the response. This information contains statistics about the call, such as duration, errors encountered, and the number of VoIP packets exchanged between the parties. At this stage of the call, the accounting gateway might be used to store the charges for the call.

Event 33: The local line is placed in an on-hook state by the local party hanging up.

Event 34: The on-hook event is relayed to the Call Agent with a Notify message.

Event 35: The Call Agent acknowledges the message.

Event 36: The Call Agent then "resets" the endpoint by informing the Gateway to monitor for an off-hook condition.

Event 37: The Gateway acknowledges the command. This operation returns the endpoint to the state it was in before event 1 took place.

SIP GENERAL DESCRIPTION

The Session Initiation Protocol (SIP) is a control protocol. Its job is to set up, modify, and tear down sessions between session users. One of its functions is to act as a signaling protocol, and another is to define the type of session for which it is signaling. The session may be a multimedia conference, a point-to-point telephone call, and so on. Table 10–4 summarizes the major aspects of SIP.

SIP has capabilities other than just signaling operations. It can support sessions via multicast or single unicast, a mesh of unicast sessions, or a combination of these choices. SIP does not act as a media gateway, in that it does not transport any media streams.

One of its more distinctive features is its ability to support mobile users. If a user registers his or her location with a SIP server, SIP will direct SIP messages to the user or invoke a proxying operation to another server to a user's current location. The mobile capability is keyed to the individual user and not to the user's terminal (telephone, computer, etc.). This aspect of SIP makes it different from other VoIP call control protocols.

SIP is an attractive support tool for IP telephony for the following reasons:

- It can operate as stateless or stateful. Thus, a stateless implementation provides good scalability, since the servers do not have to maintain information on the call state once the transaction has

Table 10–4   SIP comparison chart

What? A call processing system for voice/video/data

Where does it fit? Handset, PBX, servers

What does it do? Negotiates capabilities, defines syntaxes for traffic, sets up and clears calls, finds called parties in the Internet

Applications? Regular telco calls, conferencing

Unique Aspects? Does not use Gateway Controller concept, uses a client-server model

Pros/Cons?

+ Web-based, relatively simple, easily extensible

+ Published as RFC 2543, a formal IETF standard

Future? Market predictions show a high growth rate in the near future, with keen interest from many vendors and network providers

been processed. Moreover, the stateless approach is very robust, since the server need not remember anything about a call.

- It uses many of the formats and syntax of HTTP (Hypertext Transfer Protocol), thus providing a convenient way of operating with ongoing browsers.

- The SIP message (the message body) is opaque; it can be of any syntax. Therefore, it can be described in more than one way. As examples, it may be described with the Multipurpose Internet Mail Extension (MIME) or the Extensible Markup Language (XML).

- It identifies a user with a URL (Uniform Resource Locator), thus providing the user the ability to initiate a call by clicking on a Web link.

SIP supports these major functions:

- Determination of location of user
- Determination of media for the session
- Determination of willingness of user to participate in a session
- Call establishment, call transfer, and termination

Architecture of SIP

One aspect of SIP that differentiates it from the other three IP Call Processing Protocols is that is does not use a Gateway Controller. In fact, it does not use the Gateway Controller/Gateway concept at all but relies on a client/server model. Let's spend a moment understanding this model, and then I'll show some examples.

- *Server:* An application program that accepts request messages in order to service requests from another program, called the client, and then sends back responses to those requests to the client.
- *Proxy server:* Acts as both a server and a client for the purpose of making requests on behalf of other clients. Requests are serviced internally or by being passed on to other servers. A proxy interprets and may rewrite a SIP request message before forwarding it to another server or to a user agent (described below).
- *Redirect server:* A server that accepts a SIP request, maps the address in the request to a new address, and returns the message to the client. Unlike a proxy server, it does not initiate its own SIP request and does not "forward" SIP requests to other servers. Unlike a user agent server, it does not accept calls.
- *Registrar:* A SIP entity that accepts REGISTER requests. A registrar is typically colocated with a proxy or redirect server and may offer location services. The registrar is used to register SIP parties in a SIP domain. The domain is similar to the H.323 zone, in that it is an administrative entity for a SIP provider.
- *User agent server (UAS):* A server that contacts the user when a SIP request is received; it returns a response on behalf of the user.
- *User agent (UA):* An application containing both a user agent client (UAC) and user agent server (UAS). The UAS, user agent, and UAC are described in more detail shortly.

As Figure 10–12 shows, SIP consists of two major components: the user agent and the SIP servers. The user agent is an end system that interfaces with the user and acts on behalf of the user. As noted above, the user agent consists of two entities: a protocol client, known as the user agent client (UAC); and a protocol server, known as the user agent server (UAS). The UAC initiates the call, and the UAS answers the call. Since the user agent contains both a UAC and a UAS, SIP can operate as a peer-to-peer operation while using the client/server model.

The SIP server is implemented in two types: as a proxy server and as a redirect server. As noted, the SIP proxy server receives a request from a client and decides which next server the request goes to if indeed another server is needed. This proxy can send the request to yet another

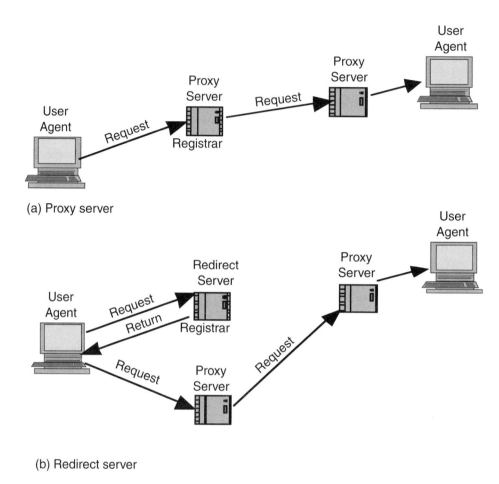

(a) Proxy server

(b) Redirect server

Figure 10–12   SIP clients and servers

server, a redirect server, or a UAS. The response to the request will travel through the same path as the request, but in reverse order. The proxy server acts as both a server and a client for making requests on behalf of other clients. A proxy server interprets the SIP message and can rewrite a request message before forwarding it to another server or a client.

The redirect server will not forward the request but will instead direct the client to contact the next server directly; its "redirect" response contains the address of the next hop server. The SIP message address is mapped into new addresses and returned to the client. A redirect server cannot act as a client, in that it does not accept calls.

Major Operations

Let's look at an example of SIP operations, depicted in Figure 10–13. It shows how the INVITE message and URLs are used by SIP and a proxy server to process a call.

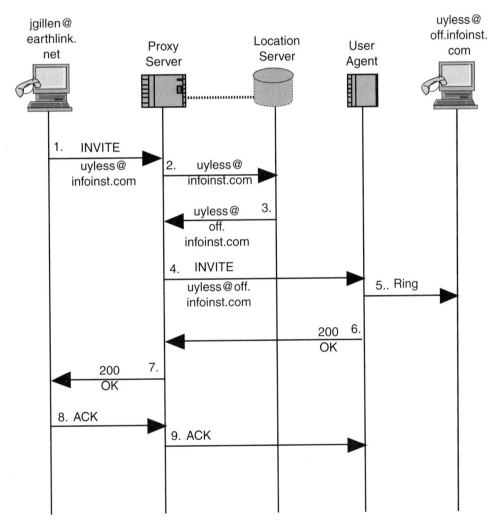

Figure 10–13   SIP operations

Event 1: Joan Gillen (jgillen@earthlink.net) is trying to reach Uyless Black at uyless@infoinst.com. The proxy server receives an INVITE message from jgillen@earthlink.net (actually, this message comes from a user agent, which is housed at jgillen's host).

Event 2: This server queries a location server to find out more information about the called party, uyless@infoinst.com.

Event 3: The location server responds and provides a more precise name (and a more precise location, when the name is associated with an IP address). It is evident that the DNS is employed by the SIP operations.[2]

Event 4: This information is then used by the proxy server to send the INVITE (with the more precise name) to the user agent that services the name (uyless@off.infoinst.com).

Event 5: The User Agent alerts the called party with a ring.

Event 6: The User Agent sends back a SIP ACK OK, (with a code of 200 [this is simply a special SIP code for a positive acknowledgment and an indication that the call request is being processed]).

Event 7: The proxy server then sends the ACK OK to the calling party.

Events 8 and 9: To complete this operation, a SIP ACK message is sent by the calling party and relayed to the called party's user agent.

SUMMARY

This chapter has covered the four major VoIP Call Processing Protocols: H.323, Megaco, MGCP, and SIP. We learned that they provide the control and management functions for telephony sessions in an internet, with the principal job of setting up and clearing calls in an IP network.

---

[2]You might want to read Internet draft draft-ietf-sip-srv-02.txt on how SIP uses location services. Go to www.ietf.org, click on IETF Working Groups, and then click on Transport Area.

We also learned that many of their operations are similar, but they are not compatible with each other.

Since it is a foregone conclusion that they will be deployed in different networks and supported by different network providers, they must be able to communicate (internetwork) with each other, as well as with SS7's ISUP. This subject is the topic for the next chapter.

11

Internetworking SS7 and Internet Call Processing

T his chapter explains how SS7 and the IP call-processing protocols can act as partners to support telephony traffic in packet networks.[1] Several Internet task forces are defining these operations and they are highlighted in this chapter. Be aware that the work is not yet finished, and some of the specifications are still in the draft stages.

Readers unfamiliar with SS7 can refer to a companion book to this series: *ISDN and SS7: Architectures for Digital Signaling Networks.* Alternatively, Appendix B provides you with enough information to understand the SS7 material in this chapter. You will need to know SS7's ISDN User Part (ISUP) protocol to understand this chapter. Additionally, it is assumed you have read the material in Chapter 10.

The subject matter of this chapter is vast and warrants an entire book. Our approach for this overview is as follows. First, we examine the reasons to interwork SS7 and VoIP systems. Then, the Internet model for internetworking IP and SS7 networks is explained. Next, specific internetworking examples that use H.323, Megago, and SIP are provided. The chapter concludes with a look at RFC 2871, titled Telephony Routing over IP (TRIP).

Because SIP is increasingly accepted as a preferred VoIP call-processing protocol, several examples in this chapter focus on this proto-

---

[1]A generic term to identify the interconnection of IP and SS7 networks is IPS7.

col. Additionally, since H.323 is currently the dominant preference, it too is highlighted.

REASONS TO COMBINE IP AND SS7

One of the criticisms of VoIP voiced by some people in the industry is the absence of the many service features that are common to telephony systems, such as call forwarding, call screening, caller ID, and so forth. These features are important to many telephone users and are a vital part of the services that produce revenue for telephony service providers.

The original IP voice protocol suite was not designed to offer these critical services, and any VoIP system that is going to succeed in the corporate environment must offer them. Certainly, there will be niche applications that run a sparse set of service features, and certain customers will be content with these services. But for VoIP to become a significant force in telephony, it must provide telephony-type services.

To provide these services, VoIP must be able to use the SS7 technology, the linchpin for telephony service features and the foundation for Advanced Intelligent Network (AIN) services. Otherwise, the services that are part of SS7 must be "reinvented" by the Internet task forces—a ridiculous alternative.

POSSIBLE CONFIGURATIONS

Much work remains to be done on the development of standards for SS7-IP gateways. However, it is evident that the configurations explained in this section will be part of the final standards mix. For example, in Figure 11–1, an SS7 network is adjacent to subnetworks that run IP (labeled internets in the figure). End users, connected to the telephone network through local loops, are serviced by SS7 at the telephone Central Office (CO), so the traffic being transferred between them is ISUP, SCCP, TCAP, etc. The SS7 nodes can be fully functioning signaling transfer points (STPs), or end points, and the full features of MTP-3, such as point code routing and recovery from failed nodes and links, are available.

Vital Telephony Databases at the Service Control Point

The important part of SS7 in regard to VoIP using SS7 resources is the service control point (SCP). It acts as the interface into the telephone

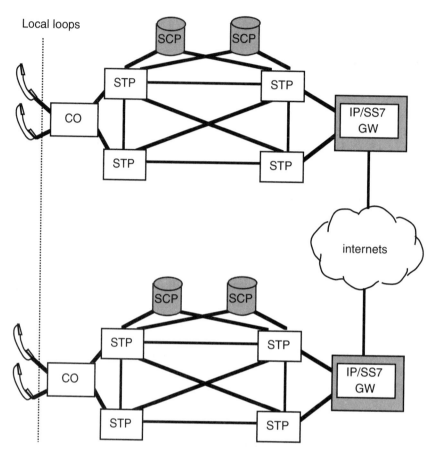

Figure 11–1   A complete SS7 topology configuration

company databases. These databases contain information on the subscriber, 800/900 numbers, calling cards, fraud data, etc. They also house the AIN features such a caller ID, call screening, and many other services. It cannot be overemphasized how vital these databases are for a full-featured VoIP system to prosper.

The principal concern with this internetworking scenario is the mapping of ISUP and the VoIP call-processing protocol messages. Assuming SIP is the VoIP call-processing protocol operating in these gateways, then the ISUP messages are mapped into the body of the SIP messages for transport across the internets.

The IETF has extended SIP to accommodate this important operation. RTP has also been extended to carry DTMF signals, as well as supervisory signals such as off-hook and on-hook. For more details, see [BLAC01a] and [SCHU00].

THE SS7-IP ARCHITECTURAL FRAMEWORK

A variety of SS7-IP components are being proposed in the Internet standards and are under development by the VoIP vendors. Figure 11–2 reflects one framework. As you can see, the entities in the "SS7-IP Gateway/Controller" are more numerous than in the model that we examined in Chapter 10.

- *Signaling gateway (SG):* The SG receives and sends public switched telephone network (PSTN) signals, and it may also receive and send SS7 messages.
- *Media gateway controller (MGC):* The MGC acts as the registration and resource management entity. It is similar to the H.323 Gatekeeper, the Megaco Media Gateway Controller, and the MGCP Call Agent, but it also can contain capabilities that establish usage of resources based on policies.
- *Media gateway (MG):* The MG acts as the physical interface for PSTN lines and trunks. It also is the interface for VoIP links.
- *Routing tables (RT):* These IP routing tables are accessed with destination IP addresses to route the IP traffic through an internet.
- *Domain Name System (DNS):* DNS is the database for domain names and associated IP addresses and SS7 point codes.

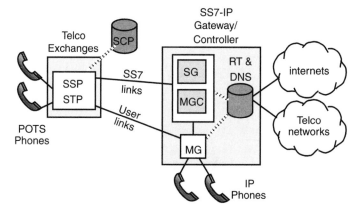

Figure 11–2   The SS7-IP architectural framework

THE IP/SS7 INTERNETWORKING MODEL (RFC 2719)

RFC 2719 defines the functions of the IP/SS7 internetworking nodes and other entities. Most of the definitions have been covered in earlier chapters, but a brief review will make certain all definitions are understood. Refer to Figure 11–3 during this discussion.

- *Switched Circuit Network (SCN):* A network that carries traffic within channelized bearers of predefined sizes, such as 64 kbit/s in 125 µs slots.
- *Signaling transport (SIG):* A protocol stack for transport of SCN signaling protocols over an IP network.
- *Media gateway (MG):* Terminates SCN media streams, packetizes the media data (if necessary) and delivers this traffic to the packet network. MG performs these functions in reverse order for media streams flowing from the packet network to the SCN.
- *Media gateway controller (MGC):* Handles the registration and management of resources at the MG. The MGC may be able to authorize resource usage based on local policy. For signaling transport purposes, the MGC serves as a possible termination and origination point for SCN application protocols, such as SS7's ISUP and Q.931.

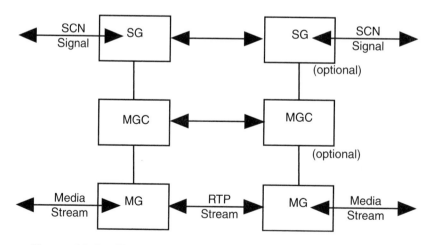

Figure 11–3   The internetworking (SIG) nodes, as defined in RFC 2719

- *Signaling Gateway (SG):* A signaling agent that receives/sends SCN native signaling at the edge of the IP network. The SG function may relay, translate, or terminate SS7 signaling in an SS7 internet gateway. The SG function may also be co-resident with the MG function to process SCN signaling associated with line or trunk terminations controlled by the MG (e.g., signaling backhaul).

The following are terms defined in RFC 2719 for physical entities relating to signaling transport in a distributed gateway model:

- *Media Gateway Unit (MGU):* A physical entity that contains the MG function. It may contain other functions, such as an SG function for handling facility-associated signaling.
- *Media Gateway Control Unit (MGCU):* A physical entity containing the MGC function.
- *Signaling Gateway Unit (SGU):* A physical entity containing the SG function.
- *Signaling End Point (SEP):* A node in an SS7 network that originates or terminates signaling messages. One example is a Central Office switch.

RFC 2719 describes the functions of these nodes by defining the signaling transport. It provides transparent transport of message-based signaling protocols over IP networks, including definition of encapsulation methods, end-to-end protocol mechanisms, and use of IP capabilities to support the functional and performance requirements for signaling.

Signaling transport is used for transporting SCN signaling between a signaling gateway unit (SGU, a physical entity in the SG), and media gateway controller unit (MGU, a physical entity in the MG). Signaling transport can also be used for transport of message-based signaling between an MGU and media gateway controller unit (MGCU, a physical entity in the MGU), between dispersed MGUs, and between two SGUs connecting signaling endpoints or signal transfer points in the SCN.

Signaling transport supports encapsulation and a variety of SCN protocols. It is defined to be independent of any SCN protocol translation functions taking place at the endpoints of the signaling, since its function is limited to the transport of the SCN protocol.

Implementations of the IP/SS7 Functions

Figure 11–4 shows examples (not all-inclusive) of three implementations of the IP/SS7 functions in physical entities as used for interworking of SS7 and IP networks for VoIP, voice over ATM, network access servers, etc. The use of signaling transport is independent of the implementation. Recall that signaling transport is used to carry SCN signaling.

For interworking with SS7-controlled SCN networks, the SG terminates the SS7 link and transfers the signaling information to the MGC by using signaling transport. The MG terminates the interswitch trunk and controls the trunk in accordance with the control signaling it receives from the MGC.

As shown in case (a), the SG, MGC and MG can be implemented in separate physical units, or as in case (b), the MG/MGC can be implemented in a single physical unit. In case (c), a facility-associated SS7 link is terminated by the same device (i.e., the MGU) that terminates the interswitch trunk. In this case, the SG function is colocated with the MG function, and signaling transport is used to "backhaul" control signaling to the MGCU.

SS7 links can also be terminated directly on the MGCU by cross-connection at the physical level before or at the MGU.

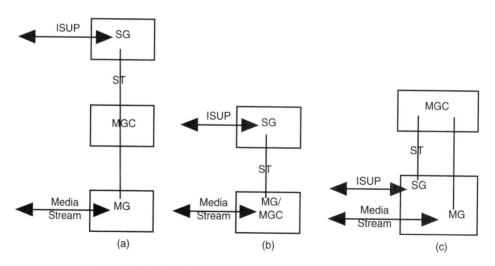

Figure 11–4   Implementations of the IP/SS7 functions

INTERWORKING H.323 AND SS7

In Chapter 10, we learned that H.323 is used to support VoIP in data networks. In addition, the H.323 Gatekeeper acts as Call Agent with a telephony network and must therefore be able to correlate H.323 and ISUP message flows. [MA99] has developed the basic scheme for the interworking of H.323 and an SS7 Gateway. In this section, we examine the major features and the protocol flow of the H.323/SS7 Gateway operations. The interworking of H.323 and ISUP is fairly straightforward because the operations of the H Recommendations are similar to those for ISUP. For example, all of these signaling protocols use the bearer capability concept, so mapping the H.225 SETUP message to the ISUP IAM message is a relatively simple procedure.

Figure 11–5 shows the operations for the setting up of a call. Notice that this example shows more details about the H.323 messages, with notations of H.225 and H.445. In Chapter 10, we noted that H.323 is a patchwork of other ITU-T specifications, and H.225 and H.445 are just such examples. H.225 is concerned with gatekeeper discovery, registration, and call management operations. H.445 is concerned with setting up logical channels and negotiating capabilities. With this background

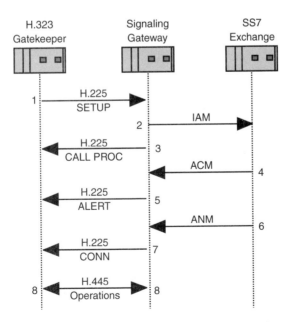

Figure 11–5   Call setup with H.323 protocols and ISUP

information, let's see how H.323 and SS7 networks communicate with each other.

> *Event 1:* The calling party on the H.323 networks makes a call to a called party who is attached to the telephone network. The H.323 Gatekeeper receives this call request from the calling party and analyzes the calling party's dialed digits. Based on this analysis, the Gatekeeper issues a SETUP message to a designated Signaling Gateway.
>
> *Event 2:* The Signaling Gateway uses the information in the SETUP message to form the ISUP IAM message. It sends this message to the next transit (and maybe final) telephony exchange (SS7 exchange in the figure).
>
> *Event 3:* The Signaling Gateway sends the CALL PROCEEDING (CALL PROC) message to the Gatekeeper.
>
> *Event 4:* The ISUP ACM message is sent by the transit exchange.
>
> *Event 5:* The receipt of the ACM message in event 5 precipitates the sending of the ALERT message by the Signaling Gateway to the Gatekeeper.
>
> *Event 6:* The transit exchange informs the Signaling Gateway that the called party has answered the call by sending the ANM message.
>
> *Event 7:* In turn, the Signaling Gateway sends the CONNECT (CONN) message to the Gatekeeper.
>
> *Event 8:* Thereafter, the H.323 Gatekeeper and the Signaling Gateway enter into the H.445 operations to perform capability exchanges and logical channel setup.

The Signaling Gateway can begin the H.445 operations immediately after receiving the H.225 SETUP message, so it need not wait for the called party to respond. This approach reduces the delay between the Gatekeeper and the Signaling Gateway after the ANM is received. The idea is shown in Figure 11–6.

The call setup obviously can be made in the opposite direction, in which case the IAM from the SS7 exchange starts the setup operations between the Gatekeeper and the Signaling Gateway. And both sides of this operation can initiate call termination operations, refuse calls, and so on.

These H.323-ISUP examples are just a few of many scenarios. I refer you to [MA99] for more details.

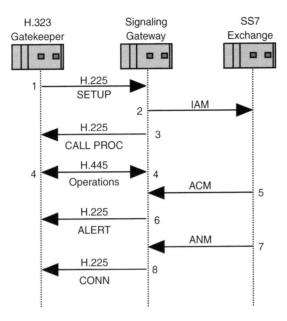

Figure 11–6   Initiating H.245 operations after receiving the SETUP message

SIP INTERNETWORKING SPECIFICATIONS

The basic SIP RFC is being enhanced considerably to provide extra capabilities. One of these is to support QOS [GIBS99]. The idea is to modify two SIP methods (a SIP method is actually a SIP message): INVITE and REGISTER. The modifications allow the INVITE method to be used to find the best path, based on QOS metrics, across a particular network. The route choice can be restricted at the network edge. The proposed modifications also allow the REGISTER method to be used as a means of disseminating information necessary to determine these QOS metrics. This information can be used to route INVITEs away from known areas of congestion or failure.

SIP QOS Model

The SIP QOS model is described as a three-layer operation, as shown in Figure 11–7.

The session control layer represents a telephony-style connection model with user connection interfaces and operations being processed by

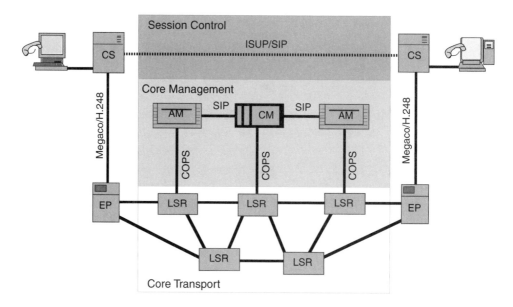

Figure 11–7   SIP QOS model

a call server (CS). The CSs interact by using either of ISUP or SIP, and the other two layers support this end-to-end user connection.

The session control layer connects directly to the core transport layer (network) with the Megaco protocol. This protocol is used by the CS to instruct its endpoint (EP) to establish a new connection for a particular session. If a session layer is not present, the EP can receive connection requests directly from the end user with, say, an RSVP path message.

The core transport layer consists of a number of links and label switching routers (LSRs) that are capable of carrying IP traffic, although a label switching backbone is not an absolute requirement.

Based on the user stimulus, such as dialing, the endpoint requests a path across the transport layer by using a Common Open Policy Service (COPS) request.[2] This message is sent to an admission manager (AM) in the core management layer. The admission managers are responsible for issuing requests for LSR paths across the network, processing these re-

---

[2]COPS is a simple query and response protocol that can be used to exchange policy information between a policy server and its clients. One example of a policy client is an RSVP router that must exercise policy-based admission control over RSVP usage. For more information on COPS, see draft-ietf-rap-cops-05.txt.

quests, and issuing responses. Only AMs can generate or terminate these message types. The COPS interface is also used to carry the response to these requests.

The core management layer also has a number of connection managers (CMs). The CMs provide administrative services to one or more LSRs. Their main job is to monitor the bandwidth along each of the MPLS tunnels emanating from the LSRs they control and to use this information to decide whether a new session can be routed through that tunnel.

When a tunnel is established from an LSR, the LSR indicates this to its associated CM by using COPS. When a session is admitted to or removed from the tunnel, its new available bandwidth is updated. This information is also forwarded to other management layer elements.

The modifications to SIP allow it to perform all messaging within the core management layer, as indicated in the figure. The modifications provide for a route selection and bandwidth reservation function between AMs and for a topology-capacity advertising function between all management layer elements.

SIP QOS Elements

There are three different elements in the core management layer: admission manager, edge connection manager, and core connection manager. A single management node might be required to perform at least two of these roles, depending upon the physical topology of the transport network.

The admission manager (AM) initiates and terminates session requests. It controls access to the network through a COPS interface to an endpoint. It receives requests for new sessions over this interface and issues decision messages based on the outcome of the resultant negotiation and any defined policies.

The AM will receive and must store the information contained within topology advertisements to determine suitable paths for INVITE messages. It does not generate any advertisements itself but manages their generation. The advertising scheme operates such that the path to each of the core CMs and the congestion on each of these paths is well known. Each of the reachable core CMs also advertises the set of domains that can be reached through it. The AM must store all of this information to enable informed path choice.

The AM can perform session request blocking at the edge of the network in the event there is not enough capacity on any of the output links. The AM must also store congestion information on incoming tunnels.

This information is used in the selection of a session path when multiple INVITEs are used.

An edge connection manager has a peer relationship with an admission manager. It is responsible for advertising a set of core CMs that is reachable by an AM. It must also advertise to its peer core CMs the set of AMs that it has connection to. This permits the core CM to build up its set of reachable domains.

In common with core CMs, an edge CM operates in a manner similar to a SIP proxy by processing and forwarding INVITEs. It uses the record-route header to ensure its continued presence in the return signaling path.

A core CM has connections only to edge CMs. A core CM must use the advertisements it receives from these edge CMs to determine the set of domains that it can reach. It must then advertise this information in a broadcast manner such that the broadcast is received by all AMs.

SIP EXTENSIONS FOR SS7 INTERNETWORKING

Many extensions to SIP are under development, some of which allow SIP to interwork gracefully with SS7's ISUP. The IETF has been working to expand the capabilities of SIP (with extensions) to make SIP more supportive of the telephone network's capabilities and other qualities (such as QOS). To that end [CAMA00] has defined the mapping (interworking) operations between SIP and ISUP.

The examples in this section show a combined gateway consisting of a joint MGC and SG. The mapping operations explained here are not affected by a joint MGC/SG. Any audio cut-through and circuit release is performed by the MG, under the control of the MGC. This audio cut-through is shown in these examples as unnumbered events since it is not performed with SIP or ISUP messages.

SIP Codes

Before proceeding further, let us pause and examine the SIP status codes that reside in the SIP messages. Variations of these codes have long been used in Internet protocols such as Telnet and FTP. The codes are three digits. SIP allows the following values for the first digit:

- *1xx: Informational:* Request received, continuing to process the request, and no problems have been encountered.

- *2xx: Success:* The action was successfully received, understood, and accepted. This code acts as an ACK.
- *3xx: Redirection:* Further action needs to be taken to complete the request. Such action may or may not entail a redirect.
- *4xx: Client Error:* The request contains bad syntax or cannot be fulfilled at this server, and the request is rejected.
- *5xx: Server Error:* The server failed to fulfill an apparently valid request. All edits on the message passed, but the server failed for internal reasons.
- *6xx: Global Failure:* The request cannot be fulfilled at any server.

Typical Call Setup

Figure 11–8 shows a typical example of a call setup that emanates from a SIP entity and is sent to a called party attached to a public switched telephone network (PSTN). The PSTN is represented by (typically) a switch.

> *Event 1:* When a SIP user wants to begin a session with a PSTN user, the SIP node issues an INVITE request message. This message is like an ISDN SETUP message; it gets the call procedures started. The Gateway starts the process of reserving resources for the call (the media stream). The resources consist of an RTP/UDP port on the IP side and an E1/T1 slot on the telco side. It is possible that the SIP node might be able to code the IAM itself; if this is the situation, the IAM is coded in the body of the SIP INVITE message.
>
> *Event 2:* The message is acknowledged with a SIP message containing the status code of 100. This message also has the effect of telling the recipient that the gateway is "trying" to complete the operation; that is, the Gateway has agreed to handle the call.
>
> *Event 3:* The INVITE message is mapped into an ISUP IAM and sent to the PSTN node, and audio is cut through.
>
> *Event 4:* This node responds with the ISUP ACM, indicating that it understands the message and knows how to set up the call.
>
> *Event 5:* The ACM contains a field called the called-party status code that is mapped to a SIP provisional response. The provisional response is 180 for subscriber free or 183 for no indication. Audio cut-through occurs.

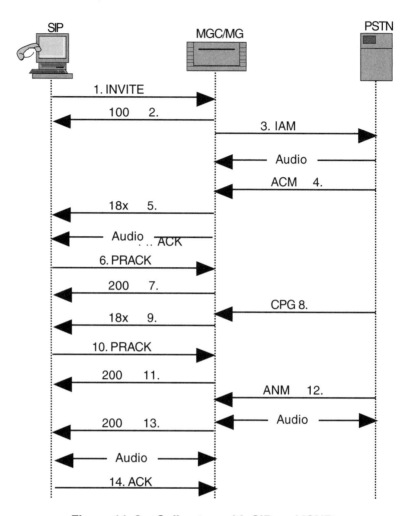

Figure 11–8   Call setup with SIP and ISUP

Event 6: The provisional response ACK (PRACK) is returned to the MGC/MG.

Event 7: A 200 code is returned in the SIP response. This code is an ACK.

Event 8: The call proceeding message (CPG) is sent back from the PSTN with codes to indicate the status of the call.

Event 9: The information in the CPG message is placed in the body of the 18x SIP response message. The ISUP event codes are mapped into the SIP status codes as follows:

ISUP Event Code	SIP Status Code
1: Alerting	180: Ringing
2: Progress	183: Call progress
3: In-band information	183: Call progress
4. Call forward; line busy	181: Call is being forwarded
5. Call forward; no reply	181: Call is being forwarded
6. Call forward; unconditional	181: Call is being forwarded

Events 10 and 11: The provisional response is returned and acknowledged.

Event 12: The called party answers the call, and the PSTN sends to the Gateway the ISUP ANM; two-way audio is cut through.

Events 13 and 14: The call is completed on the IP side of the connection.

Of course, the call might come from a party attached to the PSTN. For this situation, the IAM is received by the gateway, which reserves resources for the call and connects audio backward to the calling party. The operations then flow in the reverse manner from the example in Figure 11–8.

Call Setup Failure at ISUP   Figure 11–9 shows the procedures invoked if ISUP is unable to complete the call.

Events 1 and 2: As before, SIP initiates the call with the SIP INVITE message and its acknowledgement by the Gateway.

Event 3: The Gateway maps the INVITE request to an IAM and sends it to the SS7 network.

Event 4: However, the call cannot be completed for any number of reasons, such as the called party does not answer, no circuits are available, etc. Therefore, ISUP sends a REL message back to the Gateway.

Event 5: The Gateway acknowledges the REL with the RLC message and releases the circuit.

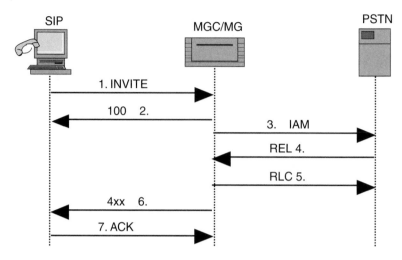

Figure 11–9   ISUP setup failure

Event 6: The reason for the failed call is coded in the cause code field in the REL message. This information is mapped into the SIP error message with a code of 4xx and sent to the SIP calling entity. The mapping of the cause code to SIP status codes is defined in the SIP standards. Here are some examples:

ISUP Cause Code	**SIP Status Code**
17: User busy	486: Busy here
18: No user responding	480: Temporarily unavailable
28: Address incomplete	484: Address incomplete
34: No circuit available	503: Service unavailable
63: Service/option not available	503: Service unavailable

Event 7: The SIP node acknowledges the status code message.

Call Failure and Playing an Error Tone/Announcement

Figure 11–10 shows the message flow for a call failure. For this operation, the ACM is used by the PSTN and the MG to generate an error tone/announcement back to the calling party. Before explaining this example, let's look at how ACM is used between the ISUP node and the Gateway.

The ACM is sent in certain situations to allow the Gateway to play back diagnostics to the SIP node and to reset timers. There are a number

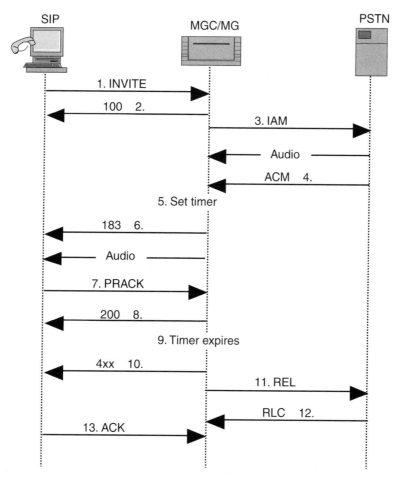

Figure 11–10   Call termination and error tones/announcements played

of reasons for resetting timers. One is when a call is being made to a mobile user and the call setup takes a long time. Another situation is that the Gateway needs to have time to interact with the SIP node before it sends back a required message to the ISUP node. For example, upon receipt of the ACM, the Gateway might have to spend some time interacting with the SIP node. Therefore, the ACM can precipitate the resetting of a network timer, allowing the Gateway to interact with the SIP node before the timer expires (which would require the Gateway to send to the ISUP node a response to the ACM). With this information in mind, we can now examine the operations shown in Figure 11–10.

Events 1, 2, and 3: Operations proceed as explained in the previous examples.

Event 4: The ISUP node is not able to complete the call and must generate an error tone/announcement. Therefore, it sends an ACM with the proper cause code.

Event 5: Upon receipt of this message, the Gateway starts a timer.

Event 6: The receipt of the ACM also causes the Gateway to send a 183 status code (Call Progress code) to the SIP node. This message contains SDP code used to establish an early media cut-through.

Events 7 and 8: The PRACK message (and ACK) are exchanged to confirm receipt of the provisional response.

Event 9: The timer expires.

Event 10: The INVITE message is sent with a SIP 4xx status code that reflects the cause code received in event 4. This action terminates the call at the SIP node.

Event 11: The expired network timer precipitates the sending of the REL to the PSTN to terminate the call. Notice that event 5 gave the Gateway sufficient time to execute events 6, 7, and 8.

Events 12 and 13: Procedures for the final clearing of the call are executed.

Termination at the Other End

Of course, call termination can occur from the SIP end as well. The operations are similar to the previous examples, except the SIP node initiates the call termination. This operation takes place if the call is terminated for reasons other than when one of the parties hangs up (the hang-up is explained shortly). In any case, the SIP node sends a special SIP message called the CANCEL, and the Gateway (a) releases any IP resources it had reserved, (b) releases the PSTN trunk, (c) and signals back to the ISP and ISUP node of these actions.

SIP Redirection

Chapter 10 introduced the concept of a SIP redirect server. Figure 11–11 shows how a call is redirected by a SIP node.

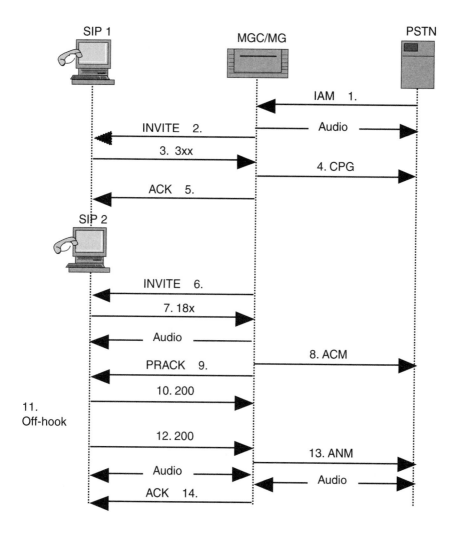

Figure 11–11   Call redirection

Event 1: The calling party is attached to the telco network, so the call is sent to a designated MGC/MC by the ISUP IAM, followed by audio cut-through by the MGC/MG.

Event 2: The INVITE message is sent to what the MGC/MG believes, based on the information it has, is the appropriate SIP node.

Event 3: The SIP node returns a 3xx message signifying that the called party is at a different location. This information is coded in the Contact field of the SIP message.

Event 4: In turn, the Gateway sends to the PSTN node an ISUP CPG with information that the call is being forwarded.

Event 5: The Gateway acknowledges the 3xx message.

Event 6: Based on the information received in event 3, the Gateway sends the INVITE message to another SIP site.

Event 7: When the receiving site has received sufficient addressing information, it returns a provisional response of 18x. The Gateway then performs audio cut-through.

Event 8: Based on receiving the 18x status code, the Gateway sends an ACM message to the PSTN node. The exact coding of the 18x code and its mapping into the ISUP message takes place as follows:

Response Received	Message Sent by Gateway
180: Ringing	ACM
181: Call is being forwarded	Early ACM and CPG
182: Queued	ACM
183: Session progress	ACM

Events 9 and 10: The PRACK message is sent to confirm the receipt of the provisional response.

Event 11: The SIP node answers the call.

Event 12: The SIP node sends a 200 message back to the gateway, signifying the call is answered, and two-way audio is cut-through by the Gateway.

Event 13: The Gateway sends the ISUP ANM to the PSTN, and cuts through two-way audio.

Event 14: The Gateway confirms the SIP node's message sent in event 12.

Caller or Callee Hangs Up

Figure 11–12 shows the operations when one of the parties in the conversation hangs up. In this example, the party attached to the PSTN hangs up, so the PSTN initiates the disconnection operations. The ISUP REL message is used by the Gateway to generate the SIP BYE message. In turn, the RLC confirms the REL and the 200 message confirms the

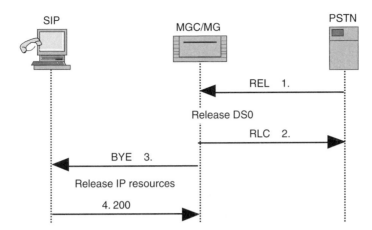

Figure 11–12   The hang-up operation

BYE. The Gateway releases the PSTN resources (a DS0 channel) and the IP resources (addresses, port numbers).

INTO THE FUTURE WITH TRIP

Jonathan Rosenberg and Henning Schulzrinne have made numerous contributions to IP telephony, notably in the SIP arena. They are the authors of RFC 2871, "Telephony Routing over IP (TRIP)," from which this section is sourced.

The Problem

As IP telephony gateways grow in terms of numbers and usage, managing their operation will become increasingly complex. One of the difficult tasks is that of gateway location and discovery. For example, assume a PC user, using a conventional phone number, calls a party residing on the circuit-switched telephone network. A gateway must be used for this connection to occur. The problem is not trivial:

- There may be a very large number of telephony gateways connecting the GSTN and the Internet. Attachment to the GSTN means that the gateway will have connectivity to the nearly one billion terminals reachable on this network. This means that every gateway could theoretically complete a call to any terminal on the GSTN.

- The owner of a gateway is unlikely to make the gateway available to any user who wants to connect to it.
- In some cases, the end user may have specific requirements regarding the gateway selection, depending, say on the capabilities of the gateway.

The Proposed Solution

The idea behind TRIP is to provide a means to disseminate information on availability of gateways that are exchanged by network providers. This would allow each provider to build up its own local database of available gateways.

TRIP is used for exchange of gateway routing information. It provides these functions:

- Establishment and maintenance of peer relationships between providers
- Exchange and synchronization of telephony gateway routing information between providers
- Prevention of stable routing loops for IP telephony signaling protocols
- Propagation of learned gateway routing information to other providers in a timely and scalable fashion
- Definition of the syntax and semantics of the data that describe telephony gateway routes

Future of TRIP

TRIP is a new endeavor, and its successful use remains to be seen. If VoIP becomes a big success, TRIP or an equivalent capability must be put in place. TRIP is a well-thought-out approach to the problem of finding a VoIP-called party. We shall have to wait to see if it is accepted in the industry.

SUMMARY

SS7 and IP must act as partners to support telephony traffic in packet networks. SS7 and H.323 are responsible for the signaling and connection management operations, and IP assumes its familiar role as the forwarding protocol for the voice traffic.

It would be a good idea for the reader to check the Internet for revisions to the specifications explained in this chapter. By the time this book is published, it is likely these drafts will have entered their final stages.

12

Other Packet Voice Alternatives

VoIP is not the only way to transport voice traffic over nontelephony networks. Indeed, the three alternatives discussed in this chapter are efficient, fast, and can yield toll-quality signals at a reasonable cost. They are voice over Frame Relay (VoFR), voice over ATM (VoATM),[1] and voice over MPLS (VoLS). A fourth alternative, voice over Ethernet, was explained in Chapter 10. In conjunction with H.323, voice over Ethernet can operate over local area networks.

USE OF OTHER ALTERNATIVES

Why use packet telephony techniques other than VoIP? The answer is that Frame Relay and ATM are widely deployed throughout the world in carrier networks, such as the telephone system and the Internet. They are deployed extensively in private internets and VPNs. For example, AT&T uses Frame Relay and ATM to operate a large VPN that supports scores of Fortune 500 companies. Moreover, ATM is often deployed at a carrier switch in the telephone office or in a PBX. Therefore, these technologies are already available to transport voice traffic.

---

[1]This series includes three books on ATM and one book on MPLS.

In addition, Frame Relay, ATM, and MPLS are designed to provide very fast service with low delay and little jitter. ATM can provide toll-quality voice calls, equal in quality to a conventional TDM-based telephone network. We have learned that IP and conventional data-oriented internets are not so designed.

One factor that has discouraged the deployment of Frame Relay and ATM for packet voice is that these technologies have not been deployed at end-user devices, such as telephones and personal computers. Historically, they have operated inside the carrier's network.

However, this situation is changing, especially for ATM. For example, many end users of DSL have ATM deployed in their DSL modem. It is an easy matter to digitize the voice at the customer site (the residence, for example) and transport the traffic to the network over the local loop through ATM. Alternatively, conventional telephones can be used, and the Central Office digitizes the traffic and relays the payload through the ATM backbone. Figure 12–1 illustrates these ideas.

(a) Conventional telephone connections to the CO

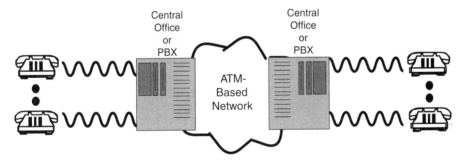

(b) Using computers and ATM modems

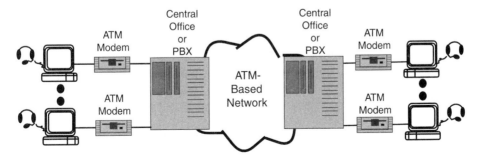

Figure 12–1   Using VoATM

FUNCTIONS OF VOICE OVER FRAME RELAY

During the years of 1996 to 1998, the Frame Relay Forum added several features to Frame Relay, principally to support real-time traffic, such as voice. The following discussion summarizes these operations and describes the three functions: PVC fragmentation, service multiplexing, and voice over Frame Relay (VoFR). We begin this discussion with an analysis of PVC fragmentation.

PVC Fragmentation

The fragmentation operation was developed by the Frame Relay Forum to support delay-sensitive traffic such as voice connections. One approach is to multiplex the shorter frames onto the same physical interface that supports longer frames. In other words, it is possible to interleave delay-sensitive traffic (in shorter frames) and non-delay-sensitive traffic (in longer frames). Obviously, this feature allows the sharing of the link by both real-time and non-real-time traffic. The size of the fragments is implementation specific, and the fragment size can be configured in accordance with the attributes of the line, interface, and local clocking mechanisms, such as a channelized or an unchannelized interface. The idea is to allow each local interface to be responsible for fragmentation.

Fragmentation operations can be implemented at (a) the user network interface (UNI), (b) network to network interface (NNI), or (c) end-to-end. Figure 12–2 shows these three fragmentation models. The term DTE stands for data terminal equipment. DTE identifies the end-user device. The term DCE stands for data circuit terminating equipment. DCE identifies a Frame Relay node, such as a router or multiplexer. The UNI fragmentation operation is local to an interface and can take advantage of transporting larger frames over the backbone network at the high bandwidths of the backbone links. The transmission of these longer frames is more efficient than the transport of a larger number of smaller fragments. In addition, in case a DTE does not implement fragmentation, this model allows the network to act as a proxy for this DTE.

Figure 12–3 shows the format for the fragmentation header for end-to-end fragmentation. The low-order bit of the first byte (byte 3) of the fragmentation header is set to 1, and the low-order bit of the Frame Relay header is set to 0 (byte 0). These bit settings distinguish the headers from each other and cause the receiver to be aware whether it is receiving the proper header. They thus act as a check that the

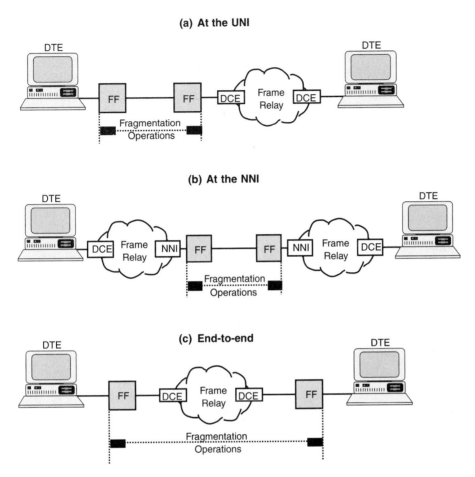

Figure 12–2   Fragmentation function (FF) operations

fragmentation peers are configured properly. The content of the header is as follows.

The first two bytes consist of the conventional Frame Relay header. Bytes 3–6 consist of the fragmentation header. Let's look at byte 5 first.

The beginning (B) bit is set to 1 for the first data fragment of the original frame. It is set to 0 for all other fragments of the frame. The ending (E) fragment bit is set to 1 for the last data fragment of the original data frame, and it is set to 0 for all other data fragments. A data fragment can be both a beginning and ending fragment, so it can have both the B and E bits set to 1.

Bit 8	Bit 7	Bit 6	Bit 5	Bit 4	Bit 3	Bit 2	Bit 1	Octet
DLCI high six bits						C/R	0	1
DLCI low four bits				F	B	DE	1	2
0	0	0	0	0	0	1	1	3
1	0	1	1	0	0	0	1	4
B	E	C	Sequence number of high-order 4 bits				R	5
Sequence number of low-order 8 bits								6
Payload								5-n
Frame Check Sequence (FCS)								5-n+2

Figure 12–3   The fragmentation header

The control (C) bit is set to 0 and is not used in the current implementation agreement. It is reserved for future operations.

The sequence number (bytes 5 and 6) is incremented for each data fragment transmitted on the link. A separate sequence number is maintained for each DLCI in the interfaces.

The end-to-end fragmentation also uses the multiprotocol encapsulation operation in accordance with Frame Relay Forum's specification FRF.3.1, titled "Multiprotocol Encapsulation Agreement." The unnumbered information (UI) byte (byte 3) is used for this process (0x03), and the Network Layer protocol ID (NLPID) value of 0xB1 has been assigned to identify the fragmentation header format (byte 4).

Fragmentation Operations

The fragmentation procedures are based on RFC 1990, titled "The Point-to-Point Protocol (PPP) Multilink Protocol (MP)," August 1996. An example of fragmentation and reassembly operations is shown in Figure 12–4. The Q.922, optional PAD, and the NLPID fields are removed by the transmitter and placed in the first fragment. Each fragment must be transmitted in the same order as its relative position in its original frame, although fragments from multiple PVCs can be interleaved with each other across one interface. The receiving machine must keep track of the incoming sequence numbers and use the beginning and ending bits for proper reassembly of traffic. If lost fragments are detected or sequence numbers skipped, the receiver must discard all currently assembled fragments and fragments subsequently received for that PVC until it receives the first fragment of a new frame (that is to say, a new beginning bit).

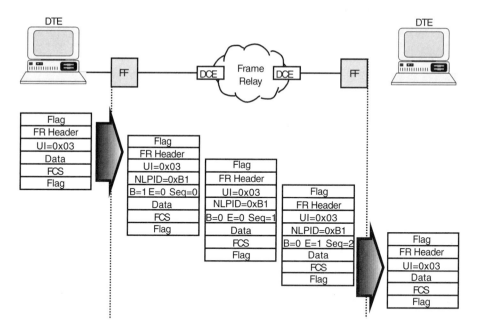

Figure 12–4   Example of end-to-end fragmentation

The data field of the original packet is broken up (fragmented) and the NLPID, B bit, E bit, and sequence number fields are all added to track the original packet. The B and E bits act as discussed in previous discussions. The sequence number is incremented for each data fragment to delineate the order of the transmission.

SERVICE MULTIPLEXING

Because of the wide-scale use of Frame Relay, considerable effort has been made in expanding Frame Relay networks to support voice traffic. The Frame Relay Forum has published a specification for this process. It is titled "Voice over Frame Relay Implementation Agreement—FRF.11."

Component of the VoFR Specification

The major components of this specification deal with analog-to-digital (A-D), digital-to-analog (D-A) voice compression operations, and the transmission of the digitized images in a Frame Relay frame. In addition to the transfer of the voice traffic, the frames can also convey data, fax images, and the signaling needed to set up, manage, and tear down

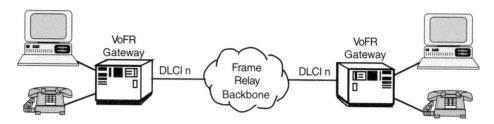

Figure 12–5   Service multiplexing

the voice or fax connection. Support is provided for dialed digits, line seizures, and other needed signals used in telephony, such as the ABCD signaling bits.

One of the key components of voice over Frame Relay (VoFR) is called service multiplexing, which supports multiple voice and data channels on a single Frame Relay connection. This concept is shown in Figure 12–5. Multiple streams of user traffic (which are called subchannels) consisting of different voice and data transmission flows are multiplexed across one DLCI (DLCI n in this example). VoFR is responsible for delivering the frames to the receiving user in the order in which they were sent from the transmitting user.

Subchannels and the DLCIs

Figure 12–6 shows the relationships of the subchannels to the DLCIs. The user applications at A and B are multiplexed into one virtual circuit,

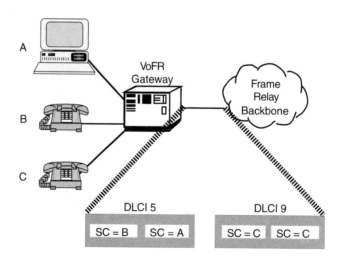

Figure 12–6   Subchannel (SC) concept

identified with DLCI 5. The user application at C is multiplexed into another virtual circuit, identified with DLCI 9. It is the job of the VoFR gateway to assemble the subchannels to the Frame Relay frame. If two users
are sending traffic that pertains to one overall traffic flow (for example, a
conversation on the telephone that discusses the data exchanged and ex-
hibited on a workstation screen), Frame Relay does not define how these
two images are played at the receiver's machines. This aspect of multiservice multiplexing is left to specific vendor implementations.

OPERATIONS OF VOICE OVER FRAME RELAY

All the operations discussed thus far in this chapter are supporting procedures to VoFR, although some of them can be used for other types of
traffic. For speech, VoFR defines several specifications on the coding of
the voice traffic. You can refer to the Annexes in FRF.11 for more detail.
For your convenience, the technologies that are supported are listed in
Table 12–1. I have added an entry in the table to include another specifi-

Table 12–1   Voice support in VoFR

Reference Document	Description
ITU G.729/ITU G.729 Annex A	Coding of speech at 8 kbit/s using Conjugate Struc- ture-Algebraic Code Excited Linear Prediction (CS-ACELP) Coding, March 1996
ITU G.711	Pulse Code Modulation of Voice Frequencies, 1988
ITU G.726	40-, 32-, 24-, 16-kbit/s Adaptive Differential Pulse Code Modulation (ADPCM), March 1996
ITU G.727	5-, 4-, 3-, and 2-bit Sample Embedded Adaptive Differ- ential Pulse Code Modulation, November 1994
ITU G.764	Voice packetization: Packetized voice protocols, De- cember 1990
ITU G.728	Coding of Speech at 16 kbit/s using Low-Delay Code Excited Linear Prediction, November 1994
ITU G.723.1	Dual Rate Speech Coder for Multimedia Communica- tions Transmitting at 5.3 and 6.3 kbit/s, March 1996
ITU G.723.1, Annex A	Silence Compression Scheme, March 1996
ITU G.723.1, Annex B	Alternative Specification Based on Floating-Point Arithmetic, March 1996
ITU G.723.1, Annex C	Scalable Channel Coding Scheme for Wireless Appli- cations, March 1996

cation (ITU-T G.723 and Annexes) that will surely be used but is not part of FRF.11 at this time. All organizations that belong to the International Media Teleconferencing Consortium (IMTC) have all selected G.723.1 for their basic coder.

Servicing the Dialed Digits

The telephone dialed digit payload contains the dialed digits entered by the calling party as well as several control parameters. The transmission occurs over an all-digital network, and the telephone signals are dual-tone, multifrequency (DTMF) signals. Because DTMF is not permitted in the VoFR specifications, binary representations are substituted for the analog signals.

In accordance with [FRF.1197], a 20 ms window is used to encode the edge when a digit is turned on and off. This is the delta time, 0 to 19 ms, from the beginning of the current frame in milliseconds. If there is no transition, the edge location will be set to 0 and the digit type of the previous windows will be repeated.

Figure 12–7 shows an example of how the dialed digits are placed into the dialed digit payload.

When the VoFR transmitter detects a dialed digit from the calling party, it starts sending a dialed digit payload that is repeated every 20 ms. Each payload covers 60 ms of digit on/off edge information. Consequently, there is redundancy of edge information. Upon the VoFR receiver receiving the dialed digit payload, it generates the dialed digits according to the location of the on and off edges. After an off edge and before an on edge, silence is applied to the duration and digits are generated after an on edge and before an off edge.

Procedure for Transmission of Dialed Digit Payloads When the transmitter detects a validated digit, it will start sending a dialed digit payload every 20 ms. Since each payload covers 60 ms of digit on/off edge information; there is redundancy of the edge information. The sequence number is incremented by one in each transmitted payload.

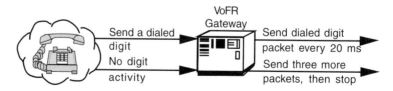

Figure 12–7   Procedure for the dialed digits

When the digit activity is off, the transmitter should continue to send three more dialed digit payloads for 60 ms.

Procedure for Interpreting Received Dialed Digit Payloads   When the receiver gets a dialed digit payload, it will generate digits according to the location of the on and off edges. Silence will be applied to the duration after an off edge and before an on edge. Digits will be generated after an on edge and before an off edge.

If the sequence number is one greater than the last received sequence number, the receiver appends the current edge information to the previously received information.

If the sequence number is two greater than the last received sequence number, the receiver appends the recent and current edge information to the previously received information.

If the sequence number is three greater than the last received sequence number, the receiver appends the previous, recent, and current edge information to the previously received information.

If the sequence number if more than three greater than the last received sequence number, the receiver appends the previous, recent, and current edge information to the previously received information. It fills in the gap with the static values based on the previously received payload.

If a voice packet is received at any time, an off edge should be appended to the previously received digits on/off edge information.

As shown in Figure 12–8, if the signaling bits do not change for 500 ms the VoFR transmitter alters the frequency that it sends the signaling packets to one every 5 s. During this period of signaling inactivity, the sequence number is not incremented, which allows the receiver to discard this packet (or use the first value to set its current values).

Fax Transmission

Fax traffic is transported by VoFR in accordance with the same concepts employed for data, dial digits, or signaling traffic. The fax traffic is

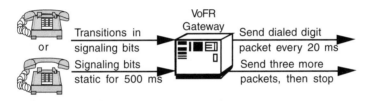

Figure 12–8   Procedures for processing the signaling bits

encapsulated into the Frame Relay subframe and remains transparent to the Frame Relay network. The VoFR gateway is responsible for handling the fax-specific operations. Figure 12–9 shows an example of VoFR fax operations.

VoFR supports the worldwide standard for Group 3 facsimile systems, which is defined in ITU-T T.4 (1993). In addition to T.4, VoFR supports several ITU-T V Series modems, as well as the V.17 fax specification for 7.2-, 9.6-, 12.0-, and 14.4-kbit/s transmission rates.

Since Frame Relay must convey fax and modem control signals between the user machines, the VoFR subframe for fax traffic is coded to identify operating parameters that are needed between the sending and receiving fax/modems. As examples, the subframe contains information on the modulation type used by the sending modem, the type of modem (V.17, V.33, etc.), and the bit/s rate (14.4 kbit/s, etc.).

The fax/modem information elements are placed in byte 2c of the payload element of the subframe. This payload packet is called the modulation turn-on packet. This packet is sent when the VoFR gateway detects a frequency tone, at which time the VoFR sends at least three of these packets. The EI1 and EI2 bits are set to 1 and 0, respectively (they are header extension bits), and the sequence number remains at 0 during this hand-shake phase. The Relay Command field is set to 011 (modulation on) to indicate that a carrier has been detected. The timestamp pro-

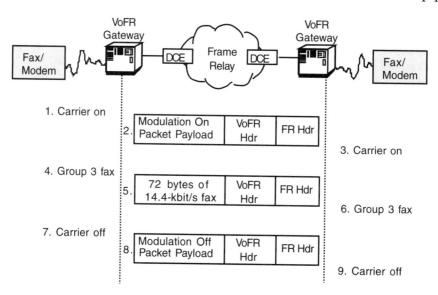

Figure 12–9 Example of VoFR support for fax transmissions

vides timing to the demodulator and is coded in 1 ms units (and must be accurate to ± 5 ms). The timing assumes free-running clocks with no synchronization between them. The HDLC bit is used if an HDLC frame is used between the modems (bit = 1, HDLC is applied).

The modulation type is set to identify the type of modem that is sending this information. This information is conveyed in analog signals to the VoFR gateway, which converts the signals to four-bit codes. For our example, the modulation type code for a 14.4 kbit/s V.17 fax/modem is 1011. A field in the frame is the frequency information element; it is coded to indicate the sending modem's frequency tone.

The VoFR gateway continues to interpret the fax/modem analog signals and maps them into the Frame Relay subframes. After the handshake, it places the fax images into the subframes and sends them to the receiving VoFR gateway. At this machine, the data fields in the subframe are mapped back to analog signals for interpretation and processing at the receiving fax/modem.

VoFR Encapsulation

Table 12–1 on page 251 lists the coder specifications that are supported by VoFR. I have selected G.723 because of its prevalent use in the industry and because it is supported as the preferred coder specification by the International Media Teleconferencing Consortium (IMTC).

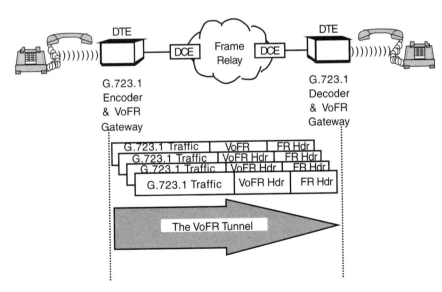

Figure 12–10   Transport of voice traffic

The coder operates on frames of 240 samples each to support the 8,000 sample per second input speech stream. Further operations (a high-pass filter to remove the DC component) result in four subframes of 60 ms each. A variety of other operations occur, such as the computation of an LPC filter and unquantized LPC filter coefficients, etc., resulting in a packetization time of 30 ms.

After the digitized frames are created by the coder, they are encapsulated into the VoFR voice information field, as shown in Figure 12–10. For MP-MLQ, the information field is 24 bytes, and for ACELP, the information field is 20 bytes. They are transported through the Frame Relay network and passed to the decoder. The decoder converts the digital images to the output voice signal, which is played out to the receiver.

VOICE OVER ATM WITH AAL 1

AAL 1 has been used for several years to transport real-time traffic in an ATM cell. The 48 bytes of the ATM cell are used by AAL 1 and the user payload, as shown in Figure 12–11. The AAL 1 PDU consists of 48 bytes with 47 bytes available for the application payload. The AAL 1 header consists of four bits in the two fields. The first field is a sequence number (SN) and is used for detection of mistakenly inserted cells or lost cells. The SN protection (SNP) field performs error detection on the SN.

AAL 1 is responsible for clock recovery for both audio and video services. The recovery operation can be accomplished through the use of real-time synchronization or through the use of timestamping.

VoATM traffic can operate in one of two modes: the unstructured data transfer (UDT) mode or the structured data transfer (SDT) mode. The former is a bit-stream operation that has an associated bit clock, and

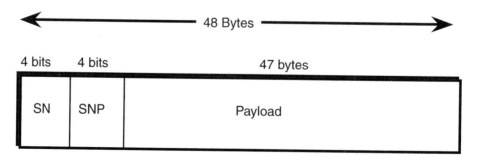

Figure 12–11   AAL 1

the latter is a byte-stream (8-bit bytes) operation with a fixed block length that has an associated clock.

In many ATM networks that support voice traffic, the voice images are encoded with the G.711 standard. The 8000 samples per second are placed in a stream of separate 53-byte cells with a technique called *single-channel adaptation* (SCA). This term conveys the idea that only one voice channel is carried in each ATM virtual circuit. SCA provides toll-quality performance for the voice call. Uncompressed G.711 VoATM adds approximately 6 ms of delay in buffering the 47 samples at 8000 samples per second ($1/8000 \times 47 = .0058$ s). Of course, as the traffic is sent across multiple nodes, each node will create additive delay degradation.

VOICE OVER ATM WITH AAL 2

The ITU-T has issued a recommendation on the ATM Adaptation Layer type 2 (AAL 2). It is published in ITU-T I.363.2. The concept of AAL 2 is to provide a mechanism for sending small packets (such as voice, since AAL 2 targets packet telephony) over an ATM network in a manner that ensures small delay. AAL 2 supports the multiplexing of multiple connections into one cell, thus avoiding the unattractive aspect of sending partially filled cells through the network. The connections are called LLCs, for logical link connections.

AAL 2 supports the multiplexing of variable-length packets, a service that is quite important in accommodating variable bit-rate coders and silence compression. Indeed, a fixed-length requirement would mean only efficient accommodation for CBR applications, all using the same coders. This method, called *position-based multiplexing and delineation,* is simply too rigid to service modern telephony requirements. Figure 12–12 shows the format for AAL 2 packets.

The fields in the 48 bytes are grouped into the start field, the CPS-packet header, the payload, and the PAD. The functions of the fields are as follows (we examine the CPS-packet header first):

- The CID value identifies the AAL type 2 CPS user of the channel. The AAL type 2 channel is a bidirectional channel. The same value of channel identification shall be used for both directions. The value 0 is not used for channel identification because the all-zero byte is used for the padding function. The values 0–7 are reserved for management operations. Therefore, 248 voice calls can be identified within each ATM virtual channel connection.

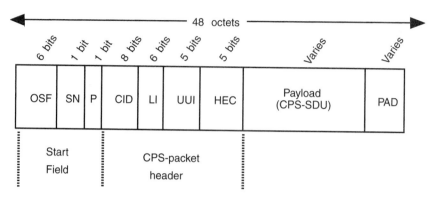

Note: CPS-packet header can exist more than once in ATM-SDU

Figure 12–12   AAL type 2

- The LI field is 1 less than the number of bytes in the CPS-packet payload. The default maximum length of the CPS-packet payload is 45 bytes; otherwise, the maximum length can be set to 64 bytes.
- The UUI field conveys information transparently between the CPS users and layer management to distinguish between the SSCS entities and management users of the CPS.
- HEC is used by the transmitter to calculate the remainder of the division (modulo 2), by the generator polynomial $x^5 + x^2 + 1$, of the product of x^5 and the contents of the first 19 bits of the CPS-PH. The coefficients of the remainder polynomial are inserted in the HEC field with the coefficient of the x^4 term in the most significant bit of the HEC field. The receiver uses the contents of the HEC field to detect errors in the CPS-PH.
- The OSF carries the binary value of the offset, measured in number of bytes, between the end of the start field and the first start of a CPS-packet or, in the absence of a first start, to the start of the PAD field. The value 47 indicates that there is no start boundary in the CPS-PDU payload. Values greater than 47 are not allowed.
- The SN bit is used to number (modulo 2) the stream of CPS-PDUs.
- The P bit is used by the receiver to detect errors in the start field.

Figure 12–13 provides an example of how AAL 2 supports voice traffic. We assume a voice over ATM (VoATM) gateway accepts analog speech at the sender and digitizes it, thus creating G.729.A voice packets, which are presented to AAL 2. At the receiving VoATM gateway, this process is reversed.

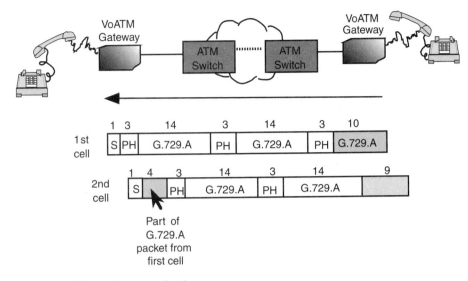

S   Start field (containing offset)
PH   Packet header

Figure 12–13   AAL 2 support of voice traffic

The G.729.A Recommendation is designed for low-bit-rate audio coders and operates at 8 kbit/s. Each G.729.A frame is 10 bytes in length. For this example, the voice packet is encapsulated with the Real-Time Protocol (RTP), thus creating a 14-byte packet (the RTP header is 4 bytes in length).

Other headers, such as UDP and IP, might exist. The use of these headers depends on where the traffic emanates from. If the VoATM speech is sent from a PC on a LAN, these extra headers are likely present. If the speech emanates from the CO, the headers are likely not present. For this example, they are not present.

The offset field points to the start of the packet. This field is placed in the first byte of the 48-byte ATM-SDU. The RTP/G.729.A packet is appended to the LL2 packet header, and these 17 bytes are placed in the cell payload. The process simply loads the ATM-SDU with contiguous 17 bytes until the 48 bytes are filled. In this example, the third packet is placed in the last part of the first cell and the first part of the second cell. The offset field in the second cell points to the first CPS packet header, which is the fourth packet in this stream. The length of the packet is indicated in the packet header; therefore, and in this example, it is used to identify the remaining bytes of the third packet residing in the second cell.

This example shows support of voice only, with fixed-length packets. AAL 2 can also support voice and data traffic by multiplexing these ap-

Table 12–2   Use of AAL 2 with standard voice coding schemes [NORT01a]

Bandwidth & Delay	10-Byte Packet		20-Byte Packet		30-Byte Packet		40-Byte Packet	
	BW	D	BW	D	BW	D	BW	D
G.711 64 kbit/s	93.8	1.25	83.0	2.5	79.4	3.75	77.6	5
G.711 64 kbit/s (SS)	46.9	1.25	41.5	2.5	39.7	3.75	38.8	5
G.726 32 kbit/s (SS)	23.4	2.5	20.7	5	19.8	7.5	10.4	10
G.728 16 kbit/s (SS)	11.7	5	10.5	10	9.9	15	9.7	20
G.729 8 kbit/s (SS)	5.9	10	5.2	20	5.0	30	4.8	40

Where BW is bandwidth, SS is silence suppressed, and D is delay in ms

plications and identifying each traffic stream (fixed-length voice and variable-length data) with a unique channel identifier (CID). The AAL 2 operations to handle these applications are like the example in this figure: The offset field identifies the packet boundaries, those packets that cannot fit into one cell are segmented, and the packet's remaining bytes are placed in the next cell.

Table 12–2 compares several VoATM/AAL 2 techniques supported by Nortel Networks with its VoATM products. Nortel's approach is to place 10 to 40 bytes in a packet and then encapsulate this packet into AAL 2 and then into the ATM cells. This large payload needs explanation.

Filling the complete cell with samples creates more delay. Indeed, a single voice call of compressed voice (say, 8 kbit/s) operating in a single cell can create delay that some listeners might find unacceptable. Therefore, AAL 2 can be used to multiplex multiple voice channels into one cell and then group them into one ATM virtual channel connection. This concept, called *multichannel adaptation* (MCA), is supported by the AAL 2 CID field.

Recall that the CID can uniquely identify up to 248 calls on an ATM connection. Therefore, the ATM VCC ID is used to traverse the ATM network. At the final destination, AAL 2 CID steers each voice channel to the correct destination, such as a TDM/PCM trunk channel or an end-user terminal.

VoFR AND VoATM: PARTNERS WITH OR COMPETITORS TO VoIP?

The VoFR and VoATM approaches do not define the details needed to develop a full telephony-supported system. Certainly, ATM furnishes the tools for carrying voice traffic through an ATM network and provides the means to negotiate the required level of service for this traffic. But it does not define the important procedures for interworking with the telephone user, for mapping the telephone signals into packets, and others. The same situation holds true for Frame Relay, although VoFR is a more complete packet-voice specification than is VoATM.

The emerging VoIP specifications provide this level of detail, as described in several chapters in this book. The VoIP standards, even though not finished, will eventually be completed and will provide sufficient detail for the designer to implement a complete standardized package.

What Resides in the User Workstation?

It is my view that Frame Relay and ATM will play a role in packet telephony for the time being, but the role will be one of supporting VoIP. Why? Because Frame Relay and ATM (with rare exceptions) do not reside in user PCs and workstations, and therefore, cannot compete with IP at the user workstation (at least at this stage of evolution of the industry). This point was made in Chapter 1 (see Figure 1–2).

However (and, again, at this stage of the game), ATM and Frame Relay can complement VoIP by acting as the high-speed transport backbone network for the VoIP traffic. With this approach, we can take advantage of the very fast label-switching techniques of ATM and Frame Relay. Moreover, with AAL 2, multiple voice calls can be carried in the ATM cell.

HERE COMES MPLS

The Multiprotocol Label Switching (MPLS) protocol is published by the Internet Engineering Task Force as RFC 3031.

MPLS is a label-swapping (mapping) and forwarding technology. Label swapping or mapping means the changing of the label value in the packet header as the packet moves from one node to another.

The idea of MPLS is to improve the performance of network layer routing and the scalability of the network layer. Several examples of MPLS have been cited in this chapter, notably the idea of constrained routing (see also Chapter 7).

The initial MPLS efforts of the Working Group focus on IPv4 and IPv6. The core technology can be extended to multiple network layer protocols, such as IPX and SNA. However, there is little interest in expanding MPLS to other network layer protocols, since IP is by far the most pervasive.

The basic idea is not to restrict MPLS to any specific link layer technology, such as ATM or Frame Relay. Most of the efforts so far are directed to the interworking of MPLS and ATM, but in the future, it is quite conceivable that MPLS could operate directly with IP over the physical layer and not use ATM at all. Indeed, it is the intent of some vendors to migrate away from ATM and use MPLS instead.

In addition, MPLS does not require one specific, label-distribution protocol (agreeing on the use of label values between neighboring LSRs). It assumes there may be more than one, such as the Resource Reservation Protocol (RSVP), BGP, or the Label Distribution Protocol (LDP). Considerable attention is on LDP since is it being designed from scratch for MPLS networks. Other protocols, such as BGP and RSVP, are also very good methods for label distribution.

FOR THE FUTURE?

For the immediate future, ATM and Frame Relay will continue to be the prevalent basic bearer services in wide area internets and the Internet. However, as MPLS matures and reaches the marketplace, the roles of ATM and Frame Relay will probably diminish. For this evolution to occur, supporting protocols, such as CR-LDP, RSVP, and DiffServ must be in place to take over the QOS and network management operations found in ATM and Frame Relay.

Eventually, VoIP will be transported without ATM and Frame Relay, probably with MPLS. But don't hold your breath. ATM and Frame Relay are deeply embedded in wide area networks today, and they will be around for some time to come.

Regardless of the basic carrier service, VoIP will continue to grow, both in the Internet and in internets. Even though I am not enamored with its performance in the Internet, I will continue to use it because it is a wonderful way for me to reach a large audience for my lectures from the many parts of the world. In addition, its use in private multiparty conferences is proving to be a very cost effective tool.

For now, I hope that you have benefited from reading this book and that you have found it a valuable addition to your library.

Appendix A

Telephony Signaling

Several discussions in this book are about the interworking of the telephone system with packet networks. This appendix provides the information you need to follow the telephony-IP internetworking discussions.

THE LOCAL LOOP

As depicted in Figure A–1, the line connecting a telephone to the telephone service provider—the Central Office (CO)—consists of two wires. The connecting point between the CPE and CO is called the point of demarcation and is usually found in a box (the protection block or station block) on the outside of a house. The outside plant facilities include the wires and supporting hardware to the CO.

At the CO, the lines enter through a cable room (aerial lines) or a cable vault (buried lines). The lines are then spliced to tip cables and directed to the main distribution frame (MDF); each wire is attached to a connector at the MDF.[1] From the MDF, the wires are directed to other equipment such as a switch.

---

[1]Even though the MDF is at the CO, it is usually considered part of the outside plant and CO performance is usually measured between the MDFs.

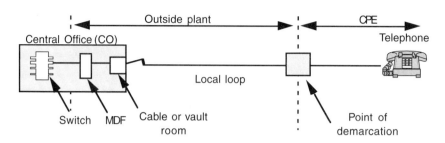

Figure A–1 The telephone plant

The two wires on the twisted pair local loop are referred to as tip and ring. As Figure A–2 shows, the terms originated during the days of the manual telephone switchboards when the conventional telephone plug was used to make the connections through the switchboard. A third wire (if present) is sometimes called a sleeve; once again, it was named for the switchboard plug. In a four-wire system the four leads are called T, R, T1, and R1.

THE OUTSIDE PLANT

Let us return to the subject of the telephone facility. Figure A–3 depicts several aspects of the subscriber loop. As shown in Figure A–3(a), the system consists of feeder plant, distribution plant, and the feeder-distribution interface. The feeder plant consists of the large number of physical wires and digital repeaters. Usually, their location is based on

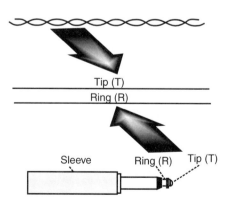

Figure A–2 Tip and ring (and their origins)

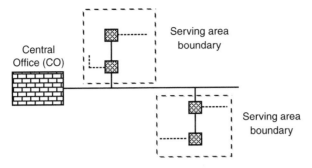

= Feeder-distribution interface (FDI), "cabinet"

Solid lines = Feeder plant

Dashed lines = Distribution plant

(a) Loop configuration of distribution plant

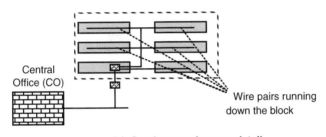

(b) Serving area in more detail

Figure A–3   The outside plant

geographical constraints and the customer locations. They often run par-
allel to roads and highways. The distribution plant consists of a smaller
number of cables and connects to the customer's network interface (NI),
which is usually located in a "box" attached to the customer's building.
The serving area interface (interface plant) is the term used to describe
the manual cross-connections between the feeder and distribution plants.
This interface is designed to allow any feeder unit to be connected to any
distribution pair.

The subscriber loop consists of sections of copper pairs (usually
about 500 ft long). The sections are joined together with electrical joints,
called splices, at the telephone poles for aerial cables and at a manhole
for underground cables. The cable pairs are bundled together in a cable
binder group.

Figure A–3(b) shows the serving area boundary in more detail. This term describes the geographical division of the outside plant into discrete parts. All wires in a serving area are connected to a single serving area interface to the feeder plant, which simplifies ongoing maintenance and record keeping.

CONNECTING THE RESIDENCE

The feeder cables provide the links from the Central Office to the local subscriber area, and then the distribution cables carry on from there to the customer sites (as depicted in Figure A–4). Since the subscriber loop system is usually installed before all the customers are connected, there will be unused distribution cables. The common practice is to connect a twisted pair from a feeder cable to more than one distribution cable. These unused distribution cables are called *bridged taps*.

Bridged taps must be set up within the loop plant rules to minimize adverse effects on the system, such as signal loss, radiation, and spectrum distortions.

The connection points in the distribution cables are in pedestals for underground cables and in terminals for aerial cables. The connection

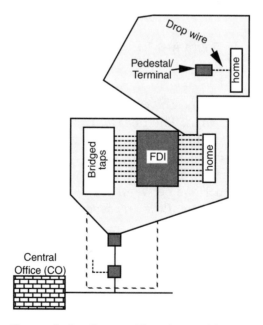

Figure A–4   Connecting the residence

into the customer site is called the drop wire. It is short and can (potentially) pick up other frequency radiations. It might also radiate signals to other devices.

TOLL OFFICES AND TRUNKS

Figure A–5 depicts several lines and types of equipment and types of "offices" found in the public network. Most of the terms in this figure are self-explanatory, but it should prove useful to amplify some of them.

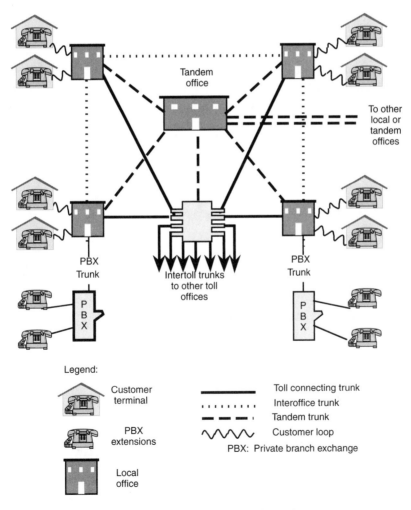

Figure A–5 Offices and trunks

- *Trunk:* A communication channel between two switching systems.
- *Tandem office:* A broad category of office that represents systems that connect trunks to trunks. Local tandem offices connect trunks within a metropolitan area. Toll offices connect trunks in the toll part of the network. With some exceptions, the end customer is not connected to a tandem.
- *Toll connecting trunk:* A trunk between an end office (local office) and a toll office.

SUBSCRIBER SYSTEMS

Subscriber-type systems are available that use the same operations as those systems that operate in the telephone network. These systems are also software programmable for voice and data circuits. The main difference is that one terminal is located in the Central Office and the other is in the field near or on the customer's location (see Figure A–6). They are also referred to as a pair gain system, a digital loop carrier, or a subscriber loop carrier. Some of them can also extend a leased digital link to the customer premise for the customer's use.

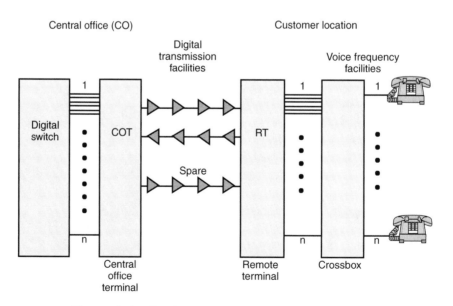

Figure A–6   Basic subscriber system arrangement

Subscriber systems support a wide variety of applications by various operating companies. One popular use is providing service to developing areas for new subdivisions where an existing cable plant is insufficient. A system can provide the service immediately and permanently, or it can be moved to another location (if growth in the area eventually justifies a Central Office). Regardless of whether the service is permanent or temporary, a subscriber system is easy to engineer and install on short notice. An example is a new industrial park experiencing sudden and unexpected growth, resulting in demands for service exceeding available loop plant. The system can be installed and operating within a few weeks. Also, many companies use these systems to provide temporary service to large functions such as business conventions or sporting events.

There are other reasons to justify the placement of a subscriber loop carrier in the loop plant. First, the copper pairs serving the subscribers will be much shorter, thus overcoming distance limitations in providing the newer services. Second, shortening the customer loop decreases the exposure to power-line interference with its resultant degradation and noise impact on these circuits. Third, electronics allow the future ability to provide new services quickly. The distance from the Central Office to the remote terminal is limited only by the performance of the copper span line. Today, most of these systems employ fiber optics, so there is very little distance limitation.

TELEPHONE SIGNALING BASICS

To keep matters simple, the telephone system was designed to perform signaling by on-hook and off-hook operations. The on-hook operation means the telephone set is not being used. The term is derived from the old days when the telephone handset was placed on a hook (later, a cradle) when it was not being used. The off-hook is just the opposite; the handset is being used—it is lifted from the telephone hook.

The off-hook and on-hook operations change the electrical state of the line between the terminal and the CO (or PBX). The signals listed in Table A–1 are on-hook or off-hook signals of various durations to convey different meanings, as summarized in the far right-hand column of the table.

Figure A–7 builds on the information provided in Table A–1 and shows the typical operations involved in the setting up of a call. One point should be made regarding the signaling between the originating office (CO) and the terminating office (CO). The example shows conven-

Table A–1   On-hook and off-hook signals

Name	Type	Direction Originating Terminating	Meaning
Connect	Off-hook	——————————>	Request service and hold connection
Disconnect	On-hook	——————————>	Release connection
Answer	Off-hook	——————————>	Terminating end has answered
Hang up	On-hook	<——————————	Message complete
Delay start	Off-hook	<——————————	Terminating end not ready for digits
Wink start	Off-hook	<——————————	Terminating end ready to receive digits
Start dialing	On-hook	<——————————	Terminating end ready for digits
Stop	Off-hook	<——————————	Terminating end not ready for further digits
Go	On-hook	<——————————	Terminating end ready for further digits
Idle trunk	On-hook	<—————————->	
Busy trunk	Off-hook	<—————————->	

tional on-hook and off-hook signaling, which has been the method used in the past. Newer systems replace this type of signaling with message-based operations. The same type of information is carried between the offices, but it is conveyed in a signaling protocol that contains digital codes (fields) in the message. This "new" type of signaling is an example of Signaling System Number 7 (SS7), discussed in Appendix B.

ACCESS-LINE SIGNALING

Access-line signaling can be implemented in a number of ways. The most common scheme used in the public telephone network is known as loop-start signaling. It is employed in the Bell Operating Companies' (BOC's) Message Telecommunications Service (MTS) for residence and business lines, the public telephone service, data/facsimile service, and private

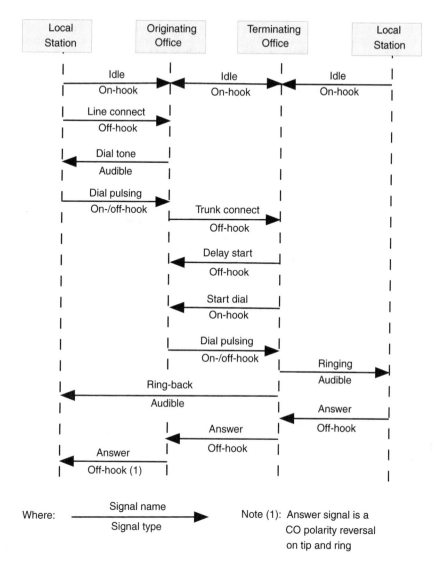

Figure A–7 Typical signaling in a connection operation

branch exchange (PBX) or automatic call distributor (ACD) service (see Figure A–8).

Loop-start signaling requires that the network connect the "tip" connector to the positive end and the "ring" connector to the negative end of the power supply for an on-hook (idle) state. Stated another way, battery is on ring and ground is on tip. The voltage supply is usually 48 volts (V),

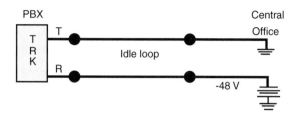

(a) Loop start: Battery always on ring and ground on tip

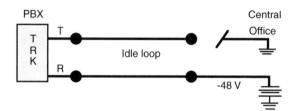

(b) Ground start: Battery always on ring and ground on/off on tip

Figure A–8   Loop start and ground start signaling

but different line conditions may cause the voltage to vary from as low as 0 V to as high as 105 V.

The Bell system imposes stringent requirements on vendors' systems with regard to access-line signaling. Nonetheless, within the confines of the standards, variations do exist. The variations are well documented and well understood and usually do not present a major problem to the end user.

Most vendors' products establish a timer upon placing dial tone on the line until the detection of the first address signal. While implementations vary, if an address signal is not received between 5–40 s, the loop is connected either to an announcement or to a receiver-on-hook (ROH) tone and then to an open-circuit condition.

After all the address signals have been sent to the network, the calling party may hear call-progress tones, and, of course, audible-ringing signals indicate a successful connection. At the calling end, the ringing signal comprises a 88 V, 20 Hz signal superimposed upon a 48-V nominal dc voltage. The ringing signal detector usually detects this signal, which is followed by about 4 seconds of silence.

Because of this operation, a Central Office line can be seized up to 4 seconds before the seizure is detected by the user station. The possible outcome of this situation is that a person may attempt to establish a call during this period. This is not a big problem since the person who originates the call from that station is the person to whom the call is intended anyway. You have experienced this situation when you pick up the phone and the party you want to call is already connected to you. It is not a poltergeist in action; there is really a practical explanation for it.

When the called party answers the call, the off-hook action removes the ringing signal and cuts through the talking path. This removal, called a tripping interval, usually lasts 200 ms, although ringing can continue for longer intervals before it is tripped.

Of course, either party can end the call by going on-hook. This forces the telephone instrument to an idle state and no dc-loop current flows to the circuit. During this disconnect operation, the network does not send any type of signal to the called or calling terminal.

The ground-start signaling for a two-way dial system is an old technology (introduced in the 1920s). It is used typically on two-way PBX Central Office trunks with direct outward dialing (DOD) and attendant-handled incoming call service. The ground-start line conductors transmit common battery-loop supervision, dual-tone multifrequency (DTMF) address signaling or loop dial pulses, alerting signals, and voiceband electrical energy.

Even though ground-start lines are an old technology, they may be used in place of loop-start lines because (a) they provide a signal that can act as a start-dial signal (it is not necessary to detect dial tone in most situations), (b) they provide a positive indication of a new call, (c) they help prevent unauthorized calls, and (d) they indicate to the calling or called party the distant-end disconnect under normal operation.

Many examples could be provided with incoming calls, outgoing calls, disconnects, and of course, ground start and loop start. Our approach here is to provide two examples to give you an understanding of the overall operations. Our examples are ground-start trunk with an incoming call sequence and a loop-start trunk with an outgoing call sequence.

Figure A–9 provides an example of an incoming call (that is, a call from the network to the subscriber) using ground-start techniques. In Figure A–9(a), the trunk is initially idle with battery on the ring with the tip open. This is called an idle state with the trunk in the high resistance.

In Figure A–9(b), the CO seizes the trunk by grounding the tip and superimposing the 20 Hz, 86-Vac ringing on the ring lead and placing ground on tip. This operation leads to a trunk seizure state on the trunk. The receiver sees a change of state and logic as the receiver reports the change of ground state; the state change makes the trunk busy to all

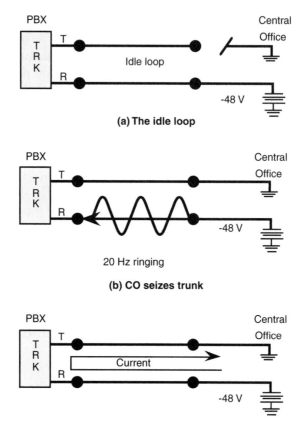

(a) The idle loop

(b) CO seizes trunk

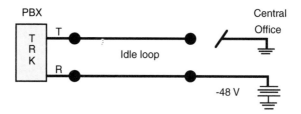

(c) Call answered, loop resistance changes, CO removes ring

(d) Parties hang up, CO disconnects by removing ground on tip

Figure A–9   Ground start signaling example

other calls. The ringing at the CO is superimposed on battery, and the call is presented to the receiver.

If the receiver is a PBX, the call is presented to an attendant, which would be a console loopkey. When the receiver answers, the loop is effectively closed, as shown in Figure A–9(c). The loop changes resistance with the current flowing across the ring and the tip (low resistance). This is an indication for the CO to remove ringing. Thereafter, the two-way voice path is established with battery on ring and ground on tip.

When a customer hangs up the handset, the CO disconnects by removing ground on tip. So, the tip is open, the battery is on ring, and the loop is once again in the idle state, as shown in Figure A–9(d).

The second example is a loop-start trunk showing an outgoing call sequence (see Figure A–10). With loop start, the idle trunk exists with battery on ring and ground on tip (Figure A–10[a]). When a call is to be processed, the PBX seizes the trunk by closing its connection from ring to tip. This changes the loop from high resistance to low resistance (Figure A–10[b]). When the CO detects low resistance, it returns dial tone to the sender (Figure A–10[c]).

Upon detecting the dial tone, the sender begins outpulsing the dialed digits (Figure A–10[d]). The CO removes the dial tone upon detecting the first pulse from the sender. The call is forwarded to the network when outpulsing is complete. The network is then responsible for forwarding the call to the called party.

When the called party answers, the network returns an "off hook" signal back to the originating CO; this CO reverses the polarity on the tip and ring leads (Figure A-10[e]). This reversal is detected by the calling end, and the call takes place.

OTHER SIGNALING EXAMPLES

Digital signaling systems must support (interwork with) the older analog signaling systems because analog is still the pervasive technology used in the local loop. The next part of this discussion shows two common operations.

These examples are not all-inclusive, but they represent common implementations. For the reader who needs information on each service option offered by the U.S. BOCs, I refer you to [BELL94].

Example One: Feature Group B

The BOCs classify several of their access arrangements with the title "feature group." This example is feature group B, which specifies an access agreement between an LEC end office (EO) and an interexchange carrier (IC) (see Figure A–11).

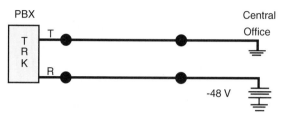

(a) High-resistance loop; battery on ring, ground on tip

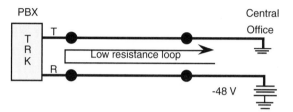

(b) High-resistance loop replaced with low-resistance loop

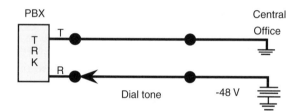

(c) CO detects low resistance and returns dial tone

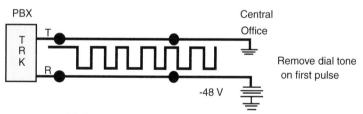

(d) Outpulsing from the calling end begins

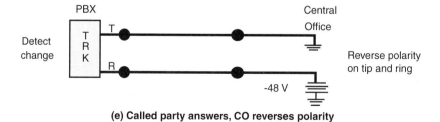

(e) Called party answers, CO reverses polarity

Figure A–10   Loop-start signaling example

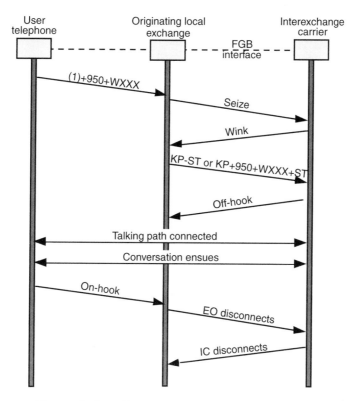

Figure A–11 Example of trunk-side access

With this arrangement, the calls to the IC must use the initial address of (I) + 950 + WXXX, where: W = 0/1.

Figure A–11 is largely self-descriptive, but some rules for the signaling sequences shown in the figure should be helpful. For calls from EOs or an access tandem: (a) the carrier returns a wink signal with 4 seconds of trunk seizure, and (b) the carrier returns an off-hook signal within 5 seconds of completion of the address outpulsing. For calls originating from a carrier to an EO or access tandem: (a) the end office or access tandem returns the wink start signal within 8 seconds of trunk seizure; (b) the carrier starts outpulsing the address with 3.5 seconds of the wink; and (c) the carrier completes sending the address sequence within 20 seconds.

Example Two: Operator Service Signaling

Operating service signaling (OSS) is similar to one of the feature groups, but it has some characteristics that may be more familiar to the reader. Figure A–12 shows these operations, with six events.

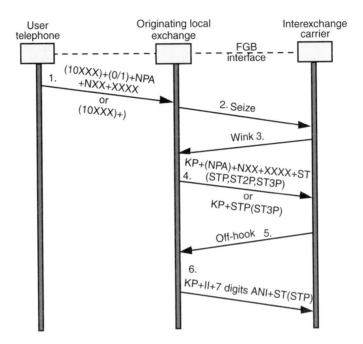

Figure A–12   Operator service signaling (OSS)

In event 1, the customer dials 10XXX + (1) + 7 or 10, or 10XXX + 0 + 7 or 10. Upon receiving these signals, the EO (event 2) seizes an outgoing trunk. In event 3, the OS facility responds with a wink. Upon receiving the wink signal the EO outpulses in event 4 the called number after a delay of 40–200 ms. The outpulsing is KP + 7 or 10 digits + ST (STP, ST2P, ST3P), or KP + STP(ST3P)

In event 5, the OS facility will go off-hook (any time after the start of the ST pulse). Off-hook indicates its ability to receive ANI.

In event 6, the EO sends the ANI (after a delay of 40–200 ms). The signals are KP + 02 + ST (STP).

Appendix B

ISDN and SS7

During the past thirty years, the telephone system has been migrating to digital, message-based signaling. Two technologies have led the way: the Integrated Services Digital Network (ISDN) and Signaling System Number 7 (SS7).

This appendix provides tutorials on these two technologies. There is also ISDN information in Chapter 7 (see Figure 7–5).

PLACEMENT OF ISDN AND SS7

It should be helpful during this introductory discussion to explain where these signaling technologies operate in relation to the customer premises equipment (CPE) and the network. Figure B–1 depicts the placement of ISDN and SS7.

The most common placement of ISDN and SS7 is to operate ISDN between the CPE (user) and the network node (such as a switch) and to run SS7 inside the network as the trunking protocol between switches. While this placement is a common practice, it does not preclude running SS7 between the CPE and the network node.

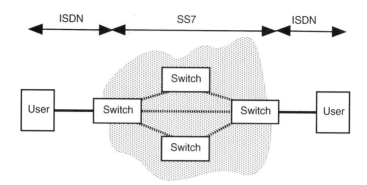

Figure B–1   System placement

ISDN is designed to operate at the boundaries of the network, but once again, no technical reason exists for not placing it inside the network. However, it is not done here because it conflicts with SS7 systems.

As we develop the analysis of ISDN and SS7, it will become evident that the two systems are designed to complement each other: ISDN at the user-network interface (UNI), and SS7 at the network node interface (NNI).

ISDN SIGNALING MESSAGES

Many of the VoIP Gateway operations entail the processing of ISDN signaling messages. These messages and their functions are defined in the ITU-T Q.931 Recommendation.

The ISDN Q.931 messages are used to manage ISDN connections on the B channels. These messages are also used (with modifications) by Frame Relay and ATM for setting up calls on demand at a UNI and for provisioning services between networks at an NNI. Table B–1 lists these messages; the functions of the more significant messages are briefly explained below.

- *ALERTING:* This message is sent as a notification that the called user party has been "alerted" and the call is being processed. This message is sent in response to an incoming SETUP message, and it is sent in the backward direction (backwards from the called end to the calling end) after the called exchange has placed ringing signals on the line to the called party.

Table B–1   ISDN layer-3 messages[1]

Call Establishment

ALERTING

CALL PROCEEDING

CONNect

CONNect ACKnowledge

PROGRESS

SETUP

SETUP ACKNOWLEDGE

Call Disestablishment

DISCONNNECT

RELEASE

RELEASE COMPLETE

RESTART

RESTART ACKNOWLEDGE

Call Information Phase

RESUME

RESUME ACKNOWLEDGE

RESUME REJECT

SUSPEND

SUSPEND ACKNOWLEDGE

SUSPEND REJECT

USER INFORMATION

Miscellaneous

CANCEL

CANCEL ACKNOWLEDGE

CANCEL REJECT

CONGESTION CONTROL

FACILITY

FACILITY ACKNOWLEDGE

FACILITY REJECT

INFORMATION

REGISTER

REGISTER ACKNOWLEDGE

REGISTER REJECT

STATUS

STATUS INQUIRY

[1]Use of these messages varies across vendors and national boundaries.

- *CALL PROCEEDING:* This message is sent to the call initiator to notify it that the call establishment procedures have been initiated. It also advises that all information necessary to set up the connection has been received and that any other call establishment information will not be accepted. In ISDN-conformant implementations, the CALL PROCEEDING message is exchanged only at the originating end of the connection.

- *CONGESTION CONTROL:* This message is employed only on USER INFORMATION messages. As the name implies, it governs the flow of USER INFORMATION messages. In most implementations, congestion control is not used, or if it is used, it is rarely invoked.

- *CONNECT:* When the called party picks up the telephone and goes off-hook, this action precipitates the invocation of this message. The message is sent in the backward direction (from the called party to the calling party) to signal the call acceptance by the called party.

- *CONNECT ACKNOWLEDGE:* This message is sent in response to the CONNECT message. Its invocation means that the parties have been awarded the call.

- *DISCONNECT:* This message is sent when either party (calling or called) hangs up the telephone (goes on-hook). It is a trigger to the network that the end-to-end connection is to be cleared and the resources reserved for the connection are to be made available for another call.

- *INFORMATION:* As the name implies, this message is sent by either the user or the network to provide more information about a connection. For example, the message can be invoked by an exchange if it is to provide additional information about a connection to another exchange.

- *NOTIFY:* This message is not often used but is available for the user or the network to provide information regarding a connection. The NOTIFY message contains a field called the notification indicator, which is described in the next section of this appendix.

- *PROGRESS:* The progress message is part of the call establishment procedure, although it is not invoked in a typical implementation. However, it is available to indicate the progress of a call and it is invoked in situations where interworking is required or where the exchanges need to provide information about in-band information. This information is provided through a field, called the process indicator, in the message. The field is described in the next section.

- *RELEASE:* This message is invoked in response to the reception of a DISCONNECT message. It is sent by the network or the user to notify its recipient that the equipment has disconnected the circuit that had been reserved for the connection. In essence, it tells the receiver that it should also release the circuit. The RELEASE message is designed also to free and make available the call reference numbers (and the associated resources) associated with the call.

- *RELEASE COMPLETE:* As the name implies, this message is sent in response to the RELEASE message. It indicates by its invocation that the sender has released the circuit, the call reference, and, of course, the resources associated with the connection. The combination of the RELEASE and RELEASE COMPLETE messages means that the circuit has been completely cleared and made available for other calls and that the call reference is no longer valid.

- *RESUME:* This message is used for a relatively simple operation, which is to request that the network resume a suspended call. The arrangements for resuming a suspended call vary among network providers, but the idea is to allow users to change their minds (within a brief period of time) upon hanging up.

- *RESUME ACKNOWLEDGE:* This message is sent by the network in response to the RESUME message. It indicates the completion of a request to RESUME a suspended call.

- *RESUME REJECT:* This message is sent by the network to report that it cannot fulfill the request to resume a suspended call.

- *SETUP:* The setup message contains more information elements than any of the other Q.931 messages. It is used to begin the call setup procedure. The SETUP message is always issued by the calling user to the network at the originating end and by the network to the called user at the terminating end.

- *SETUP ACKNOWLEDGE:* This message is sent in response to the SETUP message to acknowledge that the SETUP message has been received correctly. It signifies that call establishment has been initiated. It may also signify that additional information may be required to complete the call. For the latter case, the recipient of the SETUP ACKNOWLEDGE is required to send the additional information that is coded in an INFORMATION message.

- *STATUS:* This message is sent in response to a STATUS EN-QUIRY message. It may also be sent in the event of certain error conditions that occur at a network node.

- *STATUS ENQUIRY:* This message is sent by either the user or the network to inquire about the status of an ongoing operation, such as a call in progress. Both the STATUS and STATUS EN-QUIRY messages are intended to be flexible enough to allow the implement or latitude in the implementation. The only information element in these messages is the display information element described later in this chapter.

- *SUSPEND, SUSPEND ACKNOWLEDGE, and SUSPEND RE-JECT:* The SUSPEND message is sent from the user to request that the network suspend the call. The direction of the message is important in that the network is not allowed to send this message, so call suspension can only be initiated by the user. SUSPEND ACKNOWLEDGE is an acknowledgment by the network of the reception of the SUSPEND message; it also indicates the completion of the call suspension. SUSPEND REJECT is an acknowledgment by the network of the reception of the SUSPEND message, but it indicates that the network did not suspend the call.

  ISDN permits calls to be suspended. The reason for the suspensions are not defined in the specifications. Whatever the reasons, Q.931 supports these operations with the three methods described above.

- *USER INFORMATION:* This message is slightly different from the INFORMATION message described earlier, in that it contains parameters different from those of the INFORMATION message. The major aspect is the existence of the user-user field, which does not reside in the INFORMATION message. As the next section explains, the user-user field is passed transparently by ISDN to ISDSN users.

- *FACILITY:* This message is used by either the user or the network to provide additional information about a call. Examples are key-pad facility and display information, described in the next section.

- *RESTART:* This message is sent by the user or the network to request a restart of a connection. It returns the identified channel to an idle state.

- *RESTART ACKNOWLEDGE:* This message acknowledges the RESTART message.

EXAMPLE OF CALL SETUP WITH Q.931 MESSAGES

Q.931 Example

Figure B–2 provides an example of how a call is set up with the Q.931 messages. The two persons involved in this connection are using conventional telephone handsets that are attached to ISDN terminals, shown in this figure as the calling terminal and the called terminal. The exchange terminations (ETs) are located at the Central Offices.

The calling party goes off-hook and dials the telephone number of the called party. The calling terminal uses this information to create an ISDN SETUP message, which is sent across the ISDN line to the local ET. This ET acknowledges the message with the SETUP ACK message and initiates actions to set up a circuit to the next ET, which is shown in

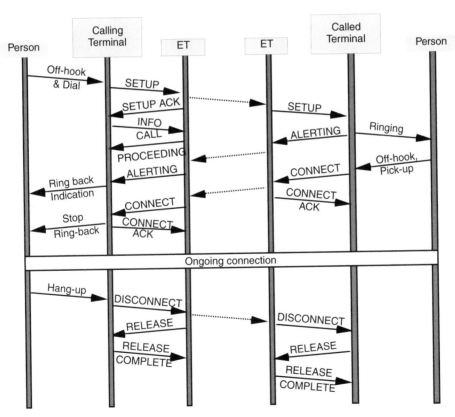

Figure B–2 ISDN signaling example (Note: use of INFO varies)

the figure with the dashed arrow. The SETUP ACK and INFORMATION messages are optional; they were described in the previous section. The local ET sends a CALL PROCEEDING message to the calling terminal to notify it that the call is being processed.

At the called end, the SETUP message is forwarded to the called terminal by the terminating ET. This terminal examines the contents of the message to determine who is being called and what services are being requested. It checks the called party's line to see if it is idle, and if so, places the ringing signal on the line. When the ringing signal is placed on the line, the called terminal transmits in the backward direction an ALERTING message, which is passed all the way to the calling terminal. This message tells the calling terminal that the called party has been signaled, and that notification allows a ring-back signal to be placed on the line to the calling party.

When the called party answers the call, the called terminal sends back a CONNECT message, which is passed to the calling terminal. Upon receipt of this message, ring-back is removed from the line and the connection is cut through to the calling party. The CONNECT messages are acknowledged with CONNECT ACK messages.

The on-hook action initiates the ISDN connection termination operations. The DISCONNECT messages are used to indicate that the connection is to be terminated. The RELEASE and RELEASE COMPLETE messages follow the DISCONNECT messages.

MAJOR FUNCTIONS OF SS7

SS7 defines the procedures for the setup, ongoing management, and clearing of a call between telephone users. It performs these functions by exchanging telephone control messages between the SS7 components that support the end-user's connection.

SS7 TOPOLOGY

Figure B–3 depicts a typical SS7 topology. The subscriber lines are connected to the SS7 network through the service switching points (SSPs). The SSPs receive the signals from the CPE and perform call processing on behalf of the user. SSPs are implemented at end offices or access tandem devices. They serve as the source and destination for SS7 messages.

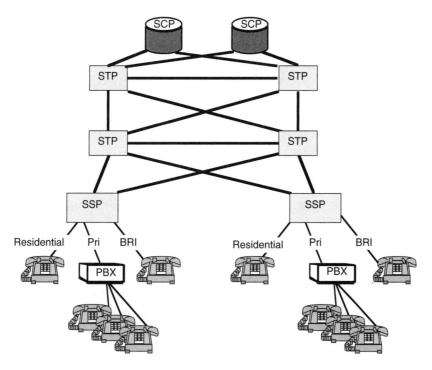

Note: Another node called the signaling point (SP) can exist between user and SSP.

Figure B–3   Typical SS7 topology

In so doing, SSP initiates SS7 messages either to another SSP or to a signaling transfer point (STP).

The STP is tasked with the translation of the SS7 messages and the routing of those messages between network nodes and databases. The STPs are switches that relay messages between SSPs, STPs, and service control points (SCPs). Their principal functions are similar to the layer-3 operations of the OSI model.

The SCPs contain software and databases for the management of the call. For example, 800 services and routing are provided by the SCP. They receive traffic (typically, requests for information) from SSPs via STPs and appropriately respond (via STPs) to the query.

Although the figure shows the SS7 components as discrete entities, they are often implemented in an integrated fashion by a vendor's equipment. For example, a Central Office can be configured with an SSP, an STP, and an SCP, or any combination of these elements. These SS7 components are explained in more detail later in this section.

The SSP

The service switching point (SSP) is the local exchange to the subscriber and the interface to the telephone network. It can be configured as a voice switch, an SS7 switch, or a computer connected to switch.

The SSP creates SS7 signal units at the sending SSP and translates them at the receiving SSP. In that way, it converts voice signaling into the SS7 signal units, and vice versa. It also supports database access queries for 800 and 900 numbers

The SSP uses the dialed telephone numbers to access a routing table to determine a final exchange and uses the outgoing trunk to reach this exchange. The SS7 connection request message is then sent to the final exchange.

The STP

The signal transfer point (STP) is a router for the SS7 network. It relays messages through the network but does not originate them. It is usually an adjunct to a voice switch and does not usually stand alone as a separate machine.

The STP is installed as a national STP, an international STP, or a gateway STP. Even though SS7 is an international standard, countries vary the way in which some of the features and options are implemented. The STP provides the conversions of the messages that flow between dissimilar systems. For example, in the United States, the STP provides conversions between ANSI SS7 and ITU-T SS7.

STPs also offer screening services, such as security checks on incoming or outgoing messages. The STP can also screen messages to make certain they are acceptable (conformant) to the specific network.

Other STP functions include the acquisition and storage of traffic and usage statistics for OAM and billing. If necessary, the STP provides an originating SCP with the address of the destination SCP.

The SCP

The service control point (SCP) acts as the interface into the telephone company databases. These databases contain information on the subscriber, 800 and 900 numbers, calling cards, fraud data, etc. The SCP is usually linked to computers and databases through X.25. The SCP address is a point code, and the address of the database is a subsystem number (addresses are explained shortly).

Bellcore provides guidance on SCP databases, but BOCs vary in how they use them. The most common databases used are:

- Business Services Database (BSDB)
- Call Management Service Database (CMSDB)
- Line Information Database (LIDB)
- Home Location Register (HLR)
- Visitor Location Register (VLR)

SS7 LAYERS

Figure B–4 provides a more detailed description of the SS7 layers and serves as an introduction to subsequent material on these levels. MTP level 1 performs the functions of a traditional OSI physical layer. It generates and receives the signals on the physical channel.

MTP level 2 relates closely to the OSI layer 2. It is a conventional data link level and is responsible for the delivery of traffic on each link

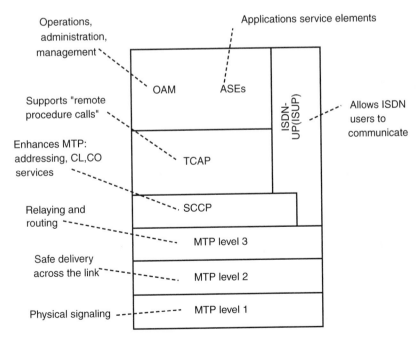

Figure B–4   The SS7 layers

between SS7 nodes. The traffic in the upper layers of SS7 are encapsulated into MTP 2 "signal units" (this term is used instead of the conventional HDLC "frame") and sent onto the channel to the receiving node. This node checks for errors that may have occurred during transmission and takes remedial action (discussed later).

MTP level 3 performs OSI layer-3 functions, notably, the routing of messages between machine and between components within a machine. It performs load sharing operations across multiple links and reconfiguration operations in the event of node or link failure.

SCCP corresponds to several of the operations associated with OSI layer 3 (and although not generally discussed in literature, OSI layer 4, as well). Some of its principal jobs are (a) supporting the MTP levels with global addressing, (b) providing connectionless or connection-oriented services, and (c) providing sequencing and flow-control operations.

The transaction capabilities application part (TCAP) corresponds to several of the functions of the OSI layer 7. It uses the remote operations service element (ROSE) with which it performs connectionless, remote procedure calls on behalf of an "application" running on top of it.

Finally, the ISDN user part (ISDN-UP or ISUP) provides the services needed to support applications running in an ISDN environment.

SS7 POINT CODES

SS7 nodes are identified with an address, and each node must have a unique address. The SS7 addresses are called point codes (PCs) (see Figure B–5). The point code is a hierarchical address consisting of a network identifier, a network cluster, and a network cluster member. The network identifier, as its name implies, identifies a unique network (123 in the example). The network cluster identifies a cluster of nodes which belong to a network (1 or 2 in the example). Typically, a cluster of signaling nodes consists of a group that home in on a mated pair of STPs. They can be addressed as a group. The network cluster member code identifies a single node operating within a cluster (1, 2, 3, or 4 in this example).

The structure of the point code fields is different in U.S., ITU-T, and other national specifications. Each country can implement its own point code structure but is expected to support an ITU-T structure at the international gateway between two countries.

In addition to the point code (PC) used by MTP for routing to a node in the network, SS7 also uses a subsystem number (SSN). This number does not pertain to a node but to entities within a node, such as an appli-

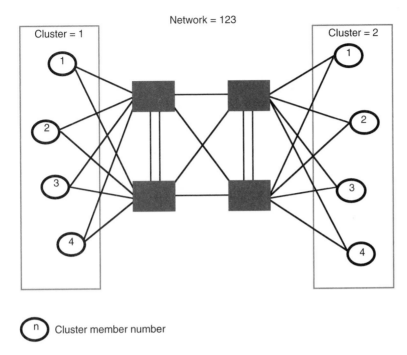

Figure B–5   SS7 numbering plan with point codes

cation or some other software entity. As examples, it could identify enhanced 800 (E800) services running in a node or an automated calling card service (ACCS) module operating in the node.

SS7 also supports the global title (GT) identifier. Perhaps the best way to view GT is that it is mapped to an SS7 network address of PC + SSN.

ISUP

This book has discussed SS7 and ISDN as separate subjects. Indeed, they are separate, and they perform different operations in a transport and signaling network architecture. However, SS7 and ISDN are "partners" in that ISDN assumes SS7 will set up the connections within a network and SS7 assumes ISDN will set up connections at network boundaries (outside the network). Therefore, we can view ISDN as a user-network interface (UNI) operating between the user device and the network node, and we can view SS7 as a network node interface (NNI) operating be-

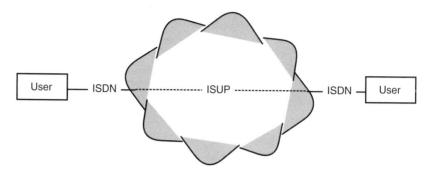

Figure B–6   ISDN user part (ISUP)

tween the nodes within the network. Of course, nothing precludes using SS7 as an internetworking interface allowing two networks to communicate with each other.

The ISDN user part (ISUP) coordinates the activities of ISDN and SS7. In effect, ISUP "bridges" the two ISDN UNIs across the SS7 network. Figure B–6 shows this relationship.

Table B–2 shows the names of the major ISUP messages, their abbreviations, and their functions. The table is self-explanatory.

Table B–2   ISUP call processing messages

Message	Name	Meaning
ACM	Address Complete Message	All information necessary to complete a call has been received.
ANM	ANswer Message	Called party has answered (used also for billing start in toll calls).
CPG	Call ProGress	An event of significance to the originator has occurred (backward direction only).
IAM	Initial Address Message	This is an invitation to establish a call.
PAM	Pass Along Message	Passes other messages; used like a "mailing envelope."
RLC	ReLease Complete	Circuit has been placed in an idle state.
RLS	ReLeaSe	Circuit is being released for reasons given (see cause value).

EXAMPLE OF ISDN AND SS7 SIGNALING

In this section, we piece together some of the information explained earlier by providing an example of how the SS7 signaling procedures and call setup occur. This example also shows the relationship of ISDN and SS7 connections.

As depicted in Figure B–7, a call setup begins when a telephone or PBX (in this example) send an ISDN setup message, which is used to create the SS7 initial address message (IAM). This message is sent to an exchange. The IAM contains all the information required to set up and route the call. All codes and digits required for the call routing through the national (and international) network will be sent in this message. Other signals can also be sent in certain situations. For example, the end of pulsing (ST) signal is sent to signify that the final digit has been sent

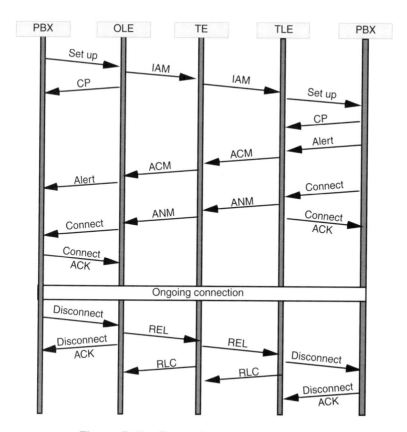

Figure B–7   Example of an ISDN/SS7 call

of the digits in the national or international numbers. Also, since the SS7 network does not pass over the speech path, it must provide facilities to provide a continuity check of the speech circuit to be used. It also makes cross-office checks to ensure the reliability of the connection through the various digital exchanges.

A call is processed by the outgoing exchange analyzing the address signals in the message. Based on these address messages, an appropriate outgoing circuit is seized and an initial address message (IAM) is forwarded to the next exchange.

This exchange analyzes the address message to determine the following information: (a) the circuit to be seized; (b) routing through another country if necessary; (c) the nature of the circuit (terrestrial or satellite); (d) whether echo control is needed; (e) the calling party's category; and, (f) the need for continuity checks. The exchanges will disable any echo suppressors (if necessary) at this time.

If all the checks are completed successfully, the network begins the call establishment (when enough address signals are received to determine routing). The address messages are analyzed to determine if all the required signals have been received, at which time the speech path setup is completed. The destination exchange provides a ringing tone back to the originator. Upon the receiving telephone user answering the call, the answer signals are returned by the originating exchange to the user.

At the receiving end, the SS7 IAM is mapped back to the ISDN Setup message and sent to the terminating PBX. Notice the Call Proceeding messages that are sent in response to the Setup messages.

Once the terminating end answers the call, an ISDN Connect message is sent to the network, which maps this message into an SS7 answer message (ANM), which is then mapped into an ISDN Connect message and given to the originating caller.

Eventually, one of the subscribers hangs up, which activates an ISDN Disconnect message, and in turn, the messages shown in the bottom part of Figure B–7 are sent. After a certain period of waiting, if no other signals emanate from the end user, additional supervisory signals are exchanged between the two exchanges to make the circuit available for new traffic.

Appendix C

Tutorial on the V.34 and V.90 Modems

Welcome to the world of intelligent modems. Just a few short years ago, modems were rather prosaic instruments and did little else but transport digital bits across the analog link. Today's modems are quite different from their predecessors, as we will see in this examination of V.34 and V.90. I have included V.34 in this discussion because the newer V.90 modem in the fallback mode uses the V.34 operations on the analog side of the modem. V.90 also uses V.34 modulation in the upstream direction (from user modem to the network.)

THE V.34 MODEM: DERIVATIONS

To begin this analysis, we see in Table C–1 an extraction of several tables in the V.34 Recommendation. (We will be using the 2400 and 3200 symbol rates and high carrier throughout this discussion.)

The symbol rate is S = (a/c) × 2400 ± 0.01% two-dimensional (2D) symbols per second. Therefore, using Table C–1, we derive the symbol rate of 3200 by (4/3) × 2400 = 3200.

The carrier frequency is C = (d/e) × S. Using Table C–1 once again, we derive a carrier frequency of 1800 by (3/4) × 2400 = 1800. A carrier frequency of 1920 is derived by (3/5) × 3200 = 1920.

Table C–1 Symbol rates and carrier frequencies

				----High Carrier----		Framing Parameter	
Symbol Rate, S	a	c	Frequency	d	e	J	P
2400	1	1	1800	3	4	7	12
3200	4	3	1920	3	5	7	16

	SWP, b.				
	----S = 2400--			----S = 3200---	
	----P = 12------			----P = 16------	
Signaling Rate	b	SWP		b	SWP
2400	8	FFF		–	–
28800	–	–		72	FFFF

(Note: Partial examples, see V.34 for complete tables)

V.34 alternates between sending b – 1 and b bits per mapping frame, based on a switching pattern SWP (of period P in the table). The result is that the transmission of a fractional number of bits per mapping frame is N/P. The value of b is the smallest integer not less than N/P.

SWP consists of 12- to 16-bit binary numbers. V.34 contains information on all combinations of signaling rate and symbol rate. For our examples of S = 2400 and 3200, the second table gives some partial examples of b, SWP. The value of SWP is shown as a hex value.

As with all V Series modems, V.34 uses a subset of the V.24 interchange circuits. Table C–2 summarizes these circuits. V.24 is a "superset" recommendation, and all the V Series modems use a subset of the V.24 interchange circuits.

THE V.34 MODEM: PHASES

The Four Phases

V.34 executes four phases before it begins sending user data (in superframes). Some of these procedures are defined in V.8. This section examines each phase. For clarity, we describe some of the V.8 and V.34 terms with a general description that you should be able to follow without having to read (at least, initially) the V.8 and V.34 recommendations. Table C–3 defines the V.8 and V.34 signals that are used in this discussion. Table C–3 does not show the bit structure for each signal. Study V.8

Table C–2   The V.34 use of V.24 interchange circuits

Interchange Circuit	Description
102	Signal ground or common return
103	Transmitted data
104	Received data
105	Request to send
106	Ready for sending
107	Data set ready
108/1 or 108/2	Data terminal ready
109	Data channel received line signal detector
113	Transmitter signal element timing (DTE source)[1]
114	Transmitter signal element timing (DCE source)[2]
115	Receiver signal element timing (DCE source)[2]
125	Calling indicator
133	Ready for receiving[3]
140	Loopback/maintenance
141	Local loopback
142	Test indicator
118	Transmitted secondary channel data[4]
119	Received secondary channel data[4]
120	Transmit secondary channel line signal[4,5]
121	Secondary channel ready[4,5]
122	Secondary channel received line signal detector[4,5,6]

[1]When the modem is not operating in a synchronous mode at the interface, any signals on this circuit shall be disregarded. Many DTEs operating in an asynchronous mode do not have a generator connected to this circuit.

[2]When the modem is not operating in a synchronous mode at the interface, this circuit shall be clamped to the OFF condition. Many DTEs operating in an asynchronous mode do not terminate this circuit.

[3]Operation of circuit 133 shall be in accordance with 7.3.1/V.42.

[4]This circuit is provided where the optional secondary channel is implemented without a separate interface.

[5]This circuit need only be provided where required by the application.

[6]This circuit is in the ON condition if circuit 109 is in the ON condition and the optional secondary channel is enabled.

Table C-3   Key V.8 and V.34 signals and their use

Notation	Name	Function
CI	Function indicator signal	Indicates a session
ANSam	Modified answer tone	Is a response to a CI signal
Te	——	Is a silent period, which begins with the termination of the call signal or after detection of ANSam. Can be used for echo canceller disabling if necessary
CM	Call menu signal	Initiates modulation-mode selection[1,2,3]
JM	Joint menu signal	Is a response to the CM signal[1,2,3]
CJ	CM terminator	Acknowledges JM signal and terminates CM signal
INFO	Information sequence	Exchanges modem capabilities, results of line probing, and data mode modulation parameters[4]
A, A	2400 Hz tone	Transmitted by answer modem, with A and A representing 180° phase reversals of 2400 Hz tone
B, B	1200 Hz tone	Transmitted by call modem, with B and B representing a 180° phase reversal of the 1200 Hz tone
L1, L2	Line probing signals	Used to analyze channel characteristics
S, S	——	Sent as part of quarter-super constellation rotation
MD	Manufacturer-defined signal	Trains a vendor-specific echo canceller
PR	——	Trains an equalizer
TRN	——	Is a sequence of symbols chosen from 4- or 16-point 2D constellation
J	——	Indicates 4- or 16-point constellation size used by remote modem
J'	——	Terminates the J sequence
MP, MP'	Modulator parameter sequences	Contains parameters to negotiate signaling rate, trellis code choice, auxiliary channel enable, amount of constellation shaping
E	——	Signals end of MP
B1	——	Sent at the end of startup

[1]Part of the signal is used to indicate the V Series modulation modes: (a) V.34 half-duplex or duplex, (b) V.32/V.32 bis, (c) V.22/V.22 bis, (d) V.17, (e) V.29 half-duplex, (f) V.27 ter, (g) V.26 ter, (h) V.26 bis, (i) V.23 half-duplex or duplex, and (j) V.21. For CM, it indicates the suggested signaling mode; for JM, it indicates the lowest signaling mode.
[2]Part of the signal is used to indicate the use of LAPM (V.42).
[3]Part of the signal is used to indicate the use of cellular access.
[4]Two sets of INFO messages are used (where a = answer modem and c = call modem): INFO0a, INFO0c and INFO1a and INFO1c.

and V.34 if you need this level of detail. The signals in the table are listed according to the order of their invocation by the V.34 modem.

As stated earlier, the V.34 modem executes four phases of operations before it is ready for data transfer. These phases are listed here and described in more detail in this section.

- Phase 1   Network interaction (see Figure C–1)
- Phase 2   Probing/ranging (see Figure C–2)
- Phase 3   Equalizer and echo canceller training (see Figure C–3)
- Phase 4   Final training (see Figure C–4)

The information in Table C–3 should be used during this analysis. Additionally, the next four sections provide a general depiction of the four phases. Be aware that these figures do not show exact timing relationships and do not show the overlapping of the signals on the duplex channel. They do show typical (but not all) sequences. This other information can be found in Section 11 of V.34.

Phase 1: Network Interaction

Figure C–1 shows the signal exchange for phase 1, network interaction. The call modem conditions its receiver to accept ANSam and then transmits CI to the answer modem. The answer modem, after it is connected to the line, remains silent for 200 ms and then transmits ANSam to the call modem and conditions its receiver to detect CM.

When the call modem receives ANSam, it remains silent for the period Te, conditions its receiver to detect JM, and sends CM to set up the categories to be used during this session (see footnotes of Table C–3).

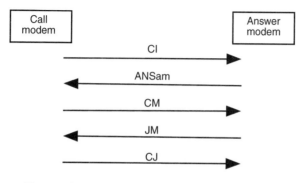

Figure C–1   Phase 1: Network interaction

The answer modem receives CM, and since CM indicates the V.34 operations, the modem sends JM and conditions its receiver to detect CJ.

The call modem, after it has sent CJ, remains silent for 75 ± 5 ms and enters phase 2. The answer modem, after receiving CJ, remains silent for 75 ± 5 ms and enters phase 2.

Phase 2: Probing and Ranging

Phase 2 is concerned with channel probing and ranging (see Figure C–2). These operations begin with the exchange of INFO0c and INFO0a, which contain the following negotiated parameters: (a) symbol rate, (b) the use of a high or low carrier, (c) maximum allowed symbol rate in the transmit and receive directions, and (d) transmit clock source.

Next, the receivers are conditioned to each other. Then, round-trip delay is calculated between the two machines by the alternate sending and receiving of Tone A and Tone B. A and B are 2400 and 1200 Hz tones, respectively, while A and B are 180° phase reversals, respectively.

The next part of phase 2 deals with the sending and receiving of L1 and L2, which are line-probing signals. They are used by the two modems to analyze the characteristics of the channel. Both L1 and L2 are a defined set of tones that enable the receiver to measure channel distortion and noise.

The final part of phase 2 deals with the exchange of INFO1c and INFO1a (see footnote 4 in Table C–3). These signals provide the following functions: (a) permissible power levels for the session and minimum power reduction that can be accepted; (b) length of MD (for phase 3); and (c) final symbol rate selection as a result of the previous probing.

Phase 3: Equalizer and Echo Canceller Training

Phase 3 is concerned with training the equalizers and the echo cancellers of both modems (see Figure C–3). The answer modem begins these procedures by sending S and S. Signal S is sent by alternating between point 0 of the quarter-superconstellation and the same point rotated counterclockwise by 90°. Signal S is sent by alternating between point 0 rotated by 180° and point 0 rotated counterclockwise by 270°.

Next, MD is sent, followed (once again) by S and S, and then PR is transmitted. The process is used to train the receiver's equalizer. The answer modem completes its phase 3 by sending TRN and J. The call modem's phase-3 procedures are identical to those of the answer modem.

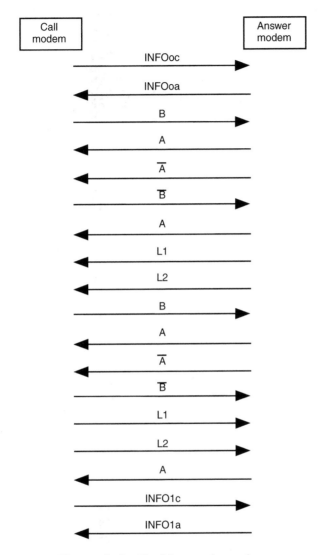

Figure C–2   Probing and ranging

Phase 4: Final Training

After the two modems have moved from phase 3 to phase 4 by exchanging J, J′, and S, S, both modems send TRN signals (discussed earlier) (see Figure C–4). Next, MP and MP′ are exchanged; they contain parameters used to negotiate a variety of the options explained in Table C–3. The E signals end the MP sequence, and the B1 signals end this phase and the overall startup procedure.

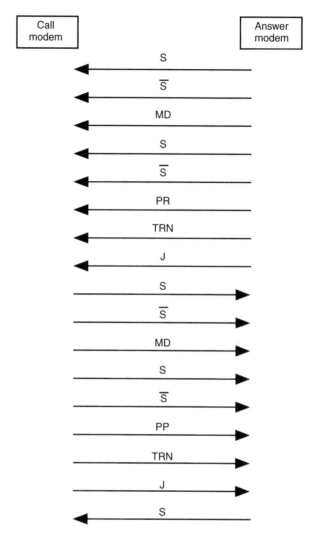

Figure C–3   Equalizer and echo canceller training

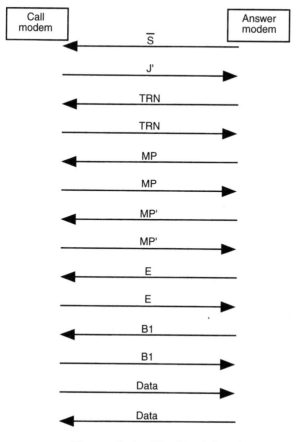

Figure C–4   Final training

THE V.90 MODEM

I have included V.34 is this discussion because the newer V.90 modem in the fallback mode uses the V.34 operations on the analog side of the modem. V.90 also uses V.34 modulation in the upstream direction (from user modem to the network).

The V.90 modem, also known as the 56-kbit/s modem, has become the dominant modem technology in the industry. It has the following characteristics:

- Operates in full duplex on telephone lines (local loops)
- Uses echo cancellation for separating channels

- Uses pulse code modulation (PCM) in the downstream direction (from network to user modem) at a symbol rate of 8000
- Has downstream data rates ranging from 28 kbit/s to 56 kbits/s

V.34 modulation is employed in the upstream direction, ranging from 4.8 kbit/s to 28.8 kbit/s, in increments of 2.4 kbit/s. It has the following characteristics:

- Optional upstream rates for 31.2 kbit/s and 33.6 kbit/s
- Adaptive signaling rate capabilities to permit the modem to operate at the maximum data rate, depending on the quality of the channel

The V.90 operates as a modem pair. The analog part of the pair is for the upstream channel, and the digital part is for the downstream channel. As stated, the analog part is based on V.34. Let us focus on the digital part.

The ITU-T G.711 Recommendation: Basis for the Digital Modem

The key to understanding the V.90 digital modem is to know about the G.711 specification. The experienced reader can skip to the next section. For the newcomer, I provide a brief tutorial on G.711 PCM.

Several methods are used to change an analog signal into a representative string of digital binary images. Even though these methods entail many processes, they are generally described in three steps: *sampling, quantizing,* and *encoding.*

The devices performing the digitizing process are called channel banks or primary multiplexers. They have two basic functions: (1) to convert analog signals to digital signals (and vice versa at the other end); and (2) to combine (multiplex) the digital signals into a single Time Division Multiplexed (TDM) data stream (and demultiplex them at the other end).

Sampling   Analog-to-digital conversion is based on Nyquist sampling theory, which states that if a signal is sampled instantaneously at regular intervals and at a rate at least twice the highest frequency in the channel, the samples will contain sufficient information to allow an accurate reconstruction of the signal.

The accepted sampling rate in the industry is 8,000 samples per second. Based on Nyquist sampling theory, this rate allows the accurate reproduction of a kHz channel, which is used as the bandwidth for a voice-grade channel. The 8,000 samples are more than sufficient to capture the signals in a telephone line if certain techniques (discussed shortly) are used.

With pulse amplitude modulation (PAM), the pulse carrier amplitude is varied with the value of the analog waveform. The pulses are fixed with respect to duration and position. PAM is classified as a modulation technique because each instantaneous sample of the wave is used to modulate the amplitude of the sampling pulse.

The 8 kHz sampling rate result in a sample pulse train of signals with a 125-microsecond (μs) time period between the pulses (1 second ÷ 8000 = .000125). Each pulse occupies 5.2 μs of this time period. Consequently, it is possible to interleave sampled pulses from other signals within the 125-μs period.

One of the problems with the conversion of an analog signal to a digital representation is that digital signals are discrete in their nature. That is, they are coded as either a binary 1 or a binary 0. In contrast, the analog signal is nondiscrete and varies continuously, displaying various levels of amplitude.

As a consequence of the nature of discrete and nondiscrete signals, it is impossible to accurately capture with digital samples the complete characteristics of the analog waveform.

Quantizing   The process of assigning values to the analog wave form is known as *quantizing* (which simply means assigning a value to something). Quantizing introduces errors into the conversion process, but their negative effects can be mitigated, as we will see shortly.

The problem illustrated in Figure C–4 is partially solved by varying the amplitude space between the quantizing values. As the figure shows, the quantizing scales are closer together for the measurement of the higher amplitude signals.

By "compression" of the quantizing scales to more accurately capture the lower amplitude signals, another goal has been achieved. Lower amplitude signals are less discernible to the human ear than are the higher amplitude signals. Therefore, it is desirable to take special actions to represent them more accurately. This goal is accomplished by the use of the varying quantizing levels.

The A-D process uses a compression technique, called *companding,* to compensate for errors in the assignment of values to each sample. (This assignment process is called companding.) Errors occur because the sampled signal may not correlate exactly to a quantizing value.

The distortion in the quantization is a function of the differences between the quantized steps. Ideally, one would like to use many quantizing steps to reduce the quantizing noise. Studies show that 2048 uniform quantizing steps provide sufficient granularity to represent the voice signal accurately. However, 2048 steps requires an 11-bit code (2^{11}), which translates to 88000 bit/s (8000×11). Since the voice signals in a telephone system can span 30 dB of variation, it makes sense to vary the distribution of the quantization steps. The variable quantizing levels reduce the quantizing noise.

The nonlinear companding is implemented in a stepwise linear process. For the μ-law, m = 255 is used and the companding value is coded by a set of eight straight-line segments that cut across the compression curve (actually eight for negative segments and eight for positive segments; since the two center segments are collinear, they are considered one).

With this approach, each segment is double the amplitude range of its preceding segment, and each segment is also one-half the slope of the preceding segment. In this manner, the segments representing the low range of PAM signals are more accurately encoded than the segments pertaining to the high range of PAM signals.

The A-law functions similarly to the μ-law characteristics. Eight positive and eight negative segments exist as in the μ-law characteristics, but the law is described as the 13-segment law.

Coding   The code of μ 255 PCM consists of (a) a one-bit polarity where 0 = positive sample value and 1 = negative sample value; (2) a three-bit segment identifier(s); and (3) a four-bit quantizing step identifier.

V.90 and the G.711 Operations

V.90 uses G.711 signals for the downstream channel. The key is the Ucord, a data unit that makes up a Ucode. The Ucodes are grouped into eight Ucords. For example, Ucord1 contains Ucodes 0–15, and Ucord8 contains Ucodes 112–127.

Table C–4   Examples of V.90 PCM codewords

Ucode	μ-law PCM	μ-law Linear	A-law PCM	A-law Linear
0	FF	0	D5	8
63	C0	1884	EA	2016
127	80	32124	AA	32256

The Ucode describes the μ-law and the A-law PCM codewords. V.90 defines the codes in a table, and Table C–4 shows several Ucodes.

The idea of the V.90 digital modem is that the values do not represent the conventional analog signal. Rather, the values are symbols. The modem generates 128 of the G.711 levels in order to send at 56 kbit/s. The proof for this rate is beyond this general discussion, but using the well-known equation of:

$$\text{Bit/s} = R_s \log_2 N_s$$
$$\text{Bit/s} \div R_s = \log_2 N_s$$
$$2^{\text{bit/s/Rs}} = N_s$$

where: R_s = symbol rate and N_s = number of symbols

The 128 value is obtained as:

$$2^{56,000/8,000} = N_s$$
$$N_s = 2^7$$
$$N_s = 1\ 28$$

The V.90 encoder creates data frames. Each data frame has a six-symbol organization. Each symbol in the data frame is called a data frame interval and is identified by a time index of i = 0 through 5.

The actual data rate is determined during the training or rate negotiation procedures. During this time, mapping parameters are established as follows:

- Six PCM code sets, one for each data frame interval 0–5, where data frame interval i has M_i members
- K, the number of modulus encoder input data bits per data frame
- S_r, the number of PCM code sign bit per data frame, used as redundancy for spectral shaping
- S, the number of spectral shaper input data bits per data frame, where $S + S_r = 6$

Based on these functions, V.90 defines the data rates achieved by different combinations of K and S during the data mode and during Phase 4 and the rate renegotiation procedures.

In some situations, the V.90 cannot achieve the 56 kbit/s rate because of a poor-quality line. Therefore, fewer levels are used. For example, a 48-kbit/s data rate requires only 2^6 levels.

For the reader who is familiar with the bandwidth theory, V.90 does not violate Shannon's Law. Furthermore, by treating the quantization levels as symbols in conventional modem symbol space (combinations of Quadrature Amplitude Modulation [QAM] amplitude and phase), we can employ many of the conventional modem techniques, such as forward error correction.

Three Reasons Not to Use a 64-kbit/s Rate

Because of FCC restrictions, the nature of codec design (DC offset problems, nonlinear distortion), and difficulty of accurately determining a quantization point, and so on, the achievable data rate is 56 kbit/s.

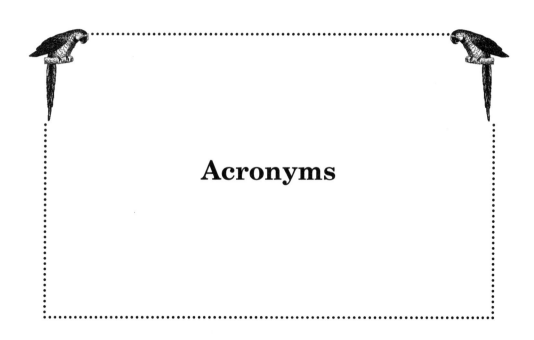

Acronyms

A

AAL	ATM adaption layer
ABR	available bit rate (service)
AbS	analysis-by-synthesis
ac	alternating current
ACCS	automated calling card service
ACK	acknowledgment (signal)
ACM	address complete message
ACELP	algebraic code excited linear prediction
A-D	analog-to-digital (conversion)
ADSL	asymmetrical digital subscriber line
ADPCM	adaptive differential pulse code modulation
ASIC	application-specific integrated circuit
AIN	advanced intelligent network
ANI	automatic number identification
ANM	answer message
ATM	asynchronous transfer mode
ATU-R	ADSL transmission unit, remote side
AVP	audio-video profile

B

BA	behavioral aggregate (classifier)
B, E	Beginning and ending bits
BGP	Border Gateway Protocol
B-ISDN	broadband-ISDN
BOC	Bell Operating Company
BRI	basic rate interface
BSDB	Business Services Database

C

CAG	Call Agent, Gatekeeper, Controller
CAP	competitive access provider
CAR	committed access rate (service)
CBR	constant bit rate
CD	compact disc
CELP	code excited linear prediction
CGMP	Cisco Group Management Protocol
CID	channel identifier
CIX	Commercial Internet Exchange

CMSDB   call management service
            database
CO   central office
CP   call proceeding
CPE   customer premise equipment
CQ   custom queuing
CPS   characters per second
CPS   cycles per second
CR   constraint-based routing
CS-ACELP   conjugate-structure-algebraic
            code excited linear
            prediction (coding)
CSB   circuit-switch bypass
cwnd   congestion window

F

FCC   Federal Communications
            Commission
FCS   Frame check sequence
FDDI   fiber distributed data interface
FEC   forward error correction
FF   fixed filter (style)
FFT   fast fourier transform
FIFO   First-in, first-out
FIR   Finite Impulse Response (filter)
FIX   Federal Internet Exchange
FM   frequency modulation
FPGA   field-programmable gate array
FR   Frame Relay
FTP   File Transfer Protocol

D

D-A   digital-to-analog (conversion)
dc   direct current
DCAR   distributed CAR
DCE   data circuit terminating
            equipment
DLCI   Data line connection ID
DNS   Domain Name System
DOD   Department of Defense
DOD   direct outward dialing
DS   differentiated services
DSL   digital subscriber line
DSP   digital signal processor
DSU   data service unit
DTE   data terminal equipment
DTMF   dual-tone multifrequency
DVMRP   Distance Vector Multicast
            Routing Protocol

G

GCF   gatekeeper confirmation
            (message)
GMT   Greenwich mean time
GPRA   generic packet rate algorithm
GR   guaranteed rate
GRJ   gatekeeper reject (message)
GRQ   gatekeeper request (message)
GSTN   general switched telephone
            network
GT   global title

H

HDLC   High level data link control
HDSL   High bit-rate DSL
HEC   header error control (field)
HF   high frequency
HFC   hybrid/fiber coax
HLR   home location register (database)
HTML   Hypertext Markup Language
HTTP   Hypertext Transfer Protocol

E

ER   explicit route
ESP   enhanced service provider
ET   exchange termination

I

IAM	initial address message
ICMP	Internet Control Message Protocol
IDC	International Data Corporation
IETF	Internet Engineering Task Force
IGMP	Internet Group Management Protocol
IP	Internet Protocol
IPDC	Internet Protocol Device Control
IPX	Internetwork Packet Exchange (protocol)
ISDN	Integrated Services Digital Network
ISO	International Standards Organization
ISP	Internet service provider
ISUP	ISDN user part
ITU-T	International Telecommunication Union-Telecommunication Standardization Bureau
IXC	interchange carrier

L

LAN	local area network
LAPB	Link Access Procedure, Balanced
LAPM	Link Access Procedure for Modems (protocol)
LD-CELP	low-delay codebook excitation linear prediction
LDP	Label Distribution Protocol
LEC	local exchange carrier
LI	length indicator (field)
LIDB	Line Information Database
LLC	logical link control
LPAS	linear prediction analysis-by-synthesis
LPC	linear prediction coding
LSP	label-switching path
LSR	label-switching router

M

MAC	media access control
MAC	multiply-and-accumulate
MAE	metropolitan area exchange
MAN	metropolitan area network
MCA	multichannel adaptation
MCU	multipoint control unit
MDF	main distribution frame
MELP	mixed-excitation LPC
MG	Media Gateway
MGC	media gateway controller
MGCP	Media Gateway Control Protocol
MIME	Multipurpose Internal Mail Extension
MIPS	millions of instructions per seconds
MOS	mean opinion score
MOSPF	Multicast OSPF (standard)
MP	modulator parameter
MP	Multilink Protocol
MPLS	Multiprotocol Label Switching
MP-MLQ	multipulse maximum likelihood quantization
MTP	message transfer part
MTS	message telecommunications service
MTU	maximum tranmission unit

N

NAP	network access point
N-ISDN	narrowband-ISDN
NISP	national Internet service provider
NIST	National Institute of Standards and Technology
NLPID	network-level protocol ID
NNI	Network network interface
NSF	National Science Foundation
NTP	Network Time Protocol

O

OAM	operations, administration and maintenance
OLE	originating local exchange
OS	operating service
OSF	Offset field
OSI	Open System Interconnection
OSPF	Open Shortest Path First (standard)
OSS	operating service signaling

P

P	Parity
PAD	Padding bytes, if needed
PAM	pulse amplitude modulation
PBR	policy-based routing
PBX	private branch exchange
PC	personal computer
PC	point code
PCM	pulse code modulation
PDN	public data network
PDU	protocol data unit
PHB	per-hop behavior
PIM	Protocol-Independent Multicast
POTS	plain old telephone system
PPP	Point-to-Point Protocol
PQ	priority queuing
PRI	primary rate interface
PSTN	public switched telephone network
PSVQ	predictive split vector quantizer
PTT	Postal, Telephone, and Telegraph Ministry
PVC	permanent virtual circuit

Q

QAM	quadrature amplitude modulation
QOS	quality of service
QPSK	quadrature phase-shift keyed

R

RBOC	Regional Bell Operating Company
RED	random early detection
RF	radio frequency
RFC	Request for Comments
RISP	regional Internet service provider
ROSE	remote operations service element
RPC	remote procedure call
RRJ	registration reject (message)
RRQ	registration request (message)
RSVP	Resource Reservation Protocol
RTCP	Real-Time Control Protocol
RTP	Real-Time Protocol
RTT	round-trip transmission time

S

SCA	single-channel adaption
SCCP	signaling connection control point
SCN	switched-circuit network
SCP	service control point
SDH	Synchronous Digital Hierarchy
SDP	Session Description Protocol
SDU	service data unit
SE	shared explicit (style)
SEQ	sequence
SG	signaling gateway
SGMP	Simple Gateway Control Protocol
SIP	Session Initiation Protocol
SLA	service level agreement
SLIP	Serial Link IP
SN	sequence number
SNA	Systems Network Architecture
SNMP	Simple Network Management Protocol
SNP	sequence number protection
SONET	synchronous optical network
SR	service representation
SS7	Signaling System Number 7
SSP	service switching point
STDM	statistical time division multiplexing

STP	signal transfer point
SWP	switching pattern

T

TA	terminal adapter
TASI	time-assigned speech interpolation
TCA	traffic conditioning agreement
TCAP	transaction capabilities application part
TCB	traffic conditioning block
TCP	Transmission Control Protocol
TDM	time division multiplexed
TDMA	time division multiple access
TE	terminal equipment
TE	traffic engineering
TE	transit exchange
TFTP	Trivial File Transfer Protocol
TLE	terminating local exchange
TOS	type of service (field)
TTL	time to live (field)

U

UAC	user agent client
UAS	user agent server
UCD	University of California at Davis
UCF	unregister confirm (message)
UDP	User Datagram Protocol
UI	unnumbered information
UIC	University of Illinois at Chicago
UNI	user-network interface

URI	uniform resource identifier
URJ	Unregister Reject (message)
URQ	Unregister Request (URQ)
URL	universal resource locator
UUI	user-to-user indicator (field)

V

VAD	voice activity detection
VBR	variable bit rate
VDSL	very high bit-rate DSL
VLR	visitor location register
VoATM	Voice over ATM
VoFR	Voice over Frame Relay
VoLS	Voice over MPLS
VPN	virtual private network
VQ	vector quantization

W

WAN	wide area network
WDM	wave division multiplexing
WF	wildcard filter (style)
WFQ	weighted fair queuing
WRED	weighted random early detection (service)

X

xDSL	X digital subscriber line
XML	Extensible Markup Language

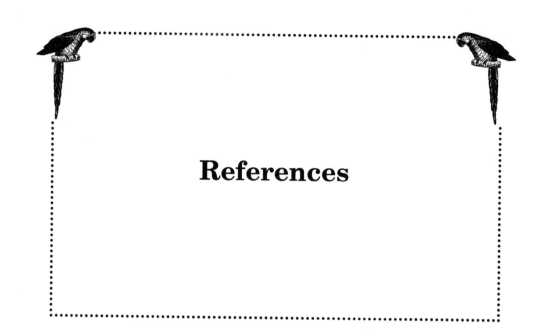

References

[ARAN98a] Arango, Mauricio, Dugan, Andrew, Elliott, Isaac, Huitema, Christian, and Pickett, Scott. "Media Gateway Control Protocol (MGCP)," Internet Engineering Task Force draft-huitema-MGCP-v0r1-01.txt, 1998.

[ARAN98] Arango, Mauricio, and Huitema, Christian. "Simple Gateway Control Protocol (SGCP)," Internet Engineering Task Force draft-huitema-sgcp-va-02.txt. 1998.

[BATE99] Bates, Bud. *Data Communications: A Business View.* TCIC International, Phoenix AZ, 1999.

[BELL94] Bellcore Document SR-TSV-002275, Issue 2, April 1994.

[BLAC93] Black, Uyless. *Data Link Protocols,* Englewood Cliffs, NJ: Prentice Hall, 1993.

[BLAC95] Black, Uyless. *The V Series Recommendations: Standards for Data Communications over the Telephone Network,* 2nd ed., McGraw Hill, 1995.

[BLAC96] Black, Uyless. *Physical Layer Protocols and Interfaces,* Washington, D.C.: IEEE Computer Society Press, 1996.

[BLAC98] Black, Uyless. *Advanced Features of the Internet,* Upper Saddle River, NJ: Prentice Hall, 1998.

[BLAC01a] Black, Uyless. *Internet Telephony: Call Processing Protocols,* ISBN 0-13-025565-3, Prentice Hall, 2001.

[BORE97] Borella, M.S., et al. "Analysis of End-to-End Internet Packet Loss: Dependence and Asymmetry," *IEEE Network,* Reprint, 1997.

[CAMA00] Camarillo, Gonzalo, and Roach, Adam. "Best Current Practice for ISUP to SIP Mapping," draft-camarillo-sip-isup-bcp-00.txt, March 2000.

[CISC99a] *Cisco IOS 12.0 Quality of Service,* Cisco Press, ISBN 1-57870-161-9, 1999.

[CISC00b] *Internetworking Technologies Handbook,* 3rd ed., Cisco Press, ISBN 1-58705-001-3, 2000.

[CISC00c] *Cisco Voice over IP Fundamentals,* ISBN 1-57870-168-6, 2000.

[COX98] Cox, R. V., Hassle, B. G., Lacuna, A., Shahraray, B., and Rabiner, L. "On the Applications of Multimedia Processing to Communications," *Proceedings of the IEEE:* 86(5), May 1998.

[CRAN97] Crandall, Richard E. "The Challenge of Large Numbers," *Scientific American,* February, 1997.

[CUER99] Cuervo, Fernando, et al. {ADD ALL AUTHORS}. "Megaco Protocol," draft-ietf-megaco-protocol-01.txt, 1999.

[DAVI00] Davie, Bruce, and Rekhter, Yakov. *MPLS: Technology and Applications,* San Diego: Academic Press, 2000.

[EYRE98] Eyre, Jennifer, and Bier, Jeff. "DSP Processors Hit the Main Stream," *Computer,* August, 1998.

[FR.1197] Voice over Frame Relay Implementation Agreement, Frame Relay Forum Document number FRF.11, 1997.

[GIBS99] Gibson, M., and Crowcroft, J. "Use of SIP for the Reservation of QoS guaranteed Paths" draft-gibson-sip-qos-resv-00.txt, October 1999.

[GORA98] Goralski, Walter. *ADSL and DSL Technologies,* New York: McGraw-Hill, 1998.

[HEND96] Henderson, P. Michael. "56kbps Data Transmission Across the PSTN," paper published by Rockwell Semiconductor Systems. No date given.

[JAMO99] Jamoussi, Belel, et al. "Constraint-Based LSP Setup Using LDP," draft-ietf-mpla-cr-ldp-03.text, September 1999.

[KRAP98] Krapf, Eric. "SDPs: Powering the Packet-Voice Revolution," *Business Communications Review's Voice 2000,* October 1998.

[LAPS97] Lapsley, Phil. *DSP Processor Fundamentals,* IEEE Press, 1997.

[MA99] Ma, Gene. "H.323 Signaling and SS7 ISUP Gateway: Procedure Interworking," Draft-ma-h323-isup-gateway-00.txt

[McCU99] McCullough, Daniel J., and Walker, John Q. "Interested in VoIP? How to Proceed," *Business Communications Review, Voice 2000,* April 1999.

[MINO98] Minoli, Daniel. *Deliver Voice over IP Networks,* John Wiley & Sons, 1998.

[NORT01a] A white paper used during a lab session between the author and Nortel Networks programmers.

[PAXS97] Paxson, Vern. "End-to-End Routing Behavior in the Internet," *IEEE/ACM Transactions on Communications:* 5(5), October 1997.

[POLE98] Poleretsky, Zoltan. "Customer interaction in an Electronic Commerce World," *Business Communications Review,* Nortel Supplement, January, 1999.

[RADI94] Radhika, R. Roy. "Networking Constraints in Multimedia Conferencing and the Role of ATM Networks," *AT&T Technical Journal,* July/August, 1994.

[RAPP98] Rappaport, David M. "The Next Wave in Do-It-Yourself Customer Service," *Business Communications Review* (BCR), June, 1998.

[RUDK97] Rudkin, S., Grace, A., and Whybray, M. W. "Real-Time Applications on the Internet," *BT Journal,* 15:(2), April 1997.

[SCHM98] Schmelling, Sarah, and Vittore, Vince. "Evolution or Revolution," *Telephony,* November 16, 1998.

[SCHU00] Schulzrinne, S. Petrack. "RTP Payload for DTMG Digits, Telephony Tones and Telephony Signals," RFC 2833, May 2000.

[STEVa98] Stevens, Jeff. "DSPs in Communications," *IEEE Spectrum,* September 1998.

[STEV94] Stevens, W. Richard. *TCP/IP Illustrated, Volume 1, The Protocols,* Addison-Wesley, 1994.

[STEVb98] Stevens, W. Richard. *TCP/IP Illustrated,* Addison-Wesley, 1998.

[STUC98] Stuck, Bart, and Weingarten, Michael. "Can Carriers Make Money on IP Telephony?", *Business Communications Review,* August, 1998.

[TAYL98] Taylor, P. Tom, Calhoun, Pat R., and Rubens, Allan C. "IPDC Base Protocol," Internet Engineering Task Force Draft-taylor-lpdc-99.txt, 1998.

[VAND98] Vandenameele, Jozef. "Requirements for the Reference Point ('N') between Media Gateway Controller and Media Gateway," Draft-vandenameele-tiphon-arch-gway-decom-00.txt, November 1988.

[WENT97] Wentworth, R. ATM Forum Contribution 97-0980, December 1997.

[WEST96] Westall, F. A., Johnston, R. D., and Lewis, A. V. "Speech Technology for Telecommunications," *BT Journal,* 14(1) January, 1996.

[WEXL98] Wexler, Joanie. "56k Modems: A Bandwidth Bird in the Hand," *Business Communications Review,* October 1998.

[WONG96] Wong, W. T. K., Mack, R. M., Cheetham, B. M. G., and Sun, X. Q. "Low Rate Speech Coding for Telecommunications," *BT Journal,* 14(1) January 1996.

[WORS98] Worster, Tom, and Wentworth, Robert. "Guaranteed Rate in Differentiated Services," draft-worster-diffserv-gr-00.txt, June 1998.

Index

Page numbers ending in "f" refer to figures; page numbers ending in "t" refer to tables.

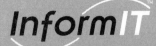

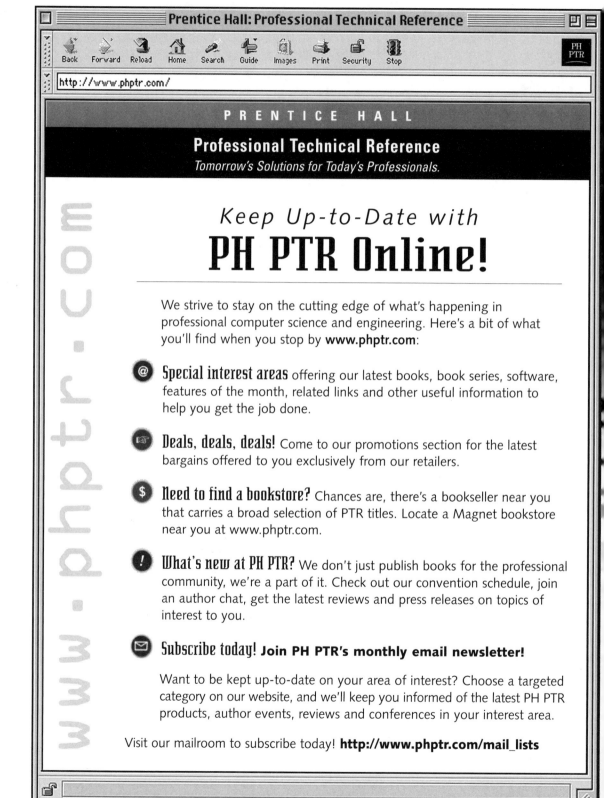